CONTENT

C000270798

New Methods for Social History

Edited by
Larry J. Griffin and
Marcel van der Linden

Introduction
Larry J. Griffin and Marcel van der Linden   3

Temporally Recursive Regression and Social Historical Inquiry:
An Example of Cross-Movement Militancy Spillover
Larry Isaac, Larry Christiansen, Jamie Miller and Tim Nickel   9

Using Event History Analysis in Historical Research:
With Illustrations from a Study of the Passage of Women's
Protective Legislation
Holly J. McCammon   33

Incorporating Space into Social Histories:
How Spatial Processes Operate and How We Observe Them
Glenn Deane, E.M. Beck and Stewart E. Tolnay   57

Narrative as Data: Linguistic and Statistical Tools for the
Quantitative Study of Historical Events
Roberto Franzosi   81

The Logic of Qualitative Comparative Analysis
Charles C. Ragin   105

Historical Social Network Analysis
Charles Wetherell   125

Historical Inference and Event-Structure Analysis
Larry J. Griffin and Robert R. Korstad   145

NOTES ON CONTRIBUTORS

E.M. Beck, Department of Sociology, University of Georgia, Athens, GA 30602–1611, USA; e-mail: wbeck@arches.uga.edu

Larry Christiansen, Department of Sociology, Florida Atlantic University, 777 Glades Road, Boca Raton, FL 33431, USA; e-mail: christia@fau.edu

Glenn D. Deane, Department of Sociology, State University of New York, Albany, NY 12222, USA; e-mail: gdd@castle.albany.edu

Roberto Franzosi, Trinity College, University of Oxford, Oxford OX1 3BH, UK; e-mail: roberto.franzosi@socres.ox.ac.uk

Larry J. Griffin, Department of Sociology, Vanderbilt University, Box 1811-B, Nashville, TN 37235, USA; e-mail: griffilj@ctrvax.vanderbilt.edu

Larry W. Isaac, Department of Sociology, Florida State University, 574 Bellamy Building, Tallahassee, FL 32306–2011, USA; e-mail: lisaac@garnet.acns.fsu.edu

Robert R. Korstad, Sanford Institute of Public Policy, Duke University, Box 90245, Durham, NC 27708, USA; e-mail: korstad@pps.pubpol.duke.edu

Marcel van der Linden, Internationaal Instituut voor Sociale Geschiedenis, Cruquiusweg 31, 1019 AT Amsterdam, The Netherlands; e-mail: mvl@iisg.nl

Holly J. McCammon, Department of Sociology, Vanderbilt University, Box 1811-B, Nashville, TN 37235, USA; e-mail: mccammhj@ctrvax.vanderbilt.edu

Jamie Miller, Department of Sociology, Florida State University, Bellamy Building, Tallahassee, FL 32306–2270, USA; e-mail: jmiller@garnet.acns.fsu.edu

Tim Nickel, Department of Sociology, Florida State University, Bellamy Building, Tallahassee, FL 32306–2270, USA; e-mail: tnickel@garnet.acns.fsu.edu

Charles Ragin, Department of Sociology, Northwestern University, 1810 Chicago Avenue, Evanston, IL 60208–1330, USA; e-mail: cragin@nwu.edu

Stewart E. Tolnay, Department of Sociology, State University of New York, Albany, NY 12222, USA; e-mail: s.tolnay@albany.edu

Charles Wetherell, Department of History, University of California, Riverside, CA 92521–0204, USA; e-mail: charles.wetherell@ucr.edu

international
review of
social history

Supplement 6

New Methods for Social History

Edited by Larry J. Griffin and Marcel van der Linden

blished by the Press Syndicate of the University of Cambridge
The Pitt Building, Trumpington Street, Cambridge, CB2 1RP
40 West 20th Street, New York, NY 10011–4211, USA
10 Stamford Road, Oakleigh, Melbourne 3166, Australia

*A catalogue record for this book is available
from the British Library*

Library of Congress Cataloguing-in-Publication Data

New methods in social history / edited by Larry Griffin
and Marcel van der Linden.
     p.   cm.—(International review of social history.
Supplement : 6)
   ISBN 0–521–65599–4 (pb)
   1. Social history—Methodology.   I. Griffin, Larry J.
II. Linden. Marcel van der, 1952–   .   III. Series.
HN28.N48   1999
361.1′01—dc21   98–40332 CIP

ISBN 0 521 655994 (paperback)

"Robot 'Victor' can play tick tack toe, and always wins".
An early version of the computer, 1950s.
Copyright Philips Company Archives.

Printed in Great Britain by the University Press, Cambridge

International Review of Social History 43 (1998), Supplement, pp. 3–8
© 1998 Internationaal Instituut voor Sociale Geschiedenis

Introduction

Our intent in publishing this collection of essays is to introduce historians to a set of quantitative and qualitative social science methods that have genuine, and as yet un- or under-explored, utility for historical inquiry. Believing that the potency of any methodology is best displayed through the analysis of actual historical cases, we called for our contributors to demonstrate their chosen method's logic and applicability by grounding their exposition in concrete historical happenings. Though we also asked them to use as expository vehicles historical cases that are significant on their own terms and of clear relevance to social historians, the essays' actual substantive pay-off is apt to be less important than their ability to display in an accessible fashion when, why and how the application of various formal methods may generate deeper, more satisfying explanations and interpretations of historical happenings.

Admittedly, a call to contemporary historians to reconsider the possible value to them of formal social science methodologies comes at a peculiar time in our intellectual life. Analytical formalism in history seems on the wane, and, at best, social science and history have shared a checkered and uneasy relationship over the last century and a half. Early sociology, for example, borrowed from, leaned on, or in other ways was in conversation with history, even if some of the discipline's founders paradoxically used history in an ahistorical manner; that is, as a "storehouse of samples" in Barrington Moore's apt phrase, a mere testing ground for grand sociological theory rather than something to be comprehended in its own right.[1] Except

---

1. See, for instance, the following English language publications: Barrington Moore, "Strategy in Social Research", in B. Moore, *Political Power and Social Theory* (Cambridge, 1958), p. 131. Published discussions of the history-social science dialogue/dilemma are extensive. Notable contributions include H. Stuart Hughes, "The Historian and the Social Scientist", in Alexander V. Riasanovsky and Barnes Riznik (eds), *Generalizations in Historical Writing* (Philadelphia, 1963), pp. 18–59; Warren Cahnman and Alvin Boskoff, "Sociology and History: Reunion and Rapprochement" (pp. 1–18) and "Sociology and History: Review and Outlook" (pp. 560–580) in their edited volume *Sociology and History* (New York, 1964); Robert Berkhofer, *A Behavioral Approach to Historical Analysis* (New York, 1969); Samuel Beer, "Political Science and History", in Melvin Richter (ed.), *Essays in Theory and History: An Approach to the Social Sciences* (Cambridge, 1970), pp. 41–73; Kai Erikson, "Sociology and the Historical Perspective", *American Sociologist*, 15 (1970), pp. 331–338; J.H. Hexter, "History and the Social Sciences", in idem, *Doing History* (Bloomington, IN, 1972), pp. 107–134; Lawrence Stone, "History and Social Sciences in the Twentieth Century", in Charles F. Delzell (ed.), *The Future of History* (Nashville, TN, 1977), pp. 3–42; Theda Skocpol, "Sociology's Historical Imagination" (pp. 1–21) and "Emerging Agendas and Recurrent Strategies in Historical Sociology" (pp. 356–391), in idem (ed.), *Vision and Method in Historical Sociology* (New York, 1984); Piotr Sztompka, "The Renaissance of Historical Orientation in Sociology", *International Sociology*, 1 (1986), pp. 321–337; Andrew Abbott, "History and Sociology: The Lost Synthesis", *Social Science History*, 15 (1991), pp. 201–238; and Jill Quadagno and Stan Knapp, "Have Historical Sociologists Forsaken Theory? Thoughts on the History/Theory Relationship", *Sociological Research and Methods*, 20 (1992), pp. 481–507.

for economic historians and the occasional institutional or Marxist maverick, economists, of course, long ago embraced marginalism and thereby jettisoned serious historical inquiry. But since the 1960s there has been a certain rapprochement between historians and social scientists, a development which has become visible in "Social Sciences History Conferences" in Europe and the US, in the blossoming of scholarship in historical sociology, in new interdisciplinary journals explicitly merging social science and history, and in the application of sociological methods by social historians.[2]

To date, however, this convergence has remained quite limited. Misunderstandings between social scientists and historians about how each actually conducts their research are part of the problem. The late historical sociologist Philip Abrams, for example, has compellingly argued that sociologists and historians share a common, if often unstated, goal, that of understanding the mutually constitutive interplay of social structure and social action, a process he has labelled "structuring" to connote its intrinsically temporal – that is to say, historical – quality.[3] But differences in the internal organization, socialization practices, overt disciplinary objectives, and so on of history and the social sciences also contribute to their intellectual separation, and to this extent complete rapprochement will never come about. What can at least be partially eliminated, though, is the isolation fed by misguided a priori dismissals of historical approaches by social scientists or of social science theories and methods by historians. This lamentable practice is all too common today.

On the one hand, many influential social scientists, such as John Gold-

2. This rapprochement, and, indeed, historical sociology's current visibility and prestige, has roots now more than a generation old: Robert Bellah, Reinhard Bendix, S.N. Eisenstadt, Norbert Elias, Seymour M. Lipset and Barrington Moore, and others, continued to infuse their sociology with history in fruitful and exciting ways throughout the 1950s and 1960s and into the 1970s. Coupled with the fact that accepted (and largely ahistorical) sociological theories and approaches were unable to anticipate or satisfactorily account for the social conflict and transformations of the 1960s, the example and influence of these scholars are likely responsible for what became a striking, perhaps even profound and possibly irreversible, turn to history in the 1970s and 1980s among sociologists. Here we should particularly acknowledge the herculean efforts of Charles Tilly – efforts seen both in his own research going back to the 1960s and his more recent programmatic statements such as *As Sociology Meets History* (New York, 1981) and *Big Structures, Large Processes, Huge Comparisons* (New York, 1984). If Tilly deserves special mention, he was clearly aided in his "subversive" quest by a whole host of others, perhaps most importantly by Theda Skocpol, again both in her own research on *States and Social Revolutions* (Cambridge, 1979) and in her influential edited volume, *Vision and Method in Historical Sociology*; by Immanuel Wallerstein in his conceptualization and analysis of *The Modern World System* (New York, 1974), and, again, by Barrington Moore, whose *Social Origins of Dictatorship and Democracy* (Boston, 1966) continues to excite and stimulate more than thirty years after it first appeared. Powerful and effective defenses of a historically oriented social science were also published by Arthur Stinchcombe, *Theoretical Methods of Social History* (New York, 1978) and Philips Abrams, "History, Sociology, Historical Sociology", *Past and Present*, 87 (1980), pp. 3–16, and *Historical Sociology* (Ithaca, NY, 1982).
3. Abrams, "History, Sociology, Historical Sociology", and *Historical Sociology*.

thorpe, argue that "history" will always remain only a "necessary residual category".[4] This view is, as we noted above, as old as academic social science itself and is especially widespread among social scientists committed to a relatively narrow "scientific" understanding of their disciplines' purposes – for example, the testing and refinement of highly abstract general theory, the empirical identification of "social laws" or law-like regularities thought operative across time and space,[5] and an unyielding commitment to quantification as the best way to summarize and analyze information.

For decades, social science research has been dominated by multivariate statistical techniques.[6] Such procedures generally require large data sets and permit the user to proceed to analysis with little, if any, in-depth knowledge of the distinct cases subject to analysis. Most sociologists using such methods, moreover, generally do not intend to limit their inferences to the specific cases they analyze. Indeed, they typically work hard to escape the spatial and temporal constraints of their studies by showing that their samples are representative of more inclusive populations, and/or that they are studying an instance or example of a theoretically general process even if the inquiry is of phenomena occurring at only one time point and/or in one place. By definition and intent, then, most sociologists do not seriously ground either the theories they use or the analyses they perform in the historical (temporal and spatial) contexts housing the sample, population, example, or instance of interest. To do so, in fact, would compromise the "timeless" and "placeless" generality of their theories, findings and inferences.[7] The effective consequence of these presuppositions and practices too often is an excessively mechanistic and ahistorical social science.[8]

On the other hand, the much-heralded quantitative revolution in history of the 1960s and 1970s, associated with such historians as Robert Fogel,

4. John H. Goldthorpe, "Current Issues in Comparative Macrosociology: A Debate on Methodological Issues", *Comparative Social Research*, 16 (1997), p. 17. Earlier, Goldthorpe made similar assertions that elicited strong commentary from historical sociologists. See Goldthorpe, "The Uses of History in Sociology: Reflections on Some Recent Tendencies", *British Journal of Sociology*, 42 (1991), pp. 211–230. Subsequent comments by Joseph Bryant (pp. 3–19), Nicky Hart (pp. 21–30), Nicos Mouzelis (pp. 31–36), and Michael Mann (pp. 37–54), and Goldthorpe's response (pp. 55–77) are found in *British Journal of Sociology*, 45 (1994).
5. See, for example, Edgar Kiser and Michael Hechter, "The Role of General Theory in Comparative-Historical Sociology", *American Journal of Sociology*, 97 (1991), pp. 1–30.
6. See, for example, Christopher Bernert, "The Career of Causal Analysis in American Sociology", *British Journal of Sociology*, 34 (1983), pp. 230–254.
7. This argument is taken from, and elaborated in, Larry J. Griffin, "Temporality, Events, and Explanation in Historical Sociology: An Introduction", *Sociological Methods and Research*, 20 (1992), pp. 403–427.
8. David Zaret, "Sociological Theory and Historical Scholarship", *American Sociologist*, 13 (1978), pp. 114–121; Larry W. Isaac and Larry J. Griffin, "Ahistoricism in Time-Series Analyses of Historical Process: Critique, Redirections, and Illustrations from U.S. Labor History", *American Sociological Review*, 54 (1989), pp. 873–890; and Norbert Elias, "The Retreat of Sociologists into the Present", *Theory, Culture and Society*, 4 (1987), pp. 223–247.

Stanley Engerman, J. Morton Kousser and Emmanuel Le Roy Ladurie, simply failed to materialize.[9] In fact, a majority of all historians, including social historians, now appears largely indifferent to most of the conventions of formal social science, particularly those calling for the development and application of codified theory stated so as to be empirically disconfirmed and the use of formal inferential techniques and methodologies.[10] Seemingly in reaction to the grandiose explanatory claims of some behaviorists and positivists, moreover, many historians increasingly turned first to Geertzian-style symbolic and interpretative anthropology for inspiration[11] and, more recently, to postmodern and linguistic constructions of history's project. In the process, cultural interpretation often has been cleaved from causal explanation, and indifference to formal social science has, in many important historical circles at least, given way to profound skepticism about its power to elucidate: when such elementary notions as "cause" and "consequence" are thought to be arbitrary, of doubtful utility, or mere intellectual fictions, historians are unlikely to concern themselves with methodological advances in the social sciences and with how those innovations can be fruitfully applied in historical research.[12]

Except for certain fields of historical research, such as historical demography and studies of social mobility, the historical utility of traditional multivariate sociological techniques undoubtedly is limited. At the risk of overgeneralizing, let us assume that most historians

(a) usually deal with a singular historical event or just a small number of cases, not dozens or hundreds of them;

9. For a relatively balanced and nuanced defense of the efficacy of a formal social science history, see Robert Fogel, "'Scientific History' and Traditional History", in R. Fogel and G.R. Elton, *Which Road to the Past?* (New Haven, 1983), pp. 5–70.

10. See, for example, the discussions of these and similar issues in Roderick Floud, "Quantitative History and People's History: Two Methods in Conflict", *Social Science History*, 8 (1984), pp. 151–168; Jürgen Kocka, "Theories and Quantification in History", *Social Science History*, 8 (1984), pp. 169–178; and Tony Judt, "A Clown in Regal Purple: Social History and the Historians", *History Workshop*, 7 (1979), pp. 66–94.

11. Clifford Geertz, *The Interpretation of Cultures* (New York, 1971); Ronald G. Walters, "Signs of the Times: Clifford Geertz and Historians", *Social Research*, XLVII (1980), pp. 537–556; Bernard S. Cohen, "Anthropology and History in the 1980s", *Journal of Interdisciplinary History*, 12 (1981), pp. 227–252.

12. See, among many others, Nancy Fitch, "Statistical Fantasies and Historical Facts: History in Crisis and Its Methodological Implication", *Historical Methods*, 17 (1984), pp. 239–254; Joan W. Scott, "History in Crisis? The Others' Side of the Story", *American Historical Review*, 94 (1989), pp. 680–692; F.R. Ankersmit, "History and Postmodernism", *History and Theory*, 28 (1989), pp. 137–153; Patrick Joyce, "The End of Social History?", *Social History*, 20 (1995), pp. 73–91; and Robert Berkhofer, *Beyond the Great Story: History as Text and Discourse* (Cambridge, 1995). Lawrence Stone initiated a sharp debate about history's postmodern turn in the journal *Past and Present*. See Stone, "History and Post–Modernism" (No. 131, 1991, pp. 217–218; No. 135, 1992, pp. 189–194) and the comments by Patrick Joyce (No. 133, 1991, pp. 204–209), Catriona Kelly (No. 133, 1991, pp. 209–213) and Gabrielle M. Spiegel (No. 135, 1992, pp. 194–208).

(b) often piece together their cases even as they analyze them rather than reach for predefined analytical units established for reasons other than historical research (e.g. census tracts, political parties);

(c) struggle with a rich variety of information that is nonetheless often too incomplete to permit statistical analysis, that cannot be easily ordered by strict criteria externally dictated by statistical rules (the so-called "crisp data partition"), that cannot be assumed to be fixed or stable in meaning through time or from one historical actor to another, and that moves across levels of analysis in a complex, apparently bewildering, fashion (from person to collectivity to institution to period);

(d) rely on and prefer explanations and interpretations that are context-dependent and causally contingent, not invariant across time and space and deterministic.

Woven throughout all of the above, of course, is the basic historical premise that "time matters" and that understanding and explaining past actions and events in time and through time is the goal of historical inquiry. "In truth", states Fernand Braudel, "the historian can never get away from the question of time in history; time sticks to his [sic] thinking like soil to a gardner's spade."[13] Given the practices and objectives of historians, given also the ahistoricism of much social science research, and given, finally, how that ahistoricism is aided and abetted by the somewhat unreflective use of multi-variate statistical procedures, it is therefore easy to understand why practising historians typically ignore formal social science methods or decry their application to real historical problems.

By virtue of the existence of this special issue, however, we clearly do not believe that this state of affairs is inevitable. During the last ten to fifteen years, social scientists themselves have discerned many of the limitations to statistical analysis and successfully historicized the application of multivariate procedures or provided analytical alternatives that permit, occasionally even coerce, greater attention to historical particularity, contingency, context and flow. Often these innovations – such as those explored in the essays to follow by Larry Isaac and his co-authors, Holly McCammon, and Glenn Deane and his co-authors – remain essentially true to the logic and

---

13. Fernand Braudel, *On History* (Chicago, 1980), p. 47. The problem is not merely that sociologists generally ignore time; it is also, and as profoundly, that the statistical analysis of time-ordered data (e.g. via time-series regression) may itself remain ahistorical. Time, that is, is not historicized; it is not transmuted in most sociological analyses of time-order data into what Braudel (*ibid.*, p. 49) calls "historical time". See the arguments and documentation put forward by Isaac and Griffin, "Ahistoricism in Time-Series Analyses of Historical Process", and Larry J. Griffin and Larry W. Isaac, "Recursive Regression and the Historical Use of 'Time' in Time-Series Analysis of Historical Process", *Historical Methods*, 25 (1992), pp. 166–179. What matters to the historical grounding of an analysis is not simply the use of over-time data, but, rather, the historical meaning those series convey and the historical purpose they can be put in the course of analysis and interpretation.

application of conventional statistical analysis, but are put to decidedly historical uses or are modified so that the inherent historicity of the data subject to analysis is magnified and exploited. Other methodological advances also illuminating historical processes – those discussed, for example, by Roberto Franzosi, Charles Ragin and Charles Wetherell in this collection – are more distant from many of the conventions of statistical analysis but are nonetheless analytically formal in that they mandate systematic and replicable routines, require strict coding rules and have an internal logic or algorithm that produces descriptive or inferential results. Finally, some formal techniques – such as that demonstrated by Larry Griffin and Robert Korstad, below – entirely leave the realm of multivariate statistics and actually merge with the type of interpretative and explanatory reasoning used by narrative historians.

Social science methodology, therefore, need not be ahistorical, whatever its track record thus far, and, as our contributors demonstrate, historically-oriented social scientists who use such methods both appreciate and advance the importance of "history" in their use of these techniques and in their interpretation of their findings. The time seems ripe, then, for social historians to examine – critically, to be sure, but with an open mind – the utility to them and to future historical inquiry of recent innovations in formal social science methodology.

Larry J. Griffin
Marcel van der Linden

International Review of Social History 43 (1998), Supplement, pp. 9–32
© 1998 Internationaal Instituut voor Sociale Geschiedenis

Temporally Recursive Regression and Social Historical Inquiry: An Example of Cross-Movement Militancy Spillover*

LARRY ISAAC, LARRY CHRISTIANSEN, JAMIE MILLER AND TIM NICKEL

Our focus here is on time-series regression as a formal analytic tool in social historical inquiry. We have three interrelated purposes. First, we argue that conventional time-series regression is typically ill-suited for social historical inquiry because ahistorical assumptions and conventions regarding time undermine the historical character of social "process-as-analyzed". Second, we present a modified time-series approach – temporally recursive regression – that takes time seriously and provides a more adequate analytic vehicle for social historical inquiry. Finally, we illustrate the promise of temporally recursive regression by using it to analyze how workplace militancy in post-war America was fueled by massive insurgency waves during successive phases of the civil rights movement.

AHISTORICAL CHARACTER OF CONVENTIONAL TIME-SERIES REGRESSION[1]

Conventional time-series regression contains a conception of time that is *ahistorical* in character.[2] It is fairly termed ahistorical, we believe, because time enters the analysis solely as a means of analysis, an instrumental marker for purposes of ordering the time unit observations (e.g. years). Treating time, and therefore history, as simply *means* rather than also *object* of analysis shapes the practice of conventional time-series regression in such a way that unduly masks significant historical context, meaning and nuance in social process. Simply put, ahistorical time severely limits what conventional

---

* We thank Larry Griffin and Marcel van der Linden for comments on prior versions of the paper. Isaac's co-authors are listed in alphabetical order.
1. This section draws on: Larry Isaac and Larry Griffin, "Ahistoricism in Time-Series Analyses of Historical Process: Critique, Redirection, and Illustrations from U.S. Labor History", *American Sociological Review*, 54 (1989), pp. 873–890; Larry Griffin and Larry Isaac, "Recursive Regression and the Historical Use of 'Time' in Time-Series Analysis of Historical Process", *Historical Methods*, 25 (1992), pp. 166–179; Larry Isaac and Kevin Leicht, "Regimes of Power and the Power of Analytic Regimes: Explaining U.S. Military Procurement Keynesianism as Historical Process", *Historical Methods*, 30 (1997), pp. 28–45.
2. On forms of temporality in social historical inquiry, see William Sewell, "Three Temporalities: Toward an Eventful Sociology", in Terrence McDonald (ed.), *The Historic Turn in the Human Sciences* (Ann Arbor, MI, 1996), pp. 245–280.

time-series regression can contribute to social historical inquiry, both in terms of mapping past historical processes and what it can offer for theoretical development.

The acceptance of ahistorical time leads to two interrelated practices that produce much of the damage. One rests on the analytical use of a single, *fixed time frame*. Data representing the process of interest are organized into and analyzed over a fixed time period without regard to historical aspects of starting, ending or intervening time points. Opening and ending dates are arbitrarily selected, then the model is estimated on a single time frame. The potential value to historical inquiry of varying the start/end points is not anticipated (usually the question is not even raised) and is, therefore, not explored.

A related convention – known as the *homogeneity assumption* – assumes that the regression coefficients linking a dependent variable to a set of independent variables are identical for each and every time point contained within the fixed time frame. Several significant ahistorical implications stem from this assumption. First, transhistorically general parameter estimates are produced as single numerical representations of causal impact over quite lengthy periods of history. Consequently historical documentation and extant analysis of how social contexts and events might condition or alter the causal processes of interest are simply ruled out by methodological fiat. The only source of social change posited within such a model occurs as quantitative variation in the dependent variable. Other, perhaps deeper, forms of social change that might register in the process structure (structural form of the model) or parameter structure (coefficients linking independent to dependent variables) are treated as historical constants.[3]

Second, the homogeneity assumption masks the existence of unusual time periods, especially active moments that form historical turning points in a particular process. "Exceptional" (or "deviant") cases are routinely treated as obstacles rather than as important theoretical-historical anomalies to be explained. As such, they are often ignored or eliminated. An image of seamless historical continuity is created, again by methodological fiat, rather than empirically detected and explained. Consequently, theories that posit important historical discontinuities and/or feature the transformative potential of events and human agency are unlikely to find inspiration or support from conventional time-series analyses. Moreover, when historical contexts and events do, in fact, affect the causal relationships between independent and dependent variables, the opposite a priori assumption is likely to generate seriously misguided inferences.

---

3. For more detail on sources of constancy and change within time-series models, see Thomas Janoski and Larry Isaac, "Introduction to Time-Series Analysis", in Thomas Janoski and Alexander Hicks (eds), *The Comparative Political Economy of the Welfare State* (Cambridge, 1994), pp. 31–53, Table 1.

Third, the homogeneity assumption licenses the analyst to "slice into" history at any convenient point. Under this assumption it makes no difference where one begins or ends the analysis since the time-series observations are understood to be manifestations of the same underlying continuous process. Encouraged by assumptions of theoretical generality and historical invariance, analyses driven exclusively by data availability can be easily justified. The findings of such studies are situated in periods defined by happenstance of data availability, or perhaps even the desire to extend the number of time points to meet technical "sample" size requirements or to enhance statistical significance. In such instances, history has been literally reduced to "merely a storehouse of samples".[4]

In combination the fixed time frame and homogeneity assumptions profoundly shape the results and, therefore, inferences drawn within conventional time-series analyses.[5] Causal models are uncritically presented as time (and therefore historically) invariant. At minimum, this leads to an underestimation of how potentially heterogeneous historical contexts, human actions and events condition social processes and alter possibilities for future action. By extension it reinforces images of seamless historical continuity already dominant in much social science theory and quantitative research.[6]

HISTORICIZING TIME-SERIES REGRESSION ANALYSIS[7]

Temporally recursive regression (TRR) – also known as "moving regression" – was originally developed to empirically examine the validity of the parameter homogeneity assumption.[8] Its procedures also necessarily relax the fixed time frame convention. Although not initially developed as a historically-oriented research tool, TRR can be historicized in a manner that allows it to be used with good result in social historical research employing time-series data. By historicization of method, we mean that

4. Barrington Moore, *Political Power and Social Theory* (Cambridge, MA, 1958), p. 113.

5. Another important temporal issue in time-series analysis of historical process is time unit (scale) aggregation: see Gary F. Jensen, "Time and Social History: Problems of Atemporality in Historical Analyses with Illustrations from Research on Early Modern Witch Hunts", *Historical Methods*, 30 (1997), pp. 46–57.

6. Larry Isaac, "Transforming Localities: Reflections on Time, Causality, and Narrative in Contemporary Historical Sociology", *Historical Methods*, 30 (1997), pp. 4–12.

7. This section draws on: Isaac and Griffin, "Ahistoricism in Time-Series Analyses", pp. 873–90; Griffin and Isaac, "Recursive Regression", pp. 166–79; Isaac and Leicht, "Regimes of Power", pp. 28–45.

8. Procedures for testing the homogeneity assumption are discussed in Richard Quandt, "The Estimation of the Parameters of a Linear Regression System Obeying Two Separate Regimes", *Journal of the American Statistical Association*, 53 (1958), pp. 873–80; and R.L. Brown, J. Durbin and J.M. Evans, "Techniques for Testing the Constancy of Regression Relations Over Time", *Journal of the Royal Statistical Society*, 37 (1975), pp. 149–192. The term "moving regression" is due to Brown *et al.*

research technique and its central premises should be subordinated to the historical and substantive terms of the analysis, not the reverse as is the case in conventional time-series practice.

TRR belongs to a family of procedures known as "time-varying" or "stochastic" parameter models[9] that are designed to allow relationships between dependent and independent variables to change through time. Such models can be estimated in a variety of different ways, some of which embody rather complex mathematics and require highly restrictive a priori theoretical assumptions about the historical process under investigation. We prefer TRR and limit our discussion to it for several important reasons: first, it is relatively simple to use and understand; second, it contains fewer restrictive assumptions than even conventional time-series regression (i.e. the fixed parameter assumption is relaxed); and third, one of its strategic forms (the "forward" version discussed below) is available as an automated routine in several regression programs (TSP, PC-GIVE, EVIEWS) while others can be programmed to do it (e.g. RATS).

While TRR has been used with increasing frequency in recent years, it is still a fringe approach relative to conventional regression analysis. Thus, several key issues should be considered by scholars contemplating the use of TRR: (1) basic procedural logics in relation to the research question of interest; (2) ability to map various dimensions of social historical change; and (3) specific contributions to social historical inquiry.

Basic procedural logics of TRR

The historicization of time-series analysis can be accomplished through TRR because it facilitates the historicization of time. It does so by presupposing the potentially unique historical value of particular temporal moments, either in terms of analytic start/end points defining the time frame of analysis or as turning points in relations governing the social historical process. This can be most clearly seen in the procedural logic of TRR. Instead of centering the analysis on a fixed time frame, TRR systematically moves the time frame through different start and/or end points bracketing the historical periods of investigation. This simple relaxation of conventional practice allows (but does not force) the estimated parameter structure to change as the time points defining historical periods are changed by the analyst.

Three different TRR strategies define how one alters the start and/or end points of the time frame containing the numerical series. An initial sub-

9. See L.W. Johnson, "Stochastic Parameter Regression: An Annotated Bibliography", *International Statistical Review*, 45 (1977), pp. 257–272; Nathaniel Beck, "Time-Varying Parameter Regression Models", *American Journal of Political Science*, 27 (1983), pp. 557–600; P. Newbold and T. Bos, *Stochastic Parameter Regression Models* (Beverly Hills, CA, 1985).

Table 1. *Structure of a hypothetical temporally recursive regression: three analytic strategies, 1948–1981*

Time frame	Panel A: Forward-moving strategy	Coefficient
1948–1960		b_{48-60}
1948–1961		b_{48-61}
1948–1962		b_{48-62}
1948–1979		b_{48-79}
1948–1980		b_{48-80}
1948–1981		b_{48-81}
Time frame	Panel B: Backward-moving strategy	Coefficient
1969–1981		b_{69-81}
1968–1981		b_{68-81}
1967–1981		b_{67-81}
1950–1981		b_{50-81}
1949–1981		b_{49-81}
1948–1981		b_{48-81}
Time frame	Panel C: Diagonal-moving strategy (using an eleven-year time frame)	Coefficient
1948–1958		b_{48-58}
1949–1959		b_{49-59}
1950–1960		b_{50-60}
1969–1979		b_{69-79}
1970–1980		b_{70-80}
1971–1981		b_{71-81}

Note: This is a restylized version of Table 1 in Griffin and Isaac, "Recursive Regression", p. 169.

period must be selected for the first estimation in each analytic strategy. Because starting and ending points are assumed to be potentially important to the analysis, the initial sub-period should be specified on the basis of sound historical-theoretical insight regarding likely homogeneity of causal relations within that sub-period. Later we illustrate an empirical application of TRR in an investigation of a social movement spillover spanning the years 1948 to 1981. Here we outline the analytic logic of TRR using those years as reference points.

The *forward-moving strategy* anchors the analysis with the first year in the series (1948), defines an initial sub-period for first estimation (1948–1960), and then repeats the estimation process seriatim by adding one new year to the time frame until the final estimation utilizes all time points in the series (1948–1961, 1948–1962, . . . , 1948–1981). The structure of the forward-moving strategy is shown in Panel A of Table 1.

Panel B displays the *backward-moving strategy*. Here the analysis is anchored at the most recent year (1981) and the start point is allowed to increment backward in time, from 1969 to 1948. In other words, the initial estimation would include the years 1969 to 1981 as the time frame, the second estimation would cover 1968 to 1981, and so on until the earliest year in the series, 1948, is part of the estimation time frame.

The third TRR strategy fixes the number of time points (i.e. years) in the time frame to be analyzed. The example in Panel C uses a period length of eleven years. The analyst then varies the start and end points simultaneously with each estimation (e.g. 1948–1958, 1949–1959, . . . , 1970–1980, 1971–1981). This is the *diagonal-moving strategy*.

In general, if the equation to be estimated contains one dependent variable and K explanatory variables to be estimated on P sub-periods, the analyst will, in effect, produce a PxK matrix of coefficients. While important practical issues will arise (discussed below), nothing extraordinary is required in terms of estimation technique *per se*: any appropriate estimator – ordinary least squares (OLS) or generalized least squares (GLS) variant – may be employed.

It is important to recognize that there is no single "truth" to be found from TRR. The three approaches – forward, backward, diagonal – posit different underlying questions and therefore generate different answers about historical processes and social change. Therefore, parameter regimes estimated by different strategies will not necessarily coincide with each other.

Because the forward strategy anchors the time frame at the historically most distant point in the series and then serially expands the time frame forward, it is most fruitfully employed when the analyst is interested in the "development" (continuous or discontinuous) of the historical process. Therefore, an example of this sort of question might be: "Given a particular structure of (causal) relations at an earlier period in history, how did subsequent historical actions and events affect (if at all) the trajectory of the relations of interest?" The backward strategy, however, is best suited to issues concerning the historical antecedents of present (any "present") historical conditions, structure and causal patterns. One type of question that might motivate this strategy would be: "At what point (if any) in the past was there a structural shift in which the current parameter structure became 'institutionalized' as a governing regime?" As the observations are expanded forward or backward in time, the analytic distinctions between these two strategies become moot as they converge on the same full time frame.

The diagonal procedure can serve as a useful check on the results obtained with either the forward or backward approaches. Unlike its counterparts, the diagonal approach will produce cross-temporal parameter stability/variability that is independent of the variability in the number of observations. Therefore, temporal stability/instability cannot be explained as a possible methodologically induced artifact of changing number of observations over time. But this method itself has the limitation that alternative sizes of the fixed temporal window (e.g. a window of eleven versus twenty-five years) could generate differing results. Each analysis may suggest something different about the general extent of stability or change as well as the particular historical location of changes in the estimated parameter structures because each time frame encompasses different historical conditions and events.

In general, because the forward and backward strategies follow a logic of expansive time periods while the diagonal approach operates with a fixed length temporal window, insights into a particular historical process gained by one approach can be buttressed by at least one of the others. Even when strong interest in either "developmental" or antecedent "structural shifts" are involved, the analyst would do well to supplement the forward or backward with the diagonal strategy. Irrespective of the particular combination of strategies, the greatest value of a TRR investigation will be achieved in conjunction with an intensive dialogue with historical sources.

Temporal patterns in parameter regimes and their uses

Because TRR allows the coefficients to change through time, the cross-temporal pattern of coefficients linking independent to dependent variables can indicate historical contingency due to changing contexts and timing of events. Any given explanatory variable in the specified model has a temporally unfolding parameter regime characterized by a shape that: (a) is relatively stable through time (parameter constancy); (b) changes abruptly at a particular moment in time (parameter shift); (c) changes in a gradual, incremental/decremental manner (parameter drift); or (d) follows a cyclical rhythm (parameter cyclicality). In multivariate models it is possible to have a mixed configuration of these patterns.

There are two basic ways in which these temporal parameter patterns may be employed: (a) as an aid in the process of periodization; and/or (b) as the object of analysis and explanation itself. The first is grounded in a contextualized version of time. If the coefficients indicate sufficiently clear discontinuities or shifts in temporal structure, they may warrant distinct periodization; that is, splitting the series into two or more distinct sub-periods on which separate, historically contextualized time-series models might be estimated and compared. However, the process of periodization should not be limited to a narrow technical exercise; rather, empirical results should be used in conjunction with theoretical-historical evidence justifying the particular historical periodization in the process of interest.

When process temporality and the trajectory of relations are of interest, TRR coefficients can be converted to temporally local (e.g. year-specific) measures of relational impact. In this approach the cross-temporal pattern of localized coefficients become the phenomena to be explained and the nature of the research question shifts from what forces induce historical variation in a dependent variable to what social processes, conditions and events produce change in the relationships themselves. Hence, drifting, shifting or cyclical parameter trajectories become the object of analysis. At this point, the explanation could proceed in a strictly historical narrative mode and/or employ a second-order model to account for the cross-temporal variability in relations. Exactly how TRR results should be used will depend on the research question and analytic context. In our subsequent example, we illustrate both uses – periodization and cross-temporal parameter trajectories – of TRR results.

Contributions to social historical inquiry

TRR has substantial value for social historical inquiry that addresses questions with time-series data. In particular, TRR can be a useful analytic device because it historicizes time and facilitates access to time-dependent processes by: (a) forcing the analyst to think seriously about time frame, starting and ending points, and thorny issues associated with periodization; (b) allowing the analyst to uncover theoretically and historically significant turning points and qualitative breaks or shifts in patterns of determination; (c) emphasizing the necessity for access to the historical record; and (d) providing a way to integrate causal processes that follow patterns of long-term (slow) change with those that occur through short-term (rapid) transformative actions and events.[10] The cross-movement impact of massive waves of insurgent actions provides a useful case in point.

ANALYZING HISTORICAL PROCESS WITH TEMPORALLY RECURSIVE REGRESSION: CIVIL RIGHTS MOVEMENT SPILLOVER ON LABOR MILITANCY

In social movement scholarship, the study of intermovement relations and cross-movement influences is still largely underdeveloped. Very little systematic attention has been given to ways in which contemporaneously occurring movements shape political environments or become resources for each other in various cooperative or even incidental ways. One recent study begins to fill this void.[11] Inspired by David Meyer and Nancy Whittier's conceptual frame for analyzing intermovement "spillover", we illustrate the potential of temporally recursive regression by examining the dynamics of militancy spillover from civil rights movement street tactics into labor movement

10. See William Sewell, "Collective Violence and Collective Loyalties in France", *Politics & Society*, 18 (1990), pp. 527–552; Isaac and Leicht, "Regimes of Power", pp. 28–45.
11. David Meyer and Nancy Whittier, "Social Movement Spillover", *Social Problems*, 41 (1994), pp. 277–298.

militancy in the form of workplace strikes. We ask how post-war civil rights insurgencies influenced (if at all) the level of labor militancy. In other words, did the civil rights movement contribute to the "labor revolt" of the 1960s and early 1970s?

Data and model specification

All data used in the subsequent analysis are annual time-series observations for the United States spanning the years 1947 through 1981. We open with 1947 because that was the year in which the passage of the Taft-Hartley Act reorganized labor-management relations in a regime that increasingly privileged management's prerogative,[12] helping to shut the window of opportunity for the labor-based civil rights movement that had emerged within parts of the dissident Congress of Industrial Organizations (CIO) during the 1930s and 1940s.[13] We close the analytic time frame with 1981 because it, too, marks another important turning point in the structure of labor-management relations. The first Reagan administration made its anti-labor position clear from the outset and quickly backed it up with a massive assault on the Professional Air Traffic Controllers Union. On more pragmatic grounds, the Reagan administration altered the standard definition employed in reporting annual aggregate strike data, with 1981 marking the last year of the continuous definition.[14]

While labor militancy is clearly multidimensional, appearing in a variety of both open and subterranean forms, we limit the scope of our analysis by focusing exclusively on strike militancy in the public sector. We have demonstrated elsewhere that some key processes that shaped labor militancy over these decades, including civil rights insurgencies, differed importantly across sectors.[15] Specifically, since the civil rights variables had no systematic influence on private sector militancy, we restrict our attention to the public sector patterns for this illustration.

Although we are primarily concerned with the spillover relations between civil rights and labor militancy, it is necessary to estimate these relations in the context of models that account for other important determinants of strikes. The major explanations for strike activity can be represented in four

12. For example, see Kim Moody, *An Injury to All* (London, 1988); Christopher Tomlins, *The State and the Unions: Labor Relations, Law, and the Organized Labor Movement in America, 1880–1960* (Cambridge, 1985).

13. See: Robert Korstad and Nelson Lichtenstein, "Opportunities Found and Lost: Labor, Radicals, and the Early Civil Rights Movement", *Journal of American History*, 75 (1988), pp. 786–811; Michael Honey, *Southern Labor and Black Civil Rights* (Urbana, 1993).

14. P.K. Edwards, "The End of American Strike Statistics", *British Journal of Industrial Relations*, 21 (1983), pp. 392–394.

15. Larry Isaac, Larry Christiansen, Jamie Miller and Tim Nickel, "Intermovement Relations: Civil Rights Movement Spillover on Labor Militancy in the Postwar United States", Paper to be presented at the American Sociological Association Meetings (San Francisco, 1998).

basic categories:[16] (1) organizational and resource strength; (2) labor market conditions and economic hardship; (3) legal-institutional framework of industrial relations; and (4) political environment or opportunity structure. In addition to constructing variables that tap each of these dimensions, we incorporate, as our central focus, measures of insurgency in the civil rights social movement field as a fifth category of partial determination. Variables associated with each theoretical category, definitions and data sources are reported in the Appendix.

Full period time-invariant patterns

We begin by presenting the regression results for the entire period under study, 1947–1981,[17] shown in the last rows of Panels A and B of Table 1. This step will aid in orienting the reader to the model structure and the general interpretation created by the conventional time-series approach. The Durbin-Watson statistic[18] from the initial OLS estimates suggested problematic serial correlation, so we re-estimated with an appropriate GLS alternative. These unstandardized coefficients and t-ratios are presented in equation 1:

$$[1] \quad PSSD_t = -10.30 + .96 \ UDEN_{t-1} + .60 \ UNEM_t + .01 \ WAGE_t +$$
$$(3.34)^* \quad (5.66)^* \qquad (.24) \qquad (.17)$$
$$1.82 \ PL330_t + .70 \ DEM_t - .02 \ PROTESTS + .03 \ REVOLTS$$
$$(.98) \qquad (.54) \qquad (-1.90) \qquad (3.02)^*$$

Period: 1948–1981; Adj R^2 = .84; Estimator = GLS-MA(1).

Equation 1 suggests that union density (UDEN) and black urban revolts (REVOLTS) contributed to strike density in the public sector (PSSD) over the whole time frame, while labor market conditions, institutional/electoral politics and protest demonstrations were all seemingly unimportant. However, this time-invariant strategy masks potential heterogeneity in causes of labor militancy. Given that protest waves are by definition highly explosive, nonlinear processes, and that the pace of insurgent actions inside movements is highly irregular, homogenizing assumptions that imply constant cross-temporal impact of urban revolts and the consistent null influence of civil rights protests appear suspect on historical grounds.

Temporally recursive regression analysis

We now relax the process homogeneity and fixed time frame assumptions that yielded the time-invariant results in equation 1. Table 2 reports TRR

16. Roberto Franzosi, *The Puzzle of Strikes* (Cambridge, 1995).
17. The first year, 1947, is lost due to the lag structure of the model.
18. OLS estimation assumes that the errors across cases (years) are independent. If that assumption is violated, the standard errors associated with the regression coefficients are biased downward and hence the t-tests for significance become biased upwards. The Durbin-Watson "d" statistic tests

estimates for our strike model. Although we draw on information from diagonal- and backward-moving strategies, we primarily employ a forward-moving approach as our central concern is the developmental sequence and temporal trajectory of the model's parameter regime. In particular, we focus on how the influence of civil rights movement militancy (both PROTESTS and REVOLTS) on labor militancy unfolded over time.

Historically contingent processes – understood as cross-temporal change in relation magnitudes – are apparent in Table 2. Note that the full period (1948–1981) results in equation 1 indicate that only union density and rebellions have significant impacts on public sector strike density. However, when we scan the temporal windows in Table 2, it is clear that none of the explanatory variables in the model show consistently significant or null effects across time. None is even consistently signed over the full time period. Hence, the full period results, constrained to be time-invariant, mask important historical contingencies in *all* processes represented in the model of public sector strikes.

Union density, for example, shows contradictory influences on public sector strike activity over time. In the early part of the period (through 1962), union density hinders strike activity. The relation is reversed when the 1970s are brought into the analytic frame as union density appears to begin fostering strike activity. Abrupt parameter shifts are also evident in the variables measuring economic conditions. Unemployment and wage deprivation show positive, significant coefficients only in very limited time periods. Both legal-institutional and electoral environments influence strikes in historically contingent ways. Throughout the 1960s, public sector labor militancy was dampened by PL 330 and promoted by Democratic party strength. By the 1970s, however, these two processes appear to lose their causal efficacy.

The parameter regimes of the civil rights movement insurgencies also shift in important ways: protests stimulate strikes (as hypothesized) but only up through 1965 (coefficients range between .005 and .007), while urban ghetto revolts foster labor militancy only when historical experience beyond 1965 (the coefficient for 1948–1966 is .38) became part of the estimation record. These patterns clearly demonstrate the historically contingent quality of processes shaping public sector strike militancy in ways that could not have been revealed (and likely would not have been considered) within a conventional regression context.

Periodization

Are these patterns representative of real historical discontinuities, real heterogeneity, or are they perhaps simply chance fluctuations? As we indicated

the null hypothesis of no first-order serial correlation among the errors. Consult any basic econometrics text for guidelines for interpreting the DW values.

Table 2. *Temporally recursive regression estimates for a model of public sector strike militancy: United States, 1948-1981*

Temporal window	Union density	Public sector unem- ployment	Wage deprivation	Public Law 330	Democratic strength	Civil rights protests	Urban rebellions	Adjusted R-squared	OLS D-W	Estimator
1948–1960	-4.04	1.88	1.06*	-6.08*	1.75*	.007*	-.76	.68	2.92	GLS
1948–1961	-3.98*	2.34	1.17*	-6.16*	1.74*	.005*	-.73	.71	3.11	GLS
1948–1962	-4.56*	1.41	.98*	-6.36*	1.83*	.005*	-.79	.73	3.15	GLS
1948–1963	-.01	.15	.63*	-3.20*	1.20*	.006*	.06	.58	2.94	GLS
1948–1964	-.04	-.38	.57*	-3.08*	1.20*	.005*	.03	.61	2.96	GLS
1948–1965	-.03	-.32	.58*	-3.05*	1.20*	.005*	.02	.64	2.96	GLS
1948–1966	-.29	-1.37	.37	-3.53*	1.18*	.002	.38*	.80	2.61	OLS
1948–1967	.05	-1.44	.41	-2.81*	1.22*	.004	.06*	.69	2.56	OLS
1948–1968	.10	-2.73	.12	-2.26*	1.17*	.002	.04*	.81	1.91	OLS
1948–1969	.14	.39	.74	-2.92*	.97	.005	.05*	.88	2.50	OLS
1948–1970	.44	3.73	.96	-1.70	.25	.001	.06*	.79	1.52	OLS
1948–1971	.64*	6.97*	1.48*	-1.51	.28	-.001	.05*	.81	1.73	OLS
1948–1972	.72*	8.03*	1.68*	-1.40	.33	-.002	.05*	.83	1.84	OLS
1948–1973	.76*	8.22*	1.73*	-1.31	.37	-.002	.05*	.86	1.86	OLS
1948–1974	.81*	4.30	.39	.61	-.71	-.010	.04*	.83	1.48	GLS
1948–1975	.85*	3.48	.19	.97	-.85	-.010	.04*	.86	1.40	GLS
1948–1976	.89*	2.30	-.01	1.43	-.96	-.015	.03*	.84	1.37	GLS
1948–1977	.90*	2.34	-.06	1.54	-1.14	-.015	.03*	.85	1.41	GLS
1948–1978	.88*	2.00	.03	1.40	-.94	-.014	.03*	.86	1.37	GLS
1948–1979	.84*	1.17	.18	1.13	-.77	-.013	.03*	.87	1.20	GLS
1948–1980	.85*	1.22	.16*	1.18	-.77	-.013	.03*	.88	1.29	GLS
1948–1981	.96*	.60	.01	1.82	.70	-.020	.03*	.84	1.34	GLS

Note: All coefficients are unstandardized regression coefficients. Statistical significance is indicated by an asterisk (*); for all periods up through 1969, * = t ≥ 1.35; for all equations beyond 1969, * = t ≥ 2.00.
Generalized least squares (GLS) estimators are: AR(1) for the periods 1948–60, . . . , 1948–65; and Robust Error MA(1) for the periods 1948–74, . . . , 1948–81.

Table 3. *Period-specific estimates for public sector strike militancy*

| Explanatory variables | Historical periods[a] | |
	1948–1969	1970–1981
Union density (t-1)	.14[b]	–3.04
Unemployment (t)	.39	6.24
Wage deprivation (t-1)	.74	– .18
Public Law 330 (t)	–2.92*	. . .[c]
Democratic Party (t)	.97	9.26*
Protests ([t]+[t-1])	.01	–.21
Urban revolts ([t]+[t-1])	.05*	.02
Constant	–14.02	104.12
Adjusted R-squared	.52	.48
Durbin-Watson d	1.83	1.99
Estimator	OLS	OLS

Notes:

[a] The Chow test for differences between period-specific parameter regimes was statistically significant: $F = 8.01$ (degrees of freedom = 7, 20) significant at $p = .0001$. F-tests for equivalence of protest and revolt slopes between periods were also significantly different.

[b] Unstandardized regression coefficients; * indicates coefficient at least twice its standard error.

[c] Public Law 330 is a constant for this period.

earlier, one of the basic uses of TRR results is to aid in the process of periodization. The issue is whether our time-series observations come from fundamentally different historical periods. Is there a point within our overall time frame in which one causal structure bifurcates into two (or more) regimes? We examined this question of structural shift using a variety of different forms of statistical evidence. Chow (F-) tests indicated statistically significant shifts (at probability levels of $p \leq .02$) for each possible break point between 1969 and 1973 with the most salient break occurring between 1969 and 1970.[19]

Table 3 reports the results of our public sector strike model estimated for the two historical periods (1948–1969 and 1970–1981) suggested by structural shift tests. Are these numerical differences historically explicable? The real

19. The Chow test is designed to test the homogeneity assumption as null hypothesis. In other words, when applied to the estimates for the two periods in Table 3, it gives an F-test statistic that gauges whether the coefficients in the two periods belong to the same overall historical period – 1948 to 1981 – or to two separate historical sub-periods. For a discussion of the Chow test, see Gregory C. Chow, "Tests of Equality Between Sets of Coefficients in Two Linear Regressions", *Econometrica*, 28 (1960), pp. 591–605, or consult any standard econometrics text. We examined other evidence for heterogeneity, including: TRR patterns for the backward- and diagonal-moving (employing 11-year windows as in Table 1, Panel C) strategies; F-tests on contrasts between protest and revolt slopes from the full period model and forward-moving TRR patterns; and Quandt's log-likelihood ratio procedure. All evidence suggested that the most significant break point was located within the 1969 to 1971 period.

issue here *is* the social historical significance of these patterns and inferences and such questions cannot be addressed by simply pointing to the coefficients themselves or even to the statistical significance of their differences across time. We believe the pronounced historical variability across the two period-specific equations in Table 3 is, in fact, historically significant and theoretically interpretable, representative of important social change in movement activity and in key institutions. We will return to the issue of social historical interpretation below.

Temporally local effect trajectories

The main question underlying the estimates presented in Table 3 continues to be what factors account for variation in public sector strike militancy within different historical contexts. But the TRR results can also be employed to gauge more temporally local influence. Such an approach is useful when the analysis focuses on the temporal trajectory of specific relations. For example, what does the trajectory of annualized influences of PROTESTS and REVOLTS on labor militancy look like over our time frame? What social processes, historical contexts and events alter the contour of these relationships?

There are a variety of ways to estimate temporally local influence. Using the forward-moving TRR results, we employ year-specific elasticities[20] as our annualized measure of militancy spillover. This strategy is simultaneously sensitive to changing parameter regimes as well as the relative *pace*[21] of insurgent activities and labor militancy at each moment (year) in time. It is especially useful for gauging historical contingency as temporally local effects in analyses where the temporal pace of collective actions matters and varies dramatically through history. The result allows an overall view

---

20. Elasticities are interpreted as the percentage increase in the dependent variable that results from a 1 per cent increase in the independent variable and are usually formed as the product of the unstandardized regression coefficient times the ratio of the mean of the independent to the mean of the dependent variable. But they can be evaluated at other points in the distributions, too. In algebraic terms, the year-specific elasticities derived from TRR results are defined as: $e_{yx(t)} = b_{yx(t)} * (x_t/y_t)$. This is a modification of the implications of nonlinear regression models discussed in Ross Stolzenberg, "The Measurement and Decomposition of Causal Effects in Nonlinear and Nonadditive Models", in Karl F. Schuessler (ed.), *Sociological Methodology 1980* (San Francisco, 1980), pp. 459–488. The year-specific elasticity scales the TRR regression coefficient in a year-specific (i.e. temporally local) manner rather than the conventional practice of scaling by the global moments of the respective distributions of X and Y (e.g. means for conventional elasticities or standard deviations for standardized regression coefficients).

21. "Pace", or the frequency of action or events within a given time period, is one of the key temporal dimensions of social action central to historical sociological inquiry: see Ron Aminzade, "Historical Sociology and Time", *Sociological Methods and Research*, 20 (1992), pp. 456–480.

of the process relations while preserving the temporally-specific elements that give protest waves their typically explosive and nonlinear qualities.[22]

Year-specific elasticities for the spillover impact of civil rights insurgencies on public sector labor militancy are mapped in Figure 1. The cross-temporal trajectories for both protests are strikingly nonlinear. For example, the peak spillover year for PROTESTS was 1961. In that year labor militancy increased approximately 1.6 per cent for each 1 per cent increase in PRO-TESTS. In many other years – those prior to 1960 and those after 1965 – the elasticities were effectively zero. Protest effects are largely concentrated between 1960 and 1965, the heyday of the Southern civil rights movement, and decline dramatically after 1965.[23] The urban ghetto revolt effect on public sector militancy explodes in 1966 and weakens gradually from 1967 through 1973,[24] the period in which the Black Power phase of the movement was strongest. The labor militancy-inducing influence dies out after that point.

The results in Figure 1 illustrate a simple but important point: for a social movement to produce substantial militancy spillover on the collective actions of other social movements, substantial levels of militant action may be required, perhaps even major waves of such action. McAdam[25] has argued that the pace of a social movement – its ability to mobilize resources, sustain critical consciousness and maintain the overall energy of the struggle – is heavily dependent on "tactical innovation", the ability of movement partici-pants to produce novel forms of collective action that catch the counter-movement forces off-balance, garner successes, and inspire continuing par-ticipation and resource flows. In tandem, PROTESTS and REVOLTS contributed significant militancy spillover from the streets into the public sector workplace for the entire decade of the 1960s and into at least the early 1970s.

22. On the wave character of movements, see Sidney Tarrow, *The Power of Movement*, (Cambridge, 1994); Doug McAdam, "Tactical Innovation and the Pace of Insurgency", *American Sociological Review*, 48 (1983), pp. 735–754; Larry W. Isaac, Debra Street and Stan Knapp, "Analyz-ing Historical Contingency with Formal Methods: The Case of the 'Relief Explosion' and 1968", *Sociological Methods and Research*, 23 (1994), pp. 114–141.

23. See Doug McAdam, *Political Process and the Development of Black Insurgency 1930–1970*, (Chicago, 1982).

24. Note that the patterning of the urban revolt effects on labor militancy die out when mapped with the year-specific elasticities (Figure 1), but appear to persist all the way through the 1970s in the forward-moving TRR results (Table 2). This difference rests on the way the year-specific elasticities rely directly on annual pace of insurgency to estimate an effect while the TRR coef-ficients alone are estimated across a series of years. The petering out of the revolt effects is also consistent with patterns from backward-moving regressions, which are not shown here except for the 1970–1981 period results shown in Table 3.

25. McAdam, "Tactical Innovation".

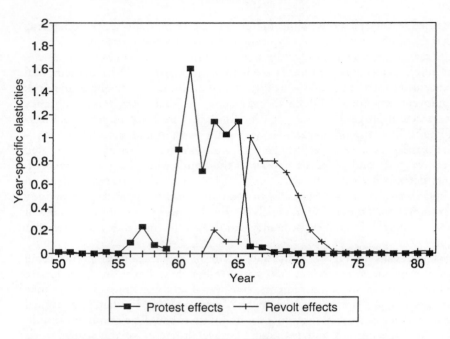

Figure 1. Civil rights movement spillover effects (US public sector strike militancy)

Periodization again

How do we interpret the preponderance of evidence to this point? To answer this question we return to the issue of periodization first raised in discussion of Table 3. The contour of the localized influences of PRO-TESTS and REVOLTS (Figure 1), the TRR results through the early 1960s (Table 2) and the historical record combine to suggest that the twofold periodization in Table 3 may be a bit too crude. In particular, we were concerned that the length of the first period (1948–1969) might jeopardize important historical change and nuance in the relations of interest as both key institutions and the civil rights movement changed through time.

Table 4 summarizes our findings on civil rights impact on labor militancy within a more refined periodization that breaks the 1948 to 1969 frame into two shorter sub-periods: 1948 to 1959 and 1960 to 1969. In addition to the statistical information, this periodization is grounded in both the institutional configuration comprising changing phases in the industrial relations regime and in the development of the civil rights movement.

During the first period (1948–1959), the industrial relations regime was marked by a general "accord" between capital and labor that was designed, among other things, to contain labor militancy. At that point, the civil rights movement was in its early stages with much of the activity centered

Table 4. *Summary of civil rights insurgency effects on public sector labor militancy in more refined historical periods*

	Historical periods		
Years[a]	1948–1959	1960–1969	1970–1981
Regime phase[b]	Accord	Accord/slowdown	Slowdown/decay
Civil rights movement phase[c]	Emergence	Heyday & Black Power	Decline & backlash
Protests[d]	−NS	+S	−NS
Revolts[d]	−NS	+S	+NS

Notes:

[a] The periodization is based on statistical and theoretical-historical information.

[b] The industrial relations "regime phases" – "accord", "accord/slowdown" and "slowdown/decay" – are based on D. Gordon, R. Edwards and M. Reich, *Segmented Work, Divided Workers* (Cambridge, 1982), ch. 5. Their periodization of the consolidation and break-up of the post-war industrial relations regime in the US is: "accord" between labor and capital (1948–1966), "slowdown" or transition phase (1967–1973), and "decay" of the regime (1974–early 1980s).

[c] These designations refer to qualitatively distinct phases in the post-war civil rights movement: "emergence" during the 1950s; the "heyday" of the movement during the first half of the 1960s; and the Black Power phase during the last half of the 1960s; by the 1970s, the movement is in serious decline with beginnings of racial backlash against movement gains.

[d] "Protest" and "urban revolt" effects are summarized for each period with qualitative designations derived from the quantitative estimates: −NS = negative but not significant; +NS = positive but not significant; −S = negative and significant; and +S = positive and significant.

on court-ordered desegregation actions and some community bus boycotts. The movement had not yet hit its massive insurgency take-off phase. Both the accord and low levels of mass insurgency account for the null PROTEST and REVOLT effects during this period.

By 1960, the mass insurgency phase of the movement had opened with the sit-ins, freedom rides, community protest tactics spreading like wildfire across the South. From 1960 to 1965, heroic civil rights protests demonstrations to dismantle the long-standing politics of Jim Crow institutions were being launched at an astounding pace. It was during these years that public sector workers, including teachers, postal employees and others, were showing signs of becoming increasingly militant.[26] In some locations it was becoming difficult to separate workers' struggles from civil rights struggles. The militant actions of municipal sanitation workers in Memphis during 1968 and the Charleston hospital workers a year later are just two of the more well-known examples of

26. Michael Goldfield, "Public Sector Union Growth", *Policy Studies Journal* (Winter 1990), pp. 404–420.

such militant fusion.[27] During the decade of the 1960s, both PROTESTS and REVOLTS had positive, significant effects on public sector labor militancy. Civil rights movement spillover was greatest when the movement was peaking and the accord was beginning to weaken.

The final period, 1970 to 1981, is marked by further decline in the accords and "decay" after 1973 as the assault on labor grew.[28] The civil rights movement itself had largely folded by 1970 and a growing racialized backlash against movement gains was beginning to appear. For example, by the early 1970s there were signs that the Republican party was mounting a racialized political strategy to foster a deeper racial division among the electorate as a way to dampen support for the Democratic party.[29] In 1971, the US Congress passed the Postal Service Reorganization Act to contain worker militancy that had spawned a massive general wildcat strike the previous year in which some of the most militant leaders were African-American men. The reorganization of the postal service contained a distinct worker fragmenting and racially divisive quality to it.[30] Overall the serious decline in movement activity coupled with the rise of a racialized backlash appear to have been sufficient to offset the favorable conditions for worker militancy provided by further decay of the accord.

We began our illustration by asking if civil rights militancy might have spilled over into public sector workplaces of America to fuel the "labor revolt" of the 1960s and early 1970s. Although partial and preliminary, our evidence suggests an affirmative answer to that question. However, this spillover effect does not appear to have been an institutionally general or temporally even outgrowth of the civil rights movement. Instead, it was profoundly contingent in quality. The unevenness of militancy diffusion was contingent on the tactical form (PROTESTS and REVOLTS) and pace of collective action waves, historical context (phase of civil rights movement and industrial regime change), and economic sector.[31] These findings should encourage further investigation and urge that a social movement hypothesis be added to the stock of standard strike theories.

27. On Memphis, see Joan Turner Beifuss, *At The River I Stand: Memphis, The 1968 Strike, and Martin Luther King* (New York, 1989); on Charleston, see Leon Fink and Brian Greenberg, *Upheaval in the Quiet Zone: A History of Hospital Workers' Union, Local 1199* (Urbana, 1989).

28. See, for example, Rick Fantasia, "The Assault on American Labor", in George Ritzer and Craig Calhoun (eds), *Social Problems* (New York, 1993).

29. On the decline of the black movement, see McAdam, *Political Process*; on racialized politics, see Thomas Edsall and Mary Edsall, *Chain Reaction* (New York, 1992); Jill Quadagno, *The Color of Welfare* (New York, 1994).

30. Peter Rachleff, "Working the Fast Lane: Jobs, Technology, and Scientific Management in the U.S. Postal Service", *Radical America*, 16, 1 and 2 (1982).

31. Other analyses, not reported here due to space limitations, indicated that militancy spillover did not take place in any systematic manner for the private sector as a whole: reported in Isaac *et al.*, "Intermovement Relations".

IMPLICATIONS FOR SOCIAL HISTORICAL INQUIRY

Relationships between social historical processes often change through time. When they are forced to be constant, when historical context and timing of important events are ignored, we miss crucial opportunities in social historical inquiry. TRR maps relationships between social processes in a way that *allows* them to change historically and pushes the analyst to be sensitive to context and timing of events.

What does this mean for social historical inquiry more broadly? We see several important implications. First, rather than reducing notions of causality to single coefficient magnitudes, TRR motivates attention to relations between quantitative variation and qualitative change, even discontinuity, in social processes. Allowing quantitative relations to change through time means removing the constraint of constant cross-temporal meaning in social actions and events. This, in turn, leads to a greater concern with the interpretive mode of social historical research.

Second, if one of the central challenges to social historical research is to integrate long-term, continuous, social processes with faster-moving, shorter-term (even explosive) events, then TRR offers one potential bridge over this analytic gulf.[32] Long-term trends, medium-term periodizations and transformative events can all be represented in TRR models.

Third, in promoting concern with the relation between the temporally general and temporally particular, TRR centers attention on specific time points as "unusual" (or "deviant") cases. Identifying such time periods creates the opportunity to theorize, for example, a particular year as a moment in which a conjuncture of events produced a transformation in a particular regime or other social arrangement. This dual focus allows generality to be informed by historical grounding in transformative moments while the uniqueness of those moments is also preserved. Within the context of quantitative time-series analyses, TRR generally allows greater access to an "eventful temporality".[33]

Fourth, the forms of causality that can be mapped with TRR afford the analyst greater opportunities for narrative flexibility in the explanation of historical processes. Theorizing historical contingency as temporally heterogeneous parameters points the narrative away from a representation of historical process as simple seamless linear continuity. TRR's potential for capturing changing nonlinear relations in historical process refocuses attention on human agency in social change by emphasizing indeterminacy and opportunities for creative action. Social movements, and the relations between them, are perhaps among the most dramatic examples of this kind of social historical process.

Finally, these methodological implications are consistent with much of

32. Sewell, "Collective Violence and Collective Loyalties"; Isaac and Leicht, "Regimes of Power".
33. Sewell, "Three Temporalities".

the redirection or "historical turn" that has marked the contemporary human sciences. This redirection has developed from the theoretical reconfiguration of time, causality and narrative in social historical inquiry. The primary achievement of TRR in this effort is, we believe, its capacity to allow concrete (i.e. temporally local) conditions of social organization to play their role in a mode of argument that integrates the determinant and contingent, the explanatory and interpretive, in the study of social historical process.[34]

Although far from resolving all the thorny issues of social historical inquiry, and in fact raising many new problems that the analyst must address, TRR strategies create opportunities that are otherwise closed-off by methodological fiat in conventional time-series practice. None of what we have identified as merits of this approach result automatically from applying a new technique. TRR has been available for over two decades and others have applied these procedures without invoking the significance of historical time nor the historicization of methods as a goal. However, by grounding its use in understandings of historical time combined with detailed forays into relevant historical records, we can exploit TRR's potential for historical exploration and explanation, thereby moderating some of the ahistorical features that plague conventional time-series analysis. We believe that this can contribute to both better quantitative social historical research and the kind of social theory that can explain and interpret concrete historical processes and events.

APPENDIX. VARIABLE DEFINITIONS AND DATA SOURCES

Public Sector Strike Density: Number of strikes per million workers in the public sector (federal, state, local) labor force. *Source:* AWS.

I. *Organizational Resource Strength*
Public Sector Union Density: Percentage of the public sector labor force unionized. *Source:* HS, SA.

II. *Labor Market Conditions and Economic Hardship*
Public Sector Unemployment: Percentage of the public sector labor force unemployed. *Source:* HS, SA.
Wage Deprivation: Public sector average annual wage as a percentage of unionized private sector average annual wage + percentage decline in public sector average annual real wages for decline years (non-decline years coded zero). *Source*: constructed from data in HS, SA, SCB.

---

34. Isaac, "Transforming Localities".

III. *Legal-Institutional Framework of Labor-Management Relations*
Public Law 330: Binary variable indicating the pre- and post-"Public Law 330" passed in 1955. PL 330 made it a felony to strike, to assert the right to strike, or to belong to an organization that asserts the right to strike; 1948–1954 = 0; 1955–1981 = 1. *Source:* constructed from Goldfield.

IV. *Electoral Political Environment*
Democratic Party Office Strength: Sum of (a) House (= proportion of non-Dixiecrat Democratic representatives + 1 if Democrats were the majority in the House; (b) Senate (= proportion of non-Dixiecrat Democratic senators + 1 if Democrats were the majority in the Senate; and (c) Presidency (= 1 for Democrat; 0 for Republican). "Dixiecrat" is defined as those legislators from Southern, "right-to-work" states. *Source:* constructed from data in HS, SA.

V. *Civil Rights Movement Field*
Protests: Two-year moving sum ($[t]+[t-1]$) of the annual pace or frequency of civil rights protest demonstrations. "Protest" is defined (following Burstein) as a "public, manifestly political action by at least five people on behalf of the rights of minorities". *Source:* NYTI.
Urban Revolts: Two-year moving sum ($[t]+[t-1]$) of the annual pace or frequency of black urban revolts ("riots"), defined (following Isaac and Kelly) as a black-initiated collective action with a minimum of thirty participants and some amount of violence and/or property damage. *Source:* NYTI.

Data Source Abbreviations:

AWS = US Bureau of Labor Statistics, *Analysis of Work Stoppages.*
Burstein = "Public Opinion, Demonstrations, and the Passage of Antidiscrimination Legislation", *Public Opinion Quarterly,* 43 (1979), pp. 157–172.
Goldfield = "Public Sector Union Growth and Public Policy", *Policy Studies Journal,* 18 (1990), pp. 404–420.
HS = US Bureau of the Census, *Historical Statistics of the United States: Colonial Times to 1970.*
Isaac and Kelly = "Racial Insurgency, the State, and Welfare Expansion", *American Journal of Sociology,* 86 (1981), pp. 1348–1386.
NYTI = *New York Times, Annual Index.*
SA = US Bureau of the Census, *Statistical Abstract of the United States.*
SCB = Bureau of Economic Analysis, *Survey of Current Business.*

ANNOTATED BIBLIOGRAPHY

This selective bibliography contains only substantive applications of various TRR strategies. Major technical expositions are cited in footnotes 8 and 9.

Beck, E.M. and Stewart Tolnay, "The Killing Fields of the Deep South: The Market for Cotton and the Lynching of Blacks, 1882–1930", *American Sociological Review*, 55 (1990), pp. 526–539.
The authors employ a diagonal-moving TRR strategy to map and interpret the temporal variability in the cotton price impact on the lynching of blacks in the deep South from 1882 to 1930.

Beck, Nathaniel, "Presidential Influence on the Federal Reserve in the 1970s", *American Journal of Political Science*, 26 (1982), pp. 415–445.
This paper examines presidential influence on Federal Reserve monetary policy in the 1970s. The author employs diagonal-moving TRR strategy as well as several tests for structural shifts.

Blau, Judith, "The Disjunctive History of U.S. Museums, 1869–1980", *Social Forces*, 70 (1991), pp. 87–106.
TRR is employed (but not presented) as an aid in periodizing the history of US museum foundings. The author uncovers and analyzes four distinct eras: 1869–1899, 1900–1930, 1931–1959 and 1960–1980.

Griffin, Larry J. and Larry W. Isaac, "Recursive Regression and the Historical Use of 'Time' in Time-Series Analysis of Historical Process", *Historical Methods*, 25 (1992), pp. 166–179.
The authors discuss the basic rationale and logic of TRR strategies. Empirical analyses of US strikes and unionization processes between 1904 and 1945 are presented to illustrate the method.

Isaac, Larry W. and Larry J. Griffin, "Ahistoricism in Time-Series Analyses of Historical Process: Critique, Redirection, and Illustrations from U.S. Labor History", *American Sociological Review*, 54 (1989), pp. 873–890.
This paper lays the foundation for taking time and temporally-moving time-series approaches seriously in historical sociology. The authors illustrate their argument by analyzing examples of historical contingency in the US strike-unionization relation from the 1880s to 1980 using temporally-moving covariance analysis.

Isaac, Larry W., Susan M. Carlson and Mary P. Mathis, "Quality of Quantity in Comparative/Historical Analysis: Temporally Changing Wage Labor Regimes in the United States and Sweden", in Thomas Janoski and Alexander Hicks (eds), *The Comparative Political Economy of the Welfare State* (Cambridge, 1994), pp. 93–135.
The authors argue that time-varying parameter approaches can be used to bridge the gulf between qualitative and quantitative analyses in comparative historical research. Empirical illustrations are presented using temporally-moving covariance analysis of the unemployment-wage

relation in the context of changing regimes in Sweden and the United States.

Isaac, Larry W., Debra Street and Stan J. Knapp, "Analyzing Historical Contingency with Formal Methods: The Case of the 'Relief Explosion' and 1968", *Sociological Methods & Research*, 23 (1994), pp. 114–141.
The authors argue that the forms of historical contingency captured by time-varying parameter models and those produced by event sequence approaches can be profitably combined. The argument is illustrated with a multi-level analysis of the "relief explosion" in the late 1960s United States: event-structure analysis is used to unpack and interpret the sequence of events behind a major quantitative turning point revealed in a TRR analysis.

Isaac, Larry W. and Kevin T. Leicht, "Regimes of Power and the Power of Analytic Regimes: Explaining U.S. Military Procurement Keynesianism as Historical Process", *Historical Methods*, 30 (1997), pp. 28–45.
The authors highlight the importance of historical context and historical timing of events in explaining key aspects of US military spending during the cold war era. The empirical analysis features a forward-moving TRR approach that links a major quantitative turning point in the corporate profit-military spending relation to the McNamara-Kennedy reorganization of the Department of Defense. A second-order regression and historical narrative are employed to explain the cross-temporal variability in the key profit-military spending relation.

McCammon, Holly J., "From Repressive Intervention to Integrative Prevention: The U.S. State's Legal Management of Labor Militancy, 1881–1978", *Social Forces*, 71 (1993), pp. 569–601.
A variety of models of labor militancy are presented with key regression coefficients estimated and plotted from both forward- and backward-moving TRRs. Tests for structural shifts are employed and major turning points in the mid-1930s are used to periodize models and explanations into pre- and post-Wagner Act eras.

Myers, Martha A., "Inequality and the Punishment of Minor Offenders in the Early 20th Century", *Law & Society Review*, 27 (1993), pp. 313–343.
The author uses a diagonal-moving TRR strategy to examine historical change in the effects of cotton price on incarceration rates in Georgia from the 1890s to the 1930s. The cross-temporal effects are presented specific to race and form (chain gang versus penitentiary) of incarceration.

Rubin, Beth and Brian Smith, "Forged Ties: Cooperation and Conflict in the Metals Industry", *Social Science Research*, 21 (1992), pp. 115–133.
The authors employ the logic of forward-moving TRR to an event-history analysis of strike settlements in the US primary metals industry from 1960 to 1977.

Woolley, John T., "Partisan Manipulation of the Economy: Another Look

at Monetary Policy with Moving Regression", *Journal of Politics*, 50 (1988), pp. 335–360.
The author studies presidential administration manipulation of economic policy employing diagonal-moving TRR. Primary focus is on the changing inflation and unemployment effects on the federal funds interest rate. The importance of timing of effects and TRR's capabilities in this regard are indicated.

International Review of Social History 43 (1998), Supplement, pp. 33–55
© 1998 Internationaal Instituut voor Sociale Geschiedenis

Using Event History Analysis in Historical Research: With Illustrations from a Study of the Passage of Women's Protective Legislation*

HOLLY J. MCCAMMON

Historians and social scientists often investigate the conditions that influence the occurrence of particular events. For instance, a researcher might be concerned with the causes of revolutionary action in some countries or the forces that unleash racial rioting in major cities. Or perhaps the researcher wishes to examine why industrial workers decide to strike or what prompts policy-makers to pass new legislation.[1] In each of these examples, a qualitative shift occurs, from a circumstance without racial rioting in a particular city, for instance, to one with racial rioting. Event history analysis can aid researchers in uncovering the conditions that lead to such a shift.

Event history analysis is a quantitative method that offers researchers a means of explaining why such events occur. A myriad of types of events can be analyzed using event history analysis. Suitable kinds of events are those marked by a definite and somewhat abrupt transition from one state to another, such as the founding or collapse of an organization or the emergence of a social movement. More gradual transitions from one state to another where there is difficulty pinpointing the moment in time of the transition are usually not amenable to event history analysis.

Event history analysis utilizes event history data which are composed of *event histories* for the nations, organizations, groups, or even individuals examined in the analysis. These event histories are over-time records that reveal when, if at all, the event being studied occurs for each of the cases included in the analysis. In addition to the event histories, additional data for each observation on a variety of factors believed to influence the occurrence of the event are included in the analysis (the specific nature of the data is discussed in greater detail below). Thus, if the event of interest is the transition of a polity from authoritarianism to democracy, not only will the researchers need information on the point in time at which the transition occurred, but they will also need longitudinal (i.e. over-time) data on the factors likely to have facilitated or even hindered this change in government. In short, then, if a researcher is interested in the question of why a historical event occurs for some cases but not for others and if the researcher

---

* I am grateful to Larry Griffin, Marcel van der Linden and Karen Campbell for comments on an earlier draft.
1. For a variety of historical studies using event history analysis concerning these and other issues, see the annotated bibliography at the end of this piece.

has longitudinal and quantifiable data on the timing of the events and similar data on the factors likely to have influenced the occurrence of the event, then event history analysis can be a useful tool for the researcher in explaining why such events occur.

Event history analysis is useful because it can explain why such events occur. But its utility also lies in the way in which it allows researchers to explain events. While focusing on a single case permits researchers to gather detailed insights into social dynamics, the case study does not usually provide a *systematic* assessment of the influences necessary for an event to occur.[2] Because event history analysis includes both cases that have and have not experienced the event, a comparison of such cases can be made to determine those conditions that are and are not necessary for the event to occur. In this sense, then, a far more systematic determination of the causes of the event is possible.[3] The "negative" cases – those for which the event did not occur – are not excluded from the analysis (this kind of exclusion occurs almost by definition in most case studies), and the valuable lessons such negative cases offer about the reasons why the event could not occur are incorporated into event history analysis.

Here I provide a discussion of how one can use event history analysis to explain, using a systematic comparison of cases in which the event occurs and cases in which the event does not occur, why the particular historical event happens. I begin with a discussion of the nature of the *data* necessary for event history analysis, then turn to the *statistical technique* used in the analysis and the *interpretation of the results*. Finally, a number of *complexities* associated with event history analysis are explored. For instance, what can be done to analyze events that repeat themselves or multiple kinds of events? Throughout this discussion, the data needs and the method are illustrated with data and an analysis concerning the passage of protective legislation for women in the United States around the turn of the century. These data, drawn from previous research,[4] are particularly suited to event history analysis given that the adoption of new law is a historical event.

2. Susan Olzak, "Analysis of Events in the Study of Collective Action", *Annual Review of Sociology*, 15 (1989), p. 121. Also, as Stanley Lieberson ("Small N's and Big Conclusions: An Examination of the Reasoning in Comparative Studies Based on a Small Number of Cases", in Charles C. Ragin and Howard S. Becker (eds), *What Is a Case? Exploring the Foundations of Social Inquiry* (New York, 1992), p. 105) discusses, studies involving a single case are best for revealing that "a given phenomenon exists in some setting" and are perhaps less useful for explaining causal processes.
3. This is true generally of methods that rely on comparative analyses such as Qualitative Comparative Analysis (see Ragin elsewhere in this volume) and Millsean methods of comparison.
4. Holly J. McCammon, "The Politics of Protection: State Minimum Wage and Maximum Hours Laws for Women in the United States, 1870–1930", *The Sociological Quarterly*, 36 (1995), pp. 217–249; idem, "Protection for Whom? Maximum Hours Laws and Women's Employment in the United States, 1880–1920", *Work and Occupations*, 23 (1996), pp. 132–164.

THE DATA FOR EVENT HISTORY ANALYSIS

A unique feature of event history analysis compared to many other quantitative methods is that it employs data that are simultaneously cross-sectional and longitudinal. Thus the method analyzes both cross-sectional and temporal variation. To put this in more concrete terms, consider data concerning the passage of women's protective legislation. To study the enactment of this legislation using event history analysis, data are needed both over time and across multiple cases. Women's protective laws, enacted – at least ostensibly – to protect women in the workplace, were passed in many states in the US around the turn of the century.[5] The event history measures, then, not only are over time, denoting the year in which a protective law was passed, but also are across observations or, in this case, across US states (i.e. the data are for Alabama, Iowa, New Jersey, etc.).

Figure 1 provides a visual representation of the general structure of the data matrix. For each measure or variable, including both the dependent variable (which indicates the year in which a protective law was enacted in a state – although see the discussion below of the precise nature of the dependent variable) and the various explanatory variables, information is given both across years and across states. The unit of analysis, then, in this study (or each cell in Figure 1) is the "state-year". The unit of analysis for event history data always designates both a cross-sectional observation and a time unit.

The level of over-time aggregation in event history data (i.e. is decade-level data used? annual data? monthly data?) ideally should be determined by the nature of the research question or by the time frame in which the event of interest occurs. For instance, the state legislatures that enacted women's protective laws met annually (or sometimes biennially) and thus annual-level data are used in this analysis. More frequently, however, the over-time level of aggregation in the data is determined by the nature of the data available to the researcher. Annual data, in particular, are frequently used in quantitative historical research because of their availability from governmental sources.[6] Researchers, however, are sometimes able to construct their own data sets or specific variables from information gleaned

---

5. Elizabeth Brandeis, "Labor Legislation", in John R. Commons (ed.), *History of Labor in the United States, 1896–1932*, vol. 4 (New York, 1935), pp. 397–697. In the research presented in this paper, women's protective legislation includes maximum hours laws (that restricted the maximum number of hours women could work), minimum wage laws and laws prohibiting night work among women.

6. See, for example: US Bureau of the Census, *Historical Statistics of the United States: Colonial Times to 1970* (Washington, DC, 1975); US Bureau of the Census, *Statistical Abstract of the United States* (Washington, DC, various years); President of the United States, *Economic Report of the President* (Washington, DC, various years); US Department of Labor, *Handbook of Labor Statistics* (Washington, DC, various years).

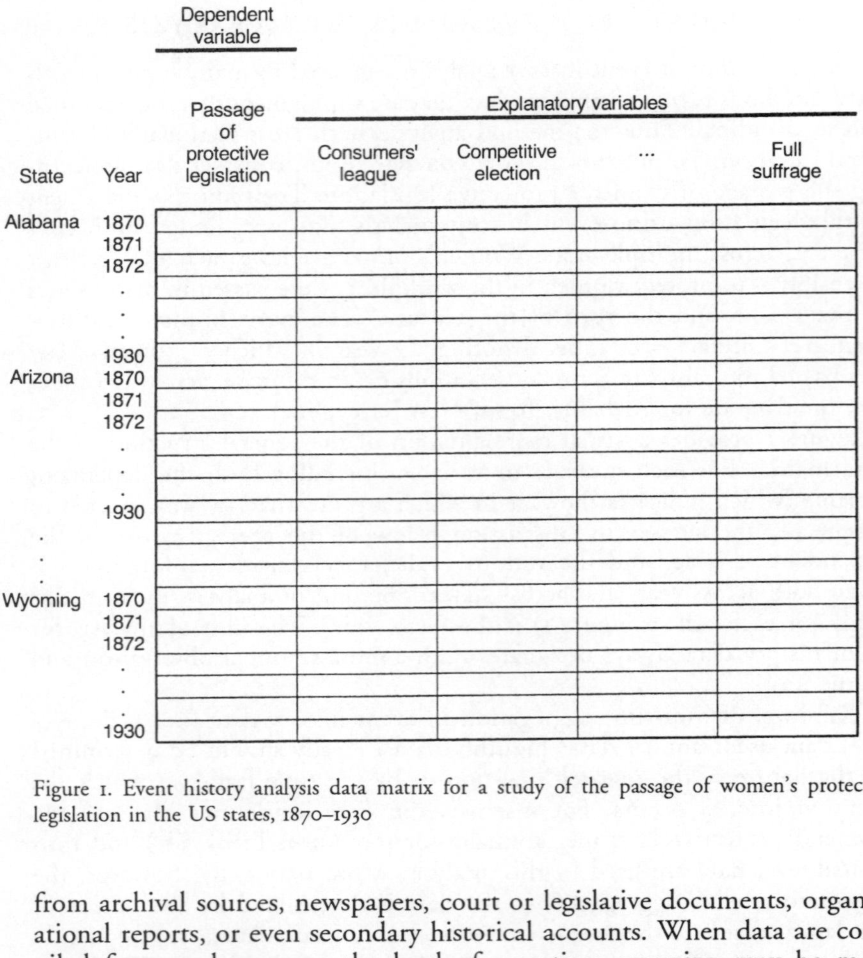

		Dependent variable	Explanatory variables			
State	Year	Passage of protective legislation	Consumers' league	Competitive election	...	Full suffrage
Alabama	1870					
	1871					
	1872					
	.					
	.					
	.					
	1930					
Arizona	1870					
	1871					
	1872					
	.					
	.					
	1930					
.						
.						
.						
Wyoming	1870					
	1871					
	1872					
	.					
	.					
	1930					

Figure 1. Event history analysis data matrix for a study of the passage of women's protective legislation in the US states, 1870–1930

from archival sources, newspapers, court or legislative documents, organizational reports, or even secondary historical accounts. When data are compiled from such sources, the level of over-time grouping may be more specific than annual-level measures. One word of caution, however. In some cases a higher level of aggregation makes more sense than data indicating the exact timing of the occurrence of the event. Consider the protective legislation data which are annual-level. Daily or even monthly data concerning the dates of passage of such laws would confound the analysis with state-to-state differences in when state legislatures meet, which is not of theoretical interest in the analysis.[7] Thus, annual-level measures for this analysis are desirable.

Given that event history analysis analyzes a shift from one condition to another, the dependent variable is coded as a binary or dichotomous vari-

7. Eliza K. Pavalko, "State Timing of Policy Adoption: Workmen's Compensation in the United States, 1909–1929", *American Journal of Sociology*, 95 (1989), p. 601.

able. That is, the measure is a simple dummy variable taking the value of "0" prior to the occurrence of the event and the value of "1" once the event occurs. The dependent variable for the event history analysis of the passage of women's protective legislation is assigned the value of "0" for all years prior to the passage of a particular state's protective law and "1" for the year in which the law is enacted. The years after the law is enacted and before the end of the period of analysis are coded as missing values on the dependent variable and thus are not included in the analysis.[8]

An example will make this clearer. The period of analysis for the protective legislation study is 1870 to 1930, and California, for instance, passed a protective law in 1911.[9] The dependent variable for this state is assigned the value of "0" from the beginning of the analysis in 1870 until 1910. A value of "1" is assigned to 1911, and missing values are assigned to all years in the 1912–1930 period. The dependent variable is constructed in a similar manner for all states. For states that did not pass a protective law (the negative cases), the value of "0" is assigned for all years from 1870 through 1930.

While the dependent variable is coded as a dichotomous variable, the actual value of the dependent variable for the event history analysis *per se* is the *hazard rate* or, as it is sometimes known, the *transition rate*. After the researcher enters the dichotomous variable into the analysis, the event history statistical software (such as SPSS or SAS) computes the hazard rate. The hazard or transition rate is the probability that the event (i.e. the passage of law) will occur at time "t" (i.e. during a particular year) given that the event has not yet occurred for that case (i.e. for that state) or, in other words, given that the case is still at risk of the event occurring.[10] In short, the hazard rate measures and the event history analyzes the likelihood of the event occurring at a particular point in time.

The hazard rate is, however, reasonably straightforward to compute by hand. For each year, one simply divides the number of events (i.e. the number of laws passed) by the number of observations at risk of the event occurring (i.e. the number of states not yet having passed a protective law). The number of observations at risk of the event occurring is the risk set.[11] Table 1 provides the annual number of laws passed (column 3) and the associated risk set (column 4) and hazard rate (column 5) for some of the years in the protective legislation data (periods when the hazard rate is constant over time are left out to simplify the table). In 1870 when no state had yet enacted protective legislation, the hazard rate is 0 (column 3) divided

---

8. Note that this also means that data on the explanatory variables are not needed for the years for which the dependent variable is assigned missing values. The explanatory variables can be assigned missing values for these years as well.

9. Below I discuss why the period 1870–1930 was chosen for the analysis.

10. Paul D. Allison, *Event History Analysis: Regression For Longitudinal Event Data* (Newbury Park, 1984), p. 16; Kazuo Yamaguchi, *Event History Analysis* (Newbury Park, 1991), pp. 3, 9–10.

11. Allison, *Event History Analysis*, p. 16.

Table 1. *The risk set and hazard rate*

(1) Year	(2) Total number of states	(3) Number of laws passed	(4) Risk set or number of states at risk of passing law	(5) Hazard rate
1870	38	0	38	.0
1871	38	0	38	.0
1872	38	0	38	.0
1873	38	0	38	.0
1874	38	1	38	.026
1875	38	0	37	.0
⋮	⋮	⋮	⋮	⋮
1884	38	0	37	.0
1885	38	1	37	.027
1886	38	1	36	.028
1887	38	3	35	.086
1888	38	0	32	.0
1889	42	0	36	.0
1890	44	1	38	.026
1891	44	0	37	.0
1892	44	1	37	.027
1893	44	0	36	.0
1894	44	0	36	.0
1895	44	0	36	.0
1896	45	0	37	.0
1897	45	1	37	.027
1898	45	0	36	.0
1899	45	3	36	.083
1900	45	0	33	.0
1901	45	1	33	.030
1902	45	0	32	.0
1903	45	2	32	.063
1904	45	0	30	.0
1905	45	0	30	.0
1906	45	0	30	.0
1907	46	2	31	.065
1908	46	0	29	.0
1909	46	3	29	.103
1910	46	0	26	.0
1911	46	5	26	.192
1912	48	3	23	.130
1913	48	6	20	.300
1914	48	1	14	.071
1915	48	3	13	.231
1916	48	0	10	.0
1917	48	1	10	.100
1918	48	0	9	.0
1919	48	1	9	.111
1920	48	0	8	.0
⋮	⋮	⋮	⋮	⋮

by 38 (column 4).[12] In 1874, when Massachusetts passed the first protective law, the hazard rate is 1 divided by 38. One can see in Table 1 that at the end of each time period (e.g. each year), the risk set is reduced by the number of observations (e.g. states) experiencing the event during that year. In addition, one can see the variation in the hazard rate over time. For these data, the probability of a state passing a protective law was highest on average in the 1910s. This is not surprising given that this was roughly the progressive era, when many such reforms were adopted.

However, while the hazard rate varies across years, as can be seen in Table 1, an assumption of event history analysis is that the rate is constant across all observations within a given year. Thus, concerning protective legislation, it is assumed that the rate is constant for all states in each year. If a researcher deems this an invalid assumption and can separate and group observations such that the assumption of constancy holds true for the subgroupings, then the researcher can analyze the separate subgroupings. So, for example, for the protective legislation data, perhaps a better assumption might be that the hazard rate for the southern, northeastern, midwestern and western states is different across these regions but relatively constant within regions. If this were the case, these subgroupings of states could be analyzed in separate event history analyses.[13]

Establishing the sample or population of observations to be included in the analysis can aid the researcher in determining the appropriate time period over which the analysis should be conducted.[14] For the analysis of protective legislation, all 48 states are included in the analysis (but see note 12). The earliest

12. There were 38 states in 1870. By the end of the period of analysis there were 48 states (see column 2 of Table 1 for the total number of states in the union). Until a territory becomes a state, it is excluded from the analysis because the territories may have had different processes by which laws were enacted. However, no territory adopted any workplace protective legislation for women.

13. See Beth A. Rubin, "Limits to Institutionalization? A Sectoral Analysis of U.S. Strike Settlements, 1960–1977", *Research in Social Stratification and Mobility*, 11 (1992), pp. 177–202; and Michael T. Hannan and John Freeman, "The Ecology of Organizational Founding: American Labor Unions, 1836–1985", *American Journal of Sociology*, 92 (1987), pp. 910–943 for other examples of subgrouping the data in this manner for event history analysis.

14. Various authors discuss the complexities associated with defining the appropriate population to be included (or sampled) in an analysis. See Larry J. Griffin, Christopher Botsko, Ana-Maria Wahl and Larry W. Isaac, "Theoretical Generality, Case Particularity: Qualitative Comparative Analysis of Trade Union Growth and Decline", *International Journal of Comparative Sociology*, 32 (1991), pp. 115–116; Charles C. Ragin, *The Comparative Method: Moving Beyond Qualitative and Quantitative Strategies* (Berkeley, 1987), pp. 41–42; Michael Burawoy, "Two Methods in Search of Science: Skocpol versus Trotsky", *Theory and Society*, 18 (1989), pp. 765–769. As these analysts point out, determining the theoretically relevant population can present difficulties because not all observations experience the event that the researcher is investigating. Such observations are the "negative cases" or the observations experiencing "non-events". Determining the theoretically relevant set of observations that experience non-events can be a challenge, and the researcher will need to rely upon a precise definition of the population at risk of the event occurring, whether or not the event actually took place for cases in the population.

year that a state passed a protective law is 1874 (a maximum hours law in Massachusetts); the latest date is 1923 (a minimum wage law in South Dakota). Noting this, the researcher could choose to analyze the period from 1870 to 1930 and be certain of including all such events in the analysis.[15]

If researchers cannot analyze a period that encompasses the occurrence of all events of interest for the sample or population being studied, researchers confront the problem of *censoring* in event history analysis. Consider a study of the onset of racial rioting in large metropolitan areas. The researcher may include in the analysis a sample of large cities and analyze the incidence of rioting in them. However, the availability of data may necessitate a particular starting date for the analysis that excludes the occurrence of an earlier riot in a particular city. Or data limitations may necessitate an ending date for the analysis that excludes a later riot in another city. For each of these cities, while the dependent variable is coded as "0" for the period of analysis (i.e. no riot occurs in the cities during the period analyzed), in actuality, the variable is censored, and the "0"s to some extent misrepresent reality. The city did experience a riot, but not within the period analyzed. Censoring of the data such as this in event history analysis introduces the possibility of sample selection bias and biased parameter estimates which can distort the conclusions drawn from the analysis. Thus, to the degree possible censored data should be avoided.[16]

Often, though, researchers are not confronted with such difficulties. In the analysis of the passage of protective legislation, eight states did not pass protective laws between 1870 and 1930, but the historical record shows that these eight states also did not pass protective laws in earlier or later years and, thus, the data are not censored. It is possible that a researcher will of necessity analyze a period that is shorter in duration that what may be ideal. The researcher may nonetheless have evidence that the events of interest did not occur outside of this period for those cases not experiencing the events during the period.

AN EVENT HISTORY ANALYSIS

Discrete-time methods

Two methods of analysis are used in event history analysis: discrete-time methods and continuous-time methods.[17] Researchers must decide which is

---

15. For detailed discussions of the theoretical and historical importance of choosing beginning and end dates for analyses, see Larry W. Isaac and Larry J. Griffin, "Ahistoricism in Time-Series Analyses of Historical Process: Critique, Redirection and Illustrations from U.S. Labor History", *American Sociological Review*, 54 (1989), pp. 873–890; Larry J. Griffin and Larry W. Isaac, "Recursive Regression and the Historical Use of 'Time' in Time-Series Analysis of Historical Process", *Historical Methods*, 25 (1992), pp. 166–179; and Isaac *et al.*, "Temporally Recursive Regression and Social Historical Inquiry: An Example of Cross-Movement Militancy Spillover" (this volume).

16. Censoring is a complex issue in event history analysis. For extended treatments of the subject see: Yamaguchi, *Event History Analysis*, pp. 3–9; Nancy Brandon Tuma and Michael T. Hannan, "Approaches to the Censoring Problem in Analysis of Event Histories", in Karl F. Schuessler (ed.), *Sociological Methodology* (San Francisco, 1979), pp. 209–240.

17. Allison, *Event History Analysis*, p. 14.

the more appropriate for their data. The decision depends largely (although not entirely) on the level of over-time aggregation in the data. Continuous-time methods should be utilized when the exact moment of the event is known and measured in the data, that is, when the data are continuous. This is often the case with individual-level data that are routinely used in biological research (e.g. in mortality research) and some sociological research (e.g. concerning marriage and divorce patterns). Discrete-time methods, on the other hand, are used when the data are aggregated or grouped over larger time units, that is, over discrete time units, such as months, years, or even decades. With quantitative historical data, given the typical nature of the available data, as discussed above, this broader level of aggregation is common. For this reason, the analyses and discussion below consider discrete-time methods.[18]

Yamaguchi lists two additional circumstances that can influence a researcher's decision to utilize discrete- or continuous-time methods.[19] First, if the data contain ties (multiple observations experiencing the event at the same point in time), then discrete methods are appropriate. Ties in the data can introduce bias in the parameter estimates when continuous-time methods are used, and ties are not at all uncommon in historical data. For example, six states passed protective laws in 1913. Second, under certain circumstances, discrete-time methods offer a reasonable approximation of continuous-time methods. This is the case when the hazard rate or the probability of an event occurring over the various time units is generally small, where small is defined as a hazard rate of less than 0.10. However, as Yamaguchi points out, this rule of thumb is somewhat flexible.[20] Analyses show that even where a moderate number of the probabilities are greater than 0.10, the discrete-time method continues to offer a reasonable approximation of the continuous-time method.

The analysis below provides an illustration of event history analysis using discrete-time methods, a technique that is appropriate to use, most importantly, when the data are over discrete time units, that is, for instance, when the data are aggregated over months or years as opposed to data that pinpoints the specific date of event occurrence. Such aggregated time units are commonly used in quantitative historical research because researchers seldom are able to design and administer a survey for data collection that allows them to collect data on the exact timing of events.

Logistic regression

Given that the dependent variable in event history analysis is a probability, discrete-time event history data can be modeled using logistic

---

18. See Nancy Brandon Tuma and Michael T. Hannan, *Social Dynamics: Models and Methods* (Orlando, 1984), *passim*; Allison, *Event History Analysis*, pp. 22–33; Yamaguchi, *Event History Analysis*, pp. 101–160; and David R. Cox and D. Oakes, *The Analysis of Survival Data* (New York, 1983), *passim* for detailed treatments of continuous-time methods.
19. Yamaguchi, *Event History Analysis*, pp. 16–17.
20. *Ibid.*, p. 42.

regression.[21] Regression allows the researcher to estimate the impact of
various explanatory variables on a dependent variable. However, because
the dependent variable for event history analysis is a probability, it
cannot be estimated to be less than 0 or greater than 1. Such an estimate
would be statistically impossible because a probability cannot be less than
0 or greater than 1. A logit transformation of the dependent variable or,
more specifically, of the hazard rate remedies this difficulty.[22] If P(t) is
the probability of the event occurring at time "t" (that is, P(t) is the
hazard rate), then a logit transformation of P(t) is:

$$\log (P(t) / (1 - P(t)),$$

or simply the log odds where the odds are the ratio of the probabilities for
two mutually exclusive states, P(t) and $1 - P(t)$. The natural base of the
logarithm is used in the equation. Thus, while P(t) varies between 0 and 1,
the log odds (or the logit) varies between negative and positive infinity.
Simply put, the log odds can take on any value generated by the regression
estimate. It need not be bounded by 0 and 1. Any standard statistical package with logistic regression capabilities (e.g. SPSS, SAS) will compute the
log odds of the dependent variable.

The regression equation then takes the form:

$$\log (P(t) / (1 - P(t)) = a + b_1 X_1 + b_2 X_2,$$

where the dependent variable (on the left-hand side of the equation) is the
logit or the log odds and b_1 and b_2 (on the right-hand side) are the parameter estimates of the impact of the explanatory variables, X_1 and X_2, on the
dependent variable. The intercept is represented by "a" on the right-hand
side. The coefficients, b_1 and b_2, generated by the logistic regression indicate
the change in the log odds for a one unit increment in X_1 and X_2 respectively.

An application

Table 2, column 1 presents parameter estimates from an event history analysis of various conditions that influence the likelihood of a state's passage of
a protective workplace law for women, where such a protective law can be
a maximum hours law, a minimum wage law, or a restriction on night work
for women.[23] A maximum likelihood estimation technique is the best

21. *Ibid.*, p. 15; Allison, *Event History Analysis*, p. 17–18.
22. Eric A. Hanushek and John E. Jackson, *Statistical Methods for Social Scientists* (New York,
1977), pp. 187–189.
23. McCammon, "The Politics of Protection", pp. 217–249 presents a more detailed analysis of
similar data.

Table 2. *Discrete-time event history analysis estimates of the effect of selected variables on the likelihood of a state adopting women's protective legislation, 1870-1930 (standard errors in parentheses)*

	(1)	(2)	(3)	(4)	(5)
Consumers' League	1.73***	1.59***	1.24***	1.01***	1.03
	(.383)	(.494)	(.324)	(.378)	(.573)
Competitive	3.23***	3.04***	2.42**	2.62**	.87
gubernatorial	(1.22)	(1.21)	(1.02)	(1.21)	(1.76)
election					
Proportion voting	8.52***	3.78	7.13***	6.77***	7.50***
for Progressive Party	(1.87)	(2.21)	(1.41)	(1.75)	(1.60)
presidential					
candidate					
Women's suffrage	1.91***	1.50***	1.93***	1.38***	1.48***
	(.510)	(.552)	(.404)	(.490)	(.510)
Percentage of	8.54***	7.20**	6.18**	4.83	1.45
workers female	(3.15)	(3.33)	(2.72)	(3.00)	(5.14)
Legislative session	3.10***	3.20***	2.93***	3.19***	2.03***
	(.748)	(.752)	(.583)	(.770)	(.769)
1870s	—[a]	−3.22***	−	−	−
		(1.10)			
1880s	−	−1.58***	−	−	−
		(.645)			
1890s	−	−1.36**	−	−	−
		(.598)			
1900s	−	−1.82***	−	−	−
		(.553)			
1920s	−	−2.16**	−	−	−
		(1.09)			
Number of past	−	−	−	11.63	−
events				(22.21)	
Time elapsed since	−	−	−	−.05	−
last event				(2.26)	
Constant	−11.10***	−9.19***	−9.65***	−9.94***	−8.64***
	(1.61)	(1.69)	(1.30)	(1.55)	(2.06)
N	1,585	1,585	1,747	1,747	2,384
Likelihood-ratio	103.8***	124.3***	145.2***	214.6***	52.4***
chi-squared					
Degrees of freedom	6	11	6	8	6

** p ≤ .05
*** p ≤ .01
[a] Variable not in the equation.

method for generating the parameter estimates and is used here.[24] The dependent variable in this analysis is coded as "0" for every year that a state did not enact a protective law and as "1" for the year, if any, in which the

24. Paul D. Allison, "Discrete-Time Methods for the Analysis of Event Histories", in Samuel Leinhardt (ed.), *Sociological Methodology* (San Francisco, 1982), pp. 73–76.

state legislated any one of these types of law. After the passage of such a law, data for the following years are coded as missing data and, therefore, these years are not included in the analysis. As discussed above, the dichotomous dependent variable is transformed into a hazard rate, and the log odds of the hazard rate is modeled with logistic regression.

As can be seen in Table 2, all of the explanatory variables entered into the equation have a significant and positive influence on the probability of a state passing a protective law. The standard errors of the coefficients are provided in parentheses, and the significance of the coefficients is determined with a Wald statistic, which is the squared ratio of the coefficient to its standard error and has a chi-squared distribution. The standard error, the Wald statistic, and its probability will usually be supplied by the event history analysis statistical package.

The results in Table 2 show that state legislatures around the turn of the century were more likely to pass protective laws for women when a Consumers' League was organized in the state. This was a middle- and upper-class women's group that lobbied for workplace protection for women. Also, states were more willing to enact protective laws when certain political conditions prevailed, for instance when a recent gubernatorial election was competitive; perhaps this made those in office unsure of their political constituencies so that they searched for ways of insuring their support in the future. Protective laws were also more likely to be adopted when there was significant support for Progressive Party presidential candidates in the state and when women possessed full voting rights in the state. In addition, the greater the percentage of the labor force that was female, the more likely law-makers were to pass protective legislation, as if a more pressing need for the law were perceived. Finally, a finding that is, of course, obvious: legislatures were more likely to pass these laws when they were in session. This measure must be included in the analysis to control for the fact that only during these years could legislatures pass laws.

One can determine the "fit" of the model or whether the model containing the explanatory variables in addition to the intercept is a significant improvement over a model with only the intercept by comparing the log likelihoods for the two equations. The log likelihoods are compared with the test statistic, the likelihood-ratio chi-square (L^2), which appears at the bottom of the table and is computed as two times the positive difference between the log likelihood for the model containing both the explanatory variables and intercept (or the "tested model") and the log likelihood for the model containing only the intercept (or the "constant rate model").[25] Typically, statistical programs compute L^2 and its significance level for the researcher (both SPSS and SAS do this) or, at a minimum, they compute −2 times the log likelihood for both the tested and constant rate models

25. Yamaguchi, *Event History Analysis*, p. 20.

which can then be used to compute L^2 by simply finding their positive difference.

The model in column 1 of Table 2 has a likelihood-ratio chi-square of 103.8 with 6 degrees of freedom. The number of degrees of freedom is determined by the difference in the number of regressors in the model with the explanatory variables and in the model without them. An L^2 of 103.8 is greater than the critical value for a .01 level of significance with 6 degrees of freedom, and thus a model including these explanatory variables is a significant improvement over a model containing only the intercept. This is not surprising given that all of the coefficients in the model are significant.[26]

The number of cases included in the analysis (N = 1,585) is also reported at the bottom of the table. Note that the N for column 1 is substantially larger than the number of states included in the analysis because the unit of analysis is the state-year. Multiple observations are included in the data for each state over the period of analysis, 1870 to 1930. However, the number of cases is not 48 times 61 (or the number of states in the analysis times the number of years in the period of analysis, which would be 2,928) because state-years are excluded from the analysis after a state passes a protective law for women.[27] Forty states passed protective laws and thus have truncated data in the analysis.

SOME MATTERS OF FURTHER INTEREST IN EVENT HISTORY ANALYSIS

Over-time variation in the hazard rate

An assumption of the model in column 1 of Table 2 is that the hazard rate is constant over time. As was seen in Table 1, this is not the case. The hazard rate is higher during some years – especially in the 1910s – because a substantial number of states passed protective laws during these years. To test the validity of the assumption concerning a constant hazard rate, a set of dummy variables can be added to the analysis, in this case, each representing a decade-long period.[28] Five such dummy variables are added

26. See Hanushek and Jackson, *Statistical Methods*, pp. 65–68 for a general discussion of statistical inference and Hubert M. Blalock, *Social Statistics* (New York, 1979), pp. 280–292 for a discussion of the chi-square statistic.

27. In addition, state-years are excluded from the analysis for years prior to a territory becoming a state (see note 12). Also, there are a few data points missing for Georgia given the unavailability of data for gubernatorial elections in that state for 1884, 1885, 1910–1917, 1920, 1921, 1928–1930. Losing data for these years, however, does not censor the data. Georgia did not pass a protective law.

28. The decade variables take the value of "0" for all years except the particular decade the variable represents. For these years, the variable equals "1". So for the 1870 measure, the variable equals "0" for all years except 1870 through 1879; for these years the value equals "1". Individual year dummies could be used instead. For this analysis, however, which contains data over 61 years, this

to the model in column 2 of Table 2. The omitted decade is the 1910s, the decade in which the greatest number of states passed protective laws. The inclusion of these measures in the model allows one to assess whether the likelihood of a state passing a protective law is significantly different in the 1910s compared to the other decades.

Indeed, the results in column 2 show that the effect for all of the dummy variables is significantly smaller than that for the 1910s, meaning that the hazard rate is significantly lower in these other decades than it was during the 1910s. States were significantly more likely to pass women's protective laws during the 1910s than during the other decades, even after the other explanatory factors (listed in the table) are statistically controlled. It does appear, however, comparing the magnitude of the coefficients for the dummy variables over time, that the likelihood of a state passing a protective law increased over time roughly until the 1910s (although the coefficient for the 1900s does not fit this trend perfectly) but then decreased substantially in the 1920s, probably due to a saturation effect given that the bulk of states had passed such laws by the 1920s.

One can also use the model log likelihoods to determine if the model including the decade dummy variables is a statistically significant improvement over the model without the dummies. Two times the positive difference between the log likelihoods for the models in columns 1 and 2 is 20.5 (this is also the simple difference between −2 log likelihood) with 5 degrees of freedom (the number of dummies added to the second model). The critical chi-squared value is 15.1 (for a .01 probability level). The computed difference is greater than this. Thus, the equation including the decade dummies significantly improves the fit of the model. (Note that the likelihood-ratio in column 2 does not represent this comparison but rather a comparison of the tested and constant rate models.)

Allowing the hazard rate to vary over time in column 2 also renders the proportion voting for Progressive Party presidential candidates insignificant. This suggests that concerning the impact of progressive period dynamics on the likelihood of states passing protective laws, the more important explanatory factor is over-time variation rather than cross-sectional variation. The over-time dummy variables had a significant effect on the passage of protec-

would be a burdensome number of variables to include in the analysis. Thus, the decade measures are used. See Allison, *Event History Analysis*, pp. 19–20 for a further description of this method. In addition, see Larry Isaac *et al.*, "Temporally Recursive Regression" and Isaac and Griffin, "Ahistoricism in Time-Series Analysis of Historical Process", pp. 873–890 for a discussion of recursive regression, another method of detecting over-time variation in quantitative analyses, specifically in the effects of the explanatory variables in time-series analysis. See Beth A. Rubin and Brian T. Smith, "Forged Ties: Cooperation and Conflict in the Metals Industries", *Social Science Research*, 21 (1992), pp. 115–133 for an application of recursive regression to event history analysis.

tive legislation in column 2 in that they capture the (over-time) difference between the progressive years (encompassed in the 1910 decade) and the other decades. On the other hand, the measure of the proportion voting for Progressive candidates for the most part is a measure of cross-state differences in Progressive Party voting in the 1912 presidential election, and it is no longer significant in the second model.[29]

Repeated events

The analyses in columns 1 and 2 of Table 2 ignore some potentially important information. The dependent variable examined in these analyses measures only a state's first passage of a protective law. While 42 states adopted some form of protective legislation, 20 of these states enacted additional protective laws concerning women's employment. That is, some states passed two or even all three types of protective law (six states, in fact, enacted all three types of law – maximum hours, minimum wage and prohibitions on night work laws). That some states passed more than one type raises the issue of *repeated events*. Many events examined with event history analysis are events that repeat themselves. For instance, workers' decision to strike and the outbreak of rioting can both occur more than once for the same workplace or the same city respectively. In the analysis of protective legislation, states can adopt more than one form of law and thus can experience the repeated event of the passage of protective legislation.

To include information on repeated events in an analysis is a reasonably straightforward procedure. The researcher must code the dependent variable so that the multiple instances of the event are indicated by the measure. For time units after the occurrence of the first event, if a later event occurs, rather than the variable taking on missing values, the variable is assigned the value "0" for the time units before the occurrence of the second event and "1" for the time unit in which the second event occurs. If a third or more events occur, this coding procedure is repeated. Thus, for California, which passed a maximum hours law in 1911, a minimum wage law in 1913, and a restriction on night work in 1918, the dependent variable is coded as follows:

---

29. Researchers could also include regional dummy variables (or the equivalent cross-sectional measure) in an analysis to determine if the hazard rate varied across regions. But, as discussed earlier, analysts could also examine separate models for the different regions. Separate models would be particularly warranted if one expects the effects of the explanatory factors to vary across regions. But also, if one expects the effects to differ across regions, interaction terms between the regional dummies and the appropriate explanatory variable could be included as an alternative to the separate regional equations. In addition to the possibility of variation in the effects over time and across regions, the pattern of results may also vary for the different types of law (i.e. maximum hours laws, minimum wage laws and night work laws). This possibility is discussed below in the section entitled "Estimating multiple types of events".

for 1870–1910 the value is "0",
for 1911 the value is "1",
for 1912 the value is "0",
for 1913 the value is "1",
for 1914–1917 the value is "0",
for 1918 the value is "1",
for 1919–1930 the value is missing because the state had passed all three measures.

A state, then, can contribute more than one passage of law to the analysis. By including all repeated events in the protective legislation data, 162 observations are added to the analysis. This information is ignored in the analysis in columns 1 and 2 of Table 2 where repeated events are not included and in which, as can now be discerned, only the adoption of a "first" protective law is analyzed.

The results of an event history analysis where all instances in which a state passed a protective law are included are shown in column 3 of Table 2. As can be seen, including the later passages of law leaves the results virtually unchanged (compare columns 1 and 3; for simplicity the decade dummy variables are left out of the analysis). All variables remain significant and positive. The standard errors for the coefficients are slightly smaller in column 3 than in column 1 given that the N for the analysis in column 3 is somewhat larger. The results suggest that a similar set of causal dynamics governs both the passage of a state's first protective law and the passage of later laws.

There are some complexities, however, associated with the inclusion of repeated events in event history analysis. The first issue that arises is the potential for a lack of independence among such events.[30] An analysis that includes repeated events must be free of dependence among such events. For the protective legislation example, this means that the passage of a second law in a state must not be dependent upon the passage of a first law (in the next section this possibility is examined further). Or, if the passage of early and later laws are correlated in some way, this relationship must be accounted for by the explanatory variables included in the analysis. If such independence between events cannot be insured, the standard errors for the coefficients may be biased.[31]

In order to minimize dependence among repeated events, the researcher can include two measures as explanatory variables in the analysis that control for the influence of a case's past event history on the present event.[32] The

30. See Daniel J. Myers, "Racial Rioting in the 1960s: An Event History Analysis of Local Conditions", *American Sociological Review*, 62 (1997), p. 101 for a discussion of this problem.
31. Allison, *Event History Analysis*, p. 54.
32. Trond Petersen, "The Statistical Analysis of Event Histories", *Sociological Methods and Research*, 19 (1991), p. 299; Allison, *Event History Analysis*, p. 54; idem, "Discrete-Time Methods", p. 93.

first is a measure of the number of past events that have occurred at the time of a repeated event. The second is a measure of the time elapsed since the occurrence of the last event (which is set equal to zero if no previous event has occurred). These two measures are included in the model in column 4 of Table 2. Here the dependent variable is the same as that in column 3 in that it indicates the passage of all protective laws in a state. However, the inclusion of the number of past events and time elapsed does not substantially alter the findings (although the impact of the percentage of the labor force that is female becomes insignificant), and neither measure is significant. This suggests that there is little interdependence among the different types of protective legislation or that the passage of one type of protective law is not likely to affect the passage of other types.

The second complexity that can occur with the inclusion of repeated events is that it is possible (and there may be sound theoretical reasons for believing) that the conditions leading to the occurrence of a first event are not the same as those producing later events.[33] In fact, the results in column 3 may be misleading if this is the case. This can easily be discerned by comparing separate analyses, one for first events (i.e. a state's first passage of a protective law) and one for later events (i.e. passage of second and even third protective laws). If the associated sets of predictors are similar across two such models, then the researcher can reasonably assume that the same causal processes govern both earlier and later events. The results in column 5 can be compared with those in column 1 to make this judgement. While column 1 provides an analysis of the passage of a state's first protective law, column 5 provides an analysis of only the passage of later laws. Some of the variables remain statistically significant across the two models (votes for Progressive candidates, women's suffrage and legislative session); others, however, are no longer significant (the presence of a Consumers' League, competitive elections and female workers). These differences suggest that the researcher would have to consider that the passage of later laws occurs under substantially different circumstances than the passage of a first protective law for women.

Estimating multiple types of events

Probably a naive assumption of the models in Table 2 is that the causal processes influencing the passage of the three types of protective legislation that are included in the dependent variable are the same. It may be, rather, that the conditions giving rise to laws restricting the number of hours that women could work, for instance, differ from the forces resulting in a state

---

33. Michael T. Hannan and Glenn R. Carroll, "Dynamics of Formal Political Structure: An Event-History Analysis", *American Sociological Review*, 46 (1981), pp. 19–35 discuss this possibility in their work on changes in political structures from military regimes to multiparty structures.

legislature adopting a minimum wage policy for women, and these dynamics, in turn, differ from those producing restrictions on night work for women.

To examine whether these different events have different causal patterns requires the construction of distinct dependent variables for each of the types of protective legislation and the estimation of separate models for each of the types of law. In estimating these separate models, one can also explicitly test the hypothesis that a state's adoption of one type of protective legislation increases the likelihood that in time a state will enact another type of protective law. Once an initial law is passed, a "policy feedback" effect may make it likelier that a state passes additional reforms.[34]

To examine these possibilities, additional models are estimated and the results are presented in Table 3.[35] Column 1 provides the results for a model estimating the effects of the various explanatory variables on the passage of maximum hours laws; column 2, the results for minimum wage laws; and column 3, the results for laws restricting night work for women. As is readily apparent, the model works well in explaining the circumstances leading to the adoption of an hours law (column 1). All coefficients continue to have a positive effect. The model is less useful in explaining the passage of minimum wage laws (column 2). Only the proportion voting for Progressive Party candidates and full suffrage for women increase the likelihood that a state will enact a minimum wage law for women. Similarly, only the presence of a Consumers' League and years in which legislatures are in session significantly increase the chances of a state passing a law regulating night work (column 3). The model does not work well for this last type of law either.

In addition, while the results in column 1 are robust for maximum hours laws, further analyses (not shown) show that the findings in columns 2 and 3 are highly sensitive to the presence or absence in the model of specific explanatory variables, suggesting that adequate specification of the processes giving rise to minimum wage laws and restrictions on night work need considerably more historical study.[36]

Many states enacted hours laws before minimum wage laws and restrictions on night work. Thus it is possible that the passage of an hours law may have eased the way for the enactment of the other two types of law. To test this idea, the minimum wage and night work models are re-estimated in columns 4 and 5 respectively, and the maximum hours law variable is

34. Theda Skocpol, *Protecting Soldiers and Mothers: The Political Origins of Social Policy in the United States* (Cambridge, 1992), pp. 57–60.

35. For a lengthier treatment of event history analysis involving multiple events, see Allison, *Event History Analysis*, pp. 42–50.

36. See McCammon, "The Politics of Protection", pp. 234–238 for an analysis of the conditions under which legislatures adopted minimum wage laws.

Table 3. *Discrete-time event history analysis estimates of the effect of selected variables on the likelihood of a state adopting women's maximum hours, minimum wage and night work legislation, 1870-1930 (standard errors in parentheses)*

Dependent variable	(1) Max. hours	(2) Min. wage	(3) Night work	(4) Min. wage	(5) Night work
Consumers'	1.38***	−.18	1.54***	−.22	1.22**
League	(.379)	(.832)	(.596)	(.829)	(.612)
Competitive	2.87***	.92	−.78	.55	−1.24
gubernatorial election	(1.17)	(2.38)	(1.27)	(2.44)	(1.33)
Proportion	8.58***	10.41***	1.54	9.91***	.90
voting for Progressive Party presidential candidate	(1.80)	(1.98)	(2.87)	(2.04)	(2.90)
Women's	1.43***	2.21***	.51	2.01***	.08
suffrage	(.474)	(.684)	(.619)	(.719)	(.649)
Percentage of	8.18***	1.91	2.50	−.46	.46
female workers	(3.11)	(3.33)	(4.97)	(8.04)	(5.41)
Legislative	3.04***	8.61	1.59**	8.62	1.63**
session	(.742)	(19.3)	(.771)	(19.3)	(.772)
Passage of	−a	−	−	.67	1.21
maximum hours law lagged 1 yr				(.811)	(.714)
Constant	−10.62***	−16.01	−6.70***	−15.54	−6.41***
	(1.55)	(19.5)	(1.65)	(19.5)	(1.68)
N	1,618	2,425	2,331	2,425	2,331
Likelihood-ratio chi-squared	93.5***	62.9***	16.8**	63.6***	19.8***
Degrees of freedom	6	6	6	7	7

** $p \le .05$
*** $p \le .01$
a Variable not in the equation.

included as an explanatory variable in both. The variable is lagged by one year because in some states hours laws were passed in the same years that the other two types of law were passed. Lagging the hours variable insures that the analyses examine only cases where an hours law was adopted prior o the enactment of either a minimum wage or night work law.[37] These

37. The same hours law variable used as a dependent variable in column 1 of Table 3 cannot be used as an explanatory variable in the analyses in columns 2 and 3 because the variable used in

findings indicate that the earlier passage of a maximum hours law did not significantly increase the likelihood that a state would adopt a minimum wage law or restrictions on night work for women, confirming the conclusions of the last section that the various types of law are not unduly dependent on one another.

CONCLUSION

Event history analysis is a quantitative method that allows researchers to investigate the causes of the occurrence or non-occurrence of historical events. This discussion has presented various instructions on how to conduct an event history analysis along with a discussion of some of the complexities associated with the method. An advantage of the method over the case study is that event history analysis allows one to compare cases in which the event occurs with cases in which the event does not occur, thereby more systematically uncovering the causal dynamics that produce or do not produce the events of interest. As is often the case in historical research, the analyst chooses a "positive" case to unravel the causal dynamics producing a particular historical outcome – that is, a case in which the historical event occurs. Event history analysis, on the other hand, is a method that requires the inclusion not only of positive cases, but negative cases as well. The method necessitates that the researcher compare cases in which the event occurs with those in which the event did not occur to more fully uncover the reasons underlying the event's occurrence.

While the data requirements are rather rigorous – both over-time and cross-sectional quantitative data are needed – the method does allow a level of analysis that is unavailable to the researcher who examines one or just a few cases. Event history analysis allows a thorough and rigorous assessment of *many* observations and the characteristics associated with those observations to gauge why the historical event of interest occurs in some of those cases and why it does not occur in others. Possibly the entire population of social entities at risk of the event occurring can be included in the analysis. In the study presented here, all of the existing US states were incorporated to examine the historical circumstances that led them to adopt or not adopt women's protective legislation. An examination of just one or even a handful

---

column 1 is assigned missing values for all years after a state passed an hours law. The hours law variable used as an explanatory variable in columns 2 and 3, rather, must be assigned the value of "0" for all years prior to the state's passage of an hours law and "1" for the year in which an hours law is passed *and* all later years as well. Note also that lagging variables with time series data pooled across states such as that found here presents a difficulty. The lagging procedure assigns the value for the year 1930 for the preceding state to the year 1870 (see Figure 1). This, however, can be corrected manually. No state passed an hours law in 1870, so "0" (rather than the 1930 value) is assigned to 1870.

of states could not offer the same scope of investigation that event history was able to offer in this case.

Event history analysis, however, is not without its disadvantages. Given the rigorous data requirements, it is possible that the researcher will not have the needed data for all observations or over the entire time period. And the work involved in collecting such information even when it is available can present a task that itself can be all-consuming. As Tilly points out concerning quantitative methods generally:

> the scale and complexity of such an investigation produce important periods when the researchers are so preoccupied with problems of coding, file construction, statistical procedure, computer techniques, and coordination of the whole effort that they practically lose contact with the people, events, places, and times they are studying.[38]

And certainly this too can be true at times of event history analysis. In the end, however, it is the researcher who must decide if enough quantifiable information exists to make the investigation viable and it is the researcher who controls whether coding and statistical technique dominate the analysis or whether event history analysis is simply a useful tool that can be utilized to reveal insights about historical change.

Event history analysis certainly is not useful in all cases of historical inquiry, but if the historical question posed by the researcher is one that seeks to uncover why particular events occur and if the appropriate data are available, even if data gathering is an arduous task, then event history analysis can be a valuable and worthy research tool.

ANNOTATED BIBLIOGRAPHY

For the most accessible discussions of discrete-time methods in event history analysis, see:

Allison, Paul D., "Discrete-time Methods for the Analysis of Event Histories", in Samuel Leinhardt (ed.), *Sociological Methodology* (San Francisco, 1982), pp. 61–98.
Allison, Paul D., *Event History Analysis: Regression For Longitudinal Event Data* (Newbury Park, 1984).
Yamaguchi, Kazuo, *Event History Analysis* (Newbury Park, 1991).

There are various recent historical studies that employ discrete-time methods. See, for example:

---

38. Charles Tilly, *As Sociology Meets History* (Orlando, 1981), p. 61. Elsewhere in this discussion, Tilly extols the virtues of quantitative methods, as well as being somewhat realistic about their shortcomings.

Kim, Chulsoo, "Determinants of the Timing of Social Policy Adoption", *Journal of Sociology and Social Welfare*, 23 (1996), pp. 5–29.

McCammon, Holly J., "The Politics of Protection: State Minimum Wage and Maximum Hours Laws for Women in the United States, 1870–1930", *The Sociological Quarterly*, 36 (1995), pp. 217–249.

Minkoff, Debra C., "The Organization of Survival: Women's and Racial-Ethnic Voluntarist and Activist Organizations, 1955–1985", *Social Forces*, 71 (1993), pp. 887–908.

Mizruchi, Mark S. and Linda Brewster Stearns, "A Longitudinal Study of the Formation of Interlocking Directorates", *Administrative Science Quarterly*, 33 (1988), pp. 194–210.

Olzak, Susan and Elizabeth West, "Ethnic Conflict and the Rise and Fall of Ethnic Newspapers", *American Sociological Review*, 56 (1991), pp. 458–474.

Pavalko, Eliza K., "State Timing of Policy Adoption: Workmen's Compensation in the United States, 1909–1929", *American Journal of Sociology*, 95 (1989), pp. 592–615.

Western, Bruce, "A Comparative Study of Working-class Disorganization: Union Decline in Eighteen Advanced Capitalist Countries", *American Sociological Review*, 60 (1995), pp. 179–201.

For detailed treatments of continuous-time methods, see:

Allison, Paul D., *Event History Analysis: Regression For Longitudinal Event Data* (Newbury Park, 1984).

Cox, David R. and D. Oakes, *The Analysis of Survival Data* (New York, 1983).

Petersen, Trond, "The Statistical Analysis of Event Histories", *Sociological Methods and Research*, 19 (1991), pp. 270–323.

Petersen, Trond, "Time-Aggregation Bias in Continuous-Time Hazard-Rate Models", in Peter V. Marsden (ed.), *Sociological Methodology* (Cambridge, 1991), pp. 263–290.

Tuma, Nancy Brandom and Michael T. Hannan, "Dynamic Analysis of Event Histories", *American Journal of Sociology*, 84 (1979), pp. 820–854.

Tuma, Nancy Brandon and Michael T. Hannan, *Social Dynamics: Models and Methods* (Orlando, 1984).

Yamaguchi, Kazuo, *Event History Analysis* (Newbury Park, 1991).

Some examples of historical research utilizing continuous-time methods are:

Carroll, Glenn R. and Yangchung Paul Huo, "Organizational and Electoral Paradoxes of the Knights of Labor", in Glenn R. Carroll (ed.), *Ecological Models of Organizations* (Cambridge, 1988), pp. 175–193.

Hannan, Michael T. and Glenn R. Carroll, "Dynamics of Formal Political

Structure: An Event-History Analysis", *American Sociological Review*, 46 (1981), pp. 19–35.

Hannan, Michael T. and John Freeman, "The Ecology of Organizational Founding: American Labor Unions, 1836–1985", *American Journal of Sociology*, 92 (1987), pp. 910–943.

McCarthy, John D., Mark Wolfson, David P. Baker and Elaine Mosakowski, "The Founding of Social Movement Organizations: Local Citizens' Groups Opposing Drunken Driving", in Glenn R. Carroll (ed.), *Ecological Models of Organizations* (Cambridge, 1988), pp. 71–84.

Myers, Daniel J., "Racial Rioting in the 1960s: An Event History Analysis of Local Conditions", *American Sociological Review*, 62 (1997), pp. 94–112.

Olzak, Susan, "The Political Context of Competition: Lynching and Urban Racial Violence, 1882–1914", *Social Forces*, 69 (1990), pp. 395–421.

Rubin, Beth A., "Limits to Institutionalization? A Sectoral Analysis of U.S. Strike Settlements, 1960–1977", *Research in Social Stratification and Mobility*, 11 (1992), pp. 177–202.

Various sources offer treatments of censoring in event history analysis. See, for example:

Tuma, Nancy Brandon and Michael T. Hannan, "Approaches to the Censoring Problem in Analysis of Event Histories", in Karl F. Schuessler (ed.), *Sociological Methodology* (San Francisco, 1979), pp. 209–240.

Yamaguchi, Kazuo, *Event History Analysis* (Newbury Park, 1991).

International Review of Social History 43 (1998), Supplement, pp. 57–80
© 1998 Internationaal Instituut voor Sociale Geschiedenis

Incorporating Space into Social Histories: How Spatial Processes Operate and How We Observe Them

GLENN DEANE, E.M. BECK and STEWART E. TOLNAY

Social historians study social, political, demographic and economic phenomena which take place in geographical space, yet "space" rarely enters historical discourse explicitly as an analytic construct. Given the recent interest among social historians in "localizing" social processes, it is unfortunate that almost all of our efforts have gone toward recognizing the significance of time, to the relative neglect of space.[1] For example, social historians typically assume that events occurring at a given point in time are affected by earlier events. In contrast, it is less widely recognized that events occurring in one location are also affected by similar events in other areas, especially those nearby. In the rare instances in which geographical space has been central, such as in Susan Watkins' treatment of western European fertility decline during the late nineteenth and early twentieth centuries, or in the evidence of the diffusion of democracy in post-war Europe that is emerging from the "Spatial and Temporal Diffusion of Democracy" project at the University of Colorado – Boulder, the payoff has been substantial.[2] Such innovative approaches to historical theorizing give reason to believe that thinking of events in the past as parts of a process moving through time and across space will become more commonplace. If so, then social historians will need an effective and accessible method to account for the spatial distributions of their study phenomena.

Spatial patterning in a dependent variable (e.g. a concentration of events in a few neighboring areas) may not be, in itself, of much interest to social historians. Clearly there is a tendency for nearby, especially contiguous, areal units to share many of the same social, demographic, economic and cultural characteristics. If those characteristics tend to facilitate (or inhibit) the occurrence of the phenomenon, then, left unaccounted for, it is possible that we would infer an unusual spatial concentration of the phenomenon that can be explained easily by the social and economic similarities of adjacent areas. For instance, it is well known that urban crime within cities is

1. The importance of incorporating space and time in historical sociology is made in Larry W. Isaac, "Transforming Localities: Reflections on Time, Causality, and Narrative in Contemporary Historical Sociology", *Historical Methods*, 30 (1997), pp. 4–12; yet even here "space" is subordinated to "time".
2. See, for example, Susan Cotts Watkins, *From Provinces Into Nations: The Demographic Integration of Western Europe, 1870–1960* (Princeton, 1991), and John O'Loughlin, Michael D. Ward, Corey L. Lofdahl, Jordin S. Cohen, David S. Brown, David Reilly, Kristian S. Gleditsch and Michael Shin, "The Diffusion of Democracy, 1946–1994", *Annals of the Association of American Geographers* (forthcoming, 1998).

concentrated in certain neighborhoods. Recent interest in "hot spots" attests to the pervasiveness of this phenomenon. But it is also well known that the social and economic antecedents of crime (e.g. poverty, unemployment, unstable families) are also geographically concentrated. Is the concentration of crime indicative of a spatial process whereby criminal activity in one neighborhood affects crime in an adjacent neighborhood? Or does it simply reflect the parallel geographic concentration of the antecedents of crime? To adjudicate between these competing interpretations, it is necessary to assess the extent to which crime continues to "cluster" within certain neighborhoods after accounting for the parallel clustering within neighborhoods of the social conditions that give rise to crime. Persistent clustering may indicate a true "spatial effect" in which the occurrence of events (e.g. crime) in one locale is causally related to events in another location, independent of shared social and economic characteristics. In the context of regression analysis, this is referred to as a *spatial-effects model*.[3]

The purpose of this essay is to motivate interest in spatial-effects models among social historians. Specifically, we will: (1) describe the common conditions under which spatial dependence arises, (2) explain a procedure (using a regression approach) through which spatial dependence can be detected and dealt with, (3) offer simple interpretations of the spatial-effects term that is produced by the procedure, as well as the coefficients for the other independent variables in the presence of spatial effects, and (4) give two illustrations of spatial processes, and their treatment, in historical research.

DIFFUSION, SPILLOVERS AND DETERRENCE AS SPATIAL PROCESSES

Spatial processes may be classified according to a simple two-dimensional scheme. Along one dimension we may identify the degree to which spatial effects diffuse over time and across space. Some processes move rapidly through time and space, e.g. epidemic diseases and their "social contagion" analog, while others are much more static, simply exerting a local influence or "spillover effect". The "Tiebout Hypothesis" of voting with one's feet (i.e. moving in or moving out) in response to local public expenditures is a classic example of highly localized "spillover".[4] Along the other dimension, spatial effects may have a *positive* impact, thereby increasing the probability

3. Even if a researcher does not infer a "causal" connection between events occurring in different areas, it is necessary to take into account the spatial clustering of social and economic characteristics in order to avoid the problem of "spatial autocorrelation". By doing so, conclusions about the relationships between a dependent variable and a set of independent variables will not be compromised by the violation of fundamental assumptions required for hypothesis testing.

4. See C.M. Tiebout, "A Pure Theory of Local Expenditures", *Journal of Political Economy*, 64 (1956), pp. 416–424; Richard J. Cebula, "The Tiebout Hypothesis of Voting With One's Feet: A Look At Recent Evidence", *Review of Regional Studies*, 11 (1981), pp. 47–50.

on the occurrence of like events, or a *negative* impact, resulting in a decreased likelihood of additional events. These dimensions are continuous and the typology produced by their intersection is one of a two-dimensional continuum where spatial effects are more or less dynamic and the strength or magnitude of these effects ranges between strong positive and strong negative.

There is a wide range of phenomena that allude to the operation of spatial processes. Diffusion processes in social history are customarily invoked to explain the impact of population contact through disease transfer and the spread of technologies, information, attitudes, beliefs and behaviors. A natural area to begin locating this imagery is in the consequences of "Old World" and "New World" population contact. Historians have amassed ample theoretical and empirical literatures on the spread of epidemic disease in "virgin populations" and considerable effort has gone into tracking the geography of epidemics in Native American populations following European contact.[5] But some of the earliest methodological work on diffusion concerned the spread of technological innovation. Several studies documented the diffusion of bovine artificial insemination in Sweden from the late 1940s through the early 1960s. More recent efforts have emphasized the spread of ideas and behaviors. We have already cited the recent scholarship on the European fertility decline in the nineteenth century and the spread of democracy in the modern world system. Social historians have also given substantial attention to the diffusion of religious group/church membership across the United States in the "Great Awakenings" of the eighteenth and nineteenth centuries and in the evangelical Protestantism movements in this century. Still other examples may be drawn from public health, crime/deviance and criminal justice as researchers in these disciplines have suggested that the rise in violent offenses in the second half of the twentieth century can be usefully regarded as a contagious social process "analogous to disease" and capable of "contagious transmission".[6] What is common to each of

---

5. For just a few representative pieces of this literature, see William H. McNeill, *Plagues and Peoples* (New York, 1976); Henry F. Dobyns, *Their Number Become Thinned: Native American Population Dynamics in Eastern North America* (Knoxville, TN, 1983); Nobel D. Cook, *Born to Die: Disease and New World Conquest, 1492–1650* (Cambridge, 1998); David P. Henige, *Numbers from Nowhere: The American Indian Contact Population Debate* (Oklahoma City, OK, 1998).

6. On the diffusion of bovine artificial insemination, see T. Hagerstrand, *Innovation Diffusion as a Spatial Process* (Chicago, 1967); and Lawrence A. Brown, Edward J. Malecki and Aron N. Spector, "Adopter Categories in a Spatial Context: Alternative Explanations for an Empirical Regularity", *Rural Sociology*, 41 (1976), pp. 99–118. On religious diffusion, see Roger Finke and Rodney Stark, *The Churching of America, 1776–1990: Winners and Losers in Our Religious Economy* (New Brunswick, NJ, 1992); Norman K. Dann, "Spatial Diffusion of a Religious Movement", *Journal for the Scientific Study of Religion*, 15 (1967), pp. 351–360; Kenneth C. Land, Glenn Deane and Judith R. Blau, "Religious Pluralism and Church Membership: A Spatial Diffusion Model", *American Sociological Review*, 56 (1991), pp. 237–249; Judith R. Blau, Kenneth C. Land and Kent Redding, "The Expansion of Religious Affiliation: An Explanation of the Growth of Church Participation in the United States, 1850–1930", *Social Science Research*, 21 (1992), pp. 329–352; and

these examples is the notion that the study phenomenon *spreads across space*, making the occurrence of the phenomenon in a given area more likely than one would predict based simply on the social, economic, demographic or political characteristics of the place.

Economists often describe another positive spatial process, a "spillover effect", that is less dynamic in nature. This too is a diffusion process, but it is characterized by an absence (or near absence) of movement across space *over time*. In other words, if we could take repeated "snapshots" of some phenomenon, the distribution across space would look the same in each snapshot. We would see geographically distributed clusters where the phenomenon occurred a lot or very little, but these clusters would be in the same place in each successive snapshot. Contrast this image with that generally evoked by contagions or epidemics. In the latter cases, the successive snapshots would show some phenomenon sweeping across space, creating new clusters in each successive snapshot. Spillovers are created when "neighbors" look to one another as they determine their appropriate behaviors, what we might call a "keeping up with the Jones' effect". Positive spillovers have been found to (partially) determine household demand for rice in Indonesia, growth rates of GNP, and county and state expenditures.[7]

In practice, evidence of spatial effects is found in a patterned distribution of a variable of interest, or better yet, the model errors (residuals) from a regression of this variable on a set of independent variables that are thought to be predictive of the outcome, or dependent, variable. Typically this connotes an observance of geographic clusters, for example, high values on a variable "clustered" together in a block of neighboring areal units and low values in some other block of areal units, that are indicative of diffusion from one areal unit to another, and which are independent of other, rel-

Judith R. Blau, Kenneth C. Land and Glenn Deane, "Religious Participation, Religious Diversity, and Social Conditions", *Program On Non-Profit Organizations Working Paper No. 162 and Institution for Social and Policy Studies Working Paper No. 2162* (New Haven, CT, 1991), pp. 1–39. In addition to the previous references to the European fertility transition, see Stewart E. Tolnay, "The Spatial Diffusion of Fertility: A Cross-Sectional Analysis of Counties in the American South, 1940", *American Sociological Review*, 60 (1995), pp. 299–308, for an extension to fertility decline in the American South. On the contagious transmission of violent offenses, see Colin Loftin, "Assaultive Violence as a Contagious Process", *Bulletin of New York Academy of Medicine*, 62 (1986), pp. 550–555; Paul C. Hollinger, Daniel Offer and Eric Ostrov, "An Epidemiologic Study of Violent Death, Population Changes, and the Potential for Prediction", *American Journal of Psychiatry*, 144 (1987), pp. 215–219; and Arthur Kellerman, *Understanding and Preventing Violence: A Public Health Perspective* (Washington, DC, 1996).

7. See respectively, Anne C. Case, "Spatial Patterns in Household Demand", *Econometrica*, 59 (1991), pp. 953–965; Timothy G. Conley and Ethan Ligon, "Economic Distance, Spillovers, and Growth", *Working Paper University of California, Berkeley* (1995); Harry H. Kelejian and Dennis P. Robinson, "A Suggested Method of Estimation for Spatial Interdependent Models with Auto-correlated Errors, and an Application to a County Expenditure Model", *Papers in Regional Science*, 72 (1993), pp. 297–312; Anne C. Case and Harvey S. Rosen, "Budget Spillovers and Fiscal Policy Interdependence", *Journal of Public Economics*, 52 (1993), pp. 285–307.

evant, similarities among the areas. But "a patterned distribution" also implies that spatial effects can be negative. The spatial process implied here is one whereby an incident in one location *is made less likely* by an incident occurring in another location. In other words, the occurrence of an event in one location has a deterrent effect on future occurrences in a different location.

Although empirical illustrations of deterrent diffusion are far less common than are cases of positive spatial effects, some examples do exist. Our examination of lynchings in ten southern states in the US between 1890 and 1919 demonstrates the operation of deterrent "spillover". We found that a lynching in one county, net of the effect of social conditions that give rise to racial violence, induces fewer lynchings in nearby counties than we would predict if lynchings were distributed randomly.[8] A recent study of population change in Chicago census tracts in the 1970s and 1980s provides another example of deterrent diffusion. In this spatial analysis, the threat of violent crime and its "mobility response", net out-migration, diffused from neighborhoods located in the ghetto core beginning in the 1970s. As the threat of violent crime spread out of the ghetto core, an increase in neighboring tracts triggered white population decline as whites fled to safer, more removed, neighborhoods.[9]

HOW DO SPATIAL PROCESSES OPERATE?

The interpretation of social diffusion relies heavily upon analogy to the spread of contagious disease in the public health literature.[10] The image, then, is one of a "contagion" that spreads through the contact of carriers ("infecteds") with uninfected members of the population ("susceptibles"). The spread of a contagion depends on the density of infecteds, the density of susceptibles, the extent of contact between the two groups, and the virulence of the disease (the probability that a carrier will infect a susceptible when contact is made). Additionally, a contagion will become epidemic if the diffusion exceeds a critical value, or "threshold". The threshold value is the rate at which new infections exceed removals, and the extent to which the threshold value is exceeded determines the rate of diffusion.

The model just described was proposed and formalized for the diffusion of a wide array of social behaviors as a "threshold model of collective

8. Stewart E. Tolnay, Glenn Deane and E.M. Beck. "Vicarious Violence: Spatial Effects on Southern Lynchings, 1890–1919", *American Journal of Sociology*, 102 (1996), pp. 788–815.

9. Jeffrey D. Morenoff and Robert J. Sampson, "Violent Crime and the Spatial Dynamics of Neighborhood Transition: Chicago, 1970–1990", *Social Forces*, 76 (1997), pp. 31–64.

10. The terminology used in this paragraph is commonplace in the public health/epidemiological literature on contagious disease. For example, see Roy M. Anderson and D.J. Nokes, "Mathematical Models of Transmission and Control", *Oxford Textbook of Public Health*, 2nd ed. (Oxford, 1991).

behavior".[11] Interpreted in this fashion, an individual's decision to adopt a technology, engage in a behavior, or adhere to a belief system depends, in part, on the behavior of other individuals. In the epidemiological literature, a contagion typically begins slowly, then accelerates rapidly until infections saturate the population-at-risk and the density of susceptibles shrinks. Thereafter, it slows and eventually falls below the critical value, at which point the epidemic collapses.

Threshold models of collective behavior include other diffusion distributions, however. Positive diffusion of social phenomena need not follow the same path as disease contagion and obviously deterrent diffusion will involve negative effects for the impact of spatial influence on a study phenomenon. While the shape of diffusion distributions may differ, each will be nonlinear and each is derived from a mixture of individual thresholds for joining. For example, the diffusion of church membership across US counties in the early twentieth century has been shown to result from strong collective behavior influence on counties with low and high church membership rates, but influence on counties with membership rates between these extremes is weak.[12] In other words, the pattern of collective influence that distributed church membership was the opposite of the pattern attributed to disease contagion, but nonetheless indicates the operation of a diffusion process.

Clearly collective behavior models, and contagion models in general, unfold over time and, as such, require repeated observations at short-time intervals to map the diffusion process. Unfortunately this type of systematic, quantitative historical data is rarely, if ever, available. Thus spatial-effects models of diffusion must take a different approach. Spatial clusters, of either a dependent variable or model errors, are "snapshots" of diffusion and are interpretable if we assume that we have captured the process at a point at which it is not changing too rapidly to quantify meaningfully.[13] In other words, diffusion may take place over time but it leaves its mark in the spatial dependence we observe as departures from randomness. We can then quantify this "mark" and interpret its magnitude and the direction of its effect.

11. Mark Granovetter, "Threshold Models of Collective Behavior", *American Journal of Sociology*, 83 (1978), pp. 1420–1443; Mark Granovetter and Roland Soong, "Threshold Models of Diffusion and Collective Behavior", *The Journal of Mathematical Sociology*, 9 (1983), pp. 165–180.
12. Documented in Land *et al.*, "Religious Pluralism and Church Membership", pp. 237–249.
13. "Spillover effects" satisfy this requirement more readily than contagion effects because they do not change over time and across space as rapidly. For example, the fact that a state's spending depends on the spending of similarly situated (in terms of economic and demographic conditions) states or that a lynching in one county diminishes the demand for lynchings in neighboring counties speaks to a lack of independence among observations, rather than the rapid unfolding of a disease or social contagion. This should not suggest, however, that spillovers are any less powerful or important than contagion effects. Indeed the methods for incorporating either of these diffusion processes are the same regardless of the source of the spatial process. We can simply be more sure when dealing with spillovers that the effect we are quantifying is accurate.

SIMPLE METHODS FOR THE DETECTION AND INCORPORATION OF SPATIAL EFFECTS

How do we know if observations in a cross-sectional sample are spatially dependent? How do we redress this dependence if it exists? The answers to both of these questions require a partitioning of the region of interest into an $N \times N$ matrix, where there are N areas in the geographic space.[14] For example, a contemporary spatial analysis of contiguous US states would result in a 48 × 48 matrix. How do we represent the relationship between areal units in the matrix? Probably the most common choice is the construction of an "adjacency" matrix, in which spatially adjacent areal units (where area i shares a common border with area j) are assigned scores of 1, and 0 otherwise (including the main diagonal). Another popular choice is the inverse of the distance between the geographic centers of the areal units (again with the main diagonal set to zero). This establishes a decay function that will weigh the effect of events in geographically closer units more heavily than those in more distant units. Inverse distance matrices are particularly useful partitions of geographic space when the phenomenon of interest involves the transfer or exchange of information. Consider, for example, the recent evidence on fertility decline. It is certainly reasonable to expect that networks spreading information about the benefits of fertility control would operate locally. Fertility limitation in distant places probably went unnoticed or, at best, carried little weight in the "numeracy" of young men and women.[15]

The choice of matrix representations is by no means limited to the two examples given here. In fact there is an infinite number of *weight matrices*, but some representations will be more substantively and historically compelling than others.[16] For example, in their analysis of southern lynching patterns, Tolnay *et al.* used the inverse of *cubed distance (in miles) between county centers* to weigh the spatial impact of lynchings. This decay function was chosen because it closely matched an impact radius of approximately 30 miles, an area judged to cover local information networks at the turn of the century in principally rural areas.[17]

14. In the language of network analysts, this matrix establishes a connection between every ego (indexed by the i rows of the matrix) and every alter (indexed by the j columns of the matrix) in the geographic space. Cells on the main diagonal of the square $N \times N$ matrix represent areal units linked to themselves. In spatial analyses, the main diagonal is always ignored.
15. See Watkins, *From Provinces Into Nations*, pp. 64–70; Pollack and Watkins, "Cultural and Economic Approaches to Fertility", pp. 482–483; Etienne van de Walle, "Fertility Transition, Conscious Choice and Numeracy", *Demography*, 29 (1992), pp. 487–502; Tolnay, "The Spatial Diffusion of Fertility", p. 301.
16. For a discussion of weights, see Keith Ord, "Estimation Methods for Models of Spatial Interaction", *Journal of the American Statistical Association*, 70 (1975), pp. 120–121; Patrick Doreian, "Estimating Linear Models with Spatially Distributed Data", in *Sociological Methodology* (San Francisco, 1981), pp. 362–364; and Case, "Spatial Patterns in Household Demand", p. 959.
17. Tolnay *et al.*, "Vicarious Violence", pp. 801–802.

With a weight matrix in hand, statistical methods designed to answer the two questions posed at the beginning of this section are readily available and easily implemented. The most common measure of spatial autocorrelation is Moran's I.[18] The presence of spatial dependence, as indicated by a significant Moran's I, is consistent with several spatially regressive models, including the spatial-effects model we are concerned with here.

The spatial-effects regression model has been available for quite some time, but the absence of computer software hindered empirical applications of the model.[19] We now have much more accessible least-squares estimators for spatial-effects models that are widely available in statistical packages such as SAS and SPSS. A detailed description of the estimators and the method of estimation is available in the articles referenced in our annotated bibliography at the end of this essay. Our goal here is simply to provide a non-technical illustration of what happens when the estimation method is applied.

The procedure involves two stages, each one requiring the regression of a dependent variable on a set of independent (predictor) variables.[20] Suppose a variable of interest, say, the number of lynching incidents per county in a given decade, is regressed on a set of independent variables, representing relevant social, economic, demographic and political characteristics of those counties. For each county, we would now have an observed number of lynchings and a predicted number of lynchings:

Matrix A

	Actual number of lynchings	Predicted number of lynchings
county A	3	2.7
county B	5	4.1
county C	2	2.2
⋮	⋮	⋮
county K	1	0.8

18. P.A.P. Moran, "A Test for the Serial Independence of Residuals", *Biometrika*, 37 (1950), pp. 178–181. See also, A.D. Cliff and Keith Ord, *Spatial Autocorrelation* (London, 1973), pp. 13–15, 29–33; and Doreian, "Estimating Linear Models with Spatially Distributed Data", pp. 371, 384–386.
19. See Ord, "Estimation Methods for Models of Spatial Interaction", pp. 120–126; Doreian, "Estimating Linear Models with Spatially Distributed Data", pp. 359–388.
20. See Luc Anselin, *Spatial Econometrics: Methods and Models* (Boston, 1988); Kenneth C. Land and Glenn Deane, "On the Large-Sample Estimation of Regression Models with Spatial- or Network-Effects Terms: A Two-Stage Least Squares Approach", in *Sociological Methodology* (Washington, DC, 1992), pp. 221–248. Anselin developed two regression estimators for spatial-effects models. The most general approach, known as an "instrumental variables" two-stage least squares (2SLS) method, was developed independently by Land.

The actual number of lynchings will be the dependent variable in the second-stage regression as well. The predicted number of lynchings is used to construct the "spatial-effects term".

Next we need a *weight matrix* that links areal unit i to every other unit j. Suppose, for the sake of simplicity, that we have a geographic space that can be subdivided into only four areal units, counties A, B, C and K, as shown above. The resulting weight matrix will be a 4 x 4 square with 16 cells – although cells on the main diagonal will always hold zero values because a unit cannot influence itself. In this example, we will place inverse distance (in miles) between units in the off-diagonal cells. For instance, in this case, the geographic center of county A is 25 miles from the center of county B; the center of county A is 30 miles from the center of county C, and so on.

Matrix B

	county A	county B	county C	county K
county A	0	1/25	1/30	1/150
county B	1/25	0	1/60	1/200
county C	1/30	1/60	0	1/120
county K	1/150	1/200	1/120	0

The spatial effects of all other j units on unit i is then given by weighting their predicted values of the dependent variables by their distance from unit i and summing over the j units. This "weighting" is accomplished by multiplying each j predicted value (in Matrix A) by its inverse distance from unit i (in Matrix B):

county A	county B	county C	county K			county A	county B	county C	county K	
2.7	4.1	2.2	0.8	×	county A	0	1/25	1/30	1/150	=
2.7	4.1	2.2	0.8	×	county B	1/25	0	1/60	1/200	=
2.7	4.1	2.2	0.8	×	county C	1/30	1/60	0	1/120	=
2.7	4.1	2.2	0.8	×	county K	1/150	1/200	1/120	0	=

and then adding the product elements in each row, resulting in a single value for each unit i:

	county A		county B		county C		county K		lynching exposure
county A	2.7×0	+	$4.1 \times 1/25$	+	$2.2 \times 1/30$	+	$0.8 \times 1/150$	=	.238
county B	.11	+	0	+	.037	+	.0040	=	.151
county C	.090	+	.068	+	0	+	.0067	=	.323
county K	.018	+	.021	+	.018	+	0	=	.05

Land and Deane refer to the spatial-effects term as a "generalized population-potential variable", acknowledging the origin of this measure in the migration research of Duncan, Cuzzort and Duncan.[21] This term aptly reflects the fact that the "potential" variable summarizes the spatial effects of the variable of interest in surrounding areal units on a particular unit i, where the influence of each of the j units is discounted by its distance from unit i. We label the *generalized population-potential variable*, "lynching exposure", in the illustration above. For example, county C is "exposed" to more lynchings than county K. Put simply, this means that, on average, the other counties that are closer to county C had experienced more lynchings than the counties that are closer to county K. Once the set of lynching exposure values has been derived, they are entered as an additional independent variable in an equation predicting the *actual number* of lynchings experienced by each county. The regression coefficient computed for the lynching exposure variable is referred to as the "spatial-effects term".

INTERPRETING EFFECTS IN A SPATIAL REGRESSION MODEL

The interpretation of effects in a spatial regression model differs from that encountered in an ordinary linear and additive regression model. Spatial regression models are *interaction models*. The presence of the spatial-effects term in a spatial regression model renders a single value for the effect of an independent variable on the dependent variable somewhat of an oversimplification. By rewriting the spatial regression model, it can be easily shown that the spatial-effects term conditions (i.e. establishes an interaction, or multiplicative, effect on) the effects of other independent variables.[22] Thus a change in an independent variable in areal unit j affects the dependent variable in unit j, which in turn affects the dependent variable in neighbor-

21. Land and Deane, "On the Large-Sample Estimation", pp. 236–238; Otis Dudley Duncan, Ray P. Cuzzort and Beverly Duncan, *Statistical Geography* (Glencoe, IL, 1961).
22. See Case, "Spatial Patterns in Household Demand", pp. 955–956.

ing units. Therefore, a dependent variable in unit i changes both because of change in the explanatory variables and change in its neighbors' dependent variable. These interaction effects are captured by the spatial-effects term and vary across areal units (as will be demonstrated below).

From an interpretive standpoint, this accomplishes exactly the "localizing" of historical process that has been recently asked of historical sociologists.[23] In practice, the product of this interaction between the spatial-effects term and an independent variable allows the effect of a change in an independent variable on the dependent variable to be unit specific and, as with nonlinear effects in general, no single estimate is sufficient to describe the effect of an independent variable throughout its entire range.[24] In these circumstances, it is preferable either to graph the (nonlinear) effect or illustrate the range of the effect, usually by selecting (at least) a low, middle and high value from the range of effects.

THE DIFFUSION OF RELIGION AND THE DETERRENCE OF LYNCHINGS: TWO ILLUSTRATIONS

To illustrate the contribution of spatial-effects models to social history, we present two examples that incorporate features of the typology developed above. The first example comes from the remarkable expansion of church membership early in the twentieth century in the United States. In this example, the diffusion process captured in the statistical analysis is *positive* and moving rapidly across geographic space. The second illustration extends the research of Tolnay and Beck on the causes of lynchings in the American South during the late nineteenth and early twentieth centuries.[25] The spatial process in this study is *negative* and interpreted as an areal *spillover*. Together, these examples incorporate all the aspects of spatial processes we have discussed in this essay.

Example 1: religious pluralism and church membership

Historians of American religion now agree that rates of church membership have risen dramatically since the eighteenth century. In *The Churching of America*, Roger Finke and Rodney Stark provide empirical documentation of the growth in American religious adherence, setting the colonial adherence rate at 17 per cent and the current rate at over 60 per cent.[26] Most

23. Isaac, "Transforming Localities", p. 5.
24. The "product of this interaction" to which we refer is not the usual product term one solves in ordinary least-squares regressions. For details, see Case, "Spatial Patterns in Household Demand", pp. 955–957.
25. Tolnay *et al.*, "Vicarious Violence", pp. 788–815. See also Stewart E. Tolnay and E.M. Beck, *A Festival of Violence: An Analysis of Southern Lynchings, 1882–1930* (Urbana, 1995).
26. Finke and Stark, *The Churching of America*, pp. 15–16.

church historians link the expansion of religious adherence to periodic "eruptions" of religious excitement, citing the occurrences of "Great Awakenings" in the second quarter of the eighteenth century and again in the first quarter of the nineteenth century, the ascendence of the Baptists in the early twentieth century, and the "explosion" of evangelical Protestantism in general since the 1970s. Other historians of religion challenge the accuracy of this imagery of "eruptions" and "explosions", preferring the more mundane notion of "religious economies" comprised of denominational competition with an organizational life course of growth, decline and periodic attempts to revive enthusiasm.[27] But whether the history of growth in American religious adherence was one of "eruptions" or "economies", the source of this expansion was the same: revivalism.

Revivalism

This has been an active and mobile enterprise in America since the exploits of the first great revivalist, George Whitefield, in the 1730s and 1740s. The importance of revivals in the expansion of religious adherence, and the way in which they are carried out, has changed little since Whitefield's campaigns.[28] For hundreds of years, revivalists have traversed the country, stopping in urban centers even more often than in the rural frontier, spreading their message of faith, community and "brotherly" love. It should come as no surprise, then, that church membership rates retain the mark of geographic diffusion.

Using the religious censuses of 1906, 1916 and 1926 for all US counties and the spatial-effects model we describe here, Land and Blau provide the first compelling empirical documentation of this process.[29] Their spatial analyses clearly establish the impact of a county's religious surroundings on its own rate of church adherence and Granovetter's model of collective influence frames the theoretical interpretation of this evidence.

Data and variables

Aggregate church membership data from the 1906, 1916 and 1926 Censuses of Religious Bodies are available for all US counties. For the sake of consistency with their independent variables, Land *et al.* relate these religious

---

27. For a summary of these positions, see *ibid.*, pp. 87–92.

28. For a summary of Whitefield's tactics, see *ibid.*, pp. 88–89; and Frank Lambert, " 'Pedlar in Divinity': George Whitefield and the Great Awakening, 1737–1745", *Journal of American History*, 77 (1990), pp. 812–837.

29. Land *et al.*, "Religious Pluralism and Church Membership", pp. 237–249. See also Land and Deane, "On the Large-Sample Estimation of Regression Models", pp. 221–248; Blau *et al.*, "Religious Participation, Religious Diversity, and Social Conditions", pp. 1–39; Blau *et al.*, "The Expansion of Religious Affiliation", pp. 329–352.

censuses to the decennial US census dates of 1910, 1920 and 1930. Although their analyses are not longitudinal, a historical county template is used to aggregate counties involved in boundary changes during the study period into approximately 1,600 county groups.[30] A 50 per cent random sample of counties stratified by percentage urban formed the initial study sample, while the remaining 50 per cent was used to assess the robustness of their conclusions in replicate analyses.

The dependent variable was defined as a *church adherence rate*, the number of church members divided by county population (multiplied by 100). In addition to the spatial-effects term, *church adherence potential*, seven independent variables were considered. Following the literature on the full set of social forces thought to affect church membership, explanatory variables included *percentage Catholic, religious diversity, percentage change in population, ethnic diversity* (using approximately 40 ethnic-origin categories available in the 1910, 1920 and 1930 decennial censuses), *percentage, urban percentage illiterate* and *economic well-being* (average manufacturing wages in county in 1920 and 1930, and average crop value in 1910).

Observing diffusion

Land *et al.* estimate their spatial-effects models (for 1910, 1920 and 1930) using a two-stage procedure similar to the method described above. Elements of the weight matrix used in these models are measured as inverse distance, in miles, from county (or county-group) centers. In the second-stage regressions, *church adherence rate* is regressed on the set of relevant independent variables described above and *church adherence potential*. These regressions are shown in Table 1. The effect of *church adherence potential*, the model's spatial-effects term, is positive and significant in all three decades (.33 in 1910; .29 in 1920; and .28 in 1930). Substantively, this means that counties that are surrounded by counties with high rates of church membership will tend to have high membership rates themselves. Statistically, this means that a one point increase in *church adherence potential* increases a county's church membership rate by about a third of a point (and a ten point increase in *adherence potential* increases a county's membership rate by about three points, and so on).

The importance of *church adherence potential* is highlighted if one compares these results with regressions in which *church adherence potential* is excluded: R^2, a summary measure of the proportion of variance in the dependent variable explained by the independent variables, declines from .52 to .38, from .49 to .39, and from .49 to .39 for 1910, 1920 and 1930 respectively. Clearly, spatial diffusion is a powerful and significant compo-

---

30. Patrick M. Horan and Peggy G. Hargis, "The County Longitudinal Template", Paper presented at the Annual Meeting of the Social Science History Association, Chicago, 1989.

Table 1. *Second-stage least squares coefficients: church adherence rate on church adherence potential and selected independent variables for US counties, 1910, 1920, 1930 (t-ratios in parentheses)*

Independent variable	1910	1920	1930
Intercept	31.47***	50.84***	54.26***
	(5.75)	(12.24)	(11.73)
Religious diversity index	−22.67***	−28.39***	−35.56***
	(−9.96)	(−9.21)	(−10.12)
Percentage Catholic	.36***	.28***	.28***
	(10.55)	(7.53)	(7.33)
Percentage change in	−1.91***	−12.58***	−15.23***
population	(−5.06)	(−6.03)	(−7.10)
Church adherence potential	(12.66)	(10.93)	(10.54)
Ethnic diversity index	−11.97***	−15.17***	−8.40***
	(−4.76)	(−5.18)	(−2.54)
Percentage urban	.04**	.00	.03
	(2.92)	(.24)	(1.52)
Percentage illiterate (log)	2.27***	1.99***	1.46***
	(6.51)	(5.46)	(3.77)
Economic well–being (log)[a]	.13	−1.22***	−.95*
	(.21)	(−3.33)	(−2.53)
N	731	697	663
R^2	.52	.49	.49

Notes:
*$p < .05$ **$p < .01$ ***$p < .001$
[a]For 1910, average crop value; for 1920 and 1930, average manufacturing wages.

nent of church adherence early in the twentieth century, although the effect of *church adherence potential* declines slightly from 1910 to 1930 suggesting that the choice of whether to be a member of an organized religious body became increasingly independent of collective behavior influences over time.

Figure 1 shows a scatterplot of church adherence rates (on the vertical axis) against church adherence potential (on the horizontal axis) for 1910.[31] As expected, the relationship is indeed nonlinear. Scatters of the type shown in Figure 1 are perhaps the best evidence available of spatial diffusion because the "best-fitting" line through this scatter (also shown in Figure 1) recalls the segments symptomatic of the collective behavior (contagion) process we discussed earlier. The shape of the scatter is indicative of a bimodal frequency distribution of thresholds for church membership in the population, with a strong collective influence at the low end of the distribution of church membership (indicated by the steep slope of the polynomial near the origin) followed by a lower level of influence in the middle part of the

31. Results for 1920 and 1930 were practically identical.

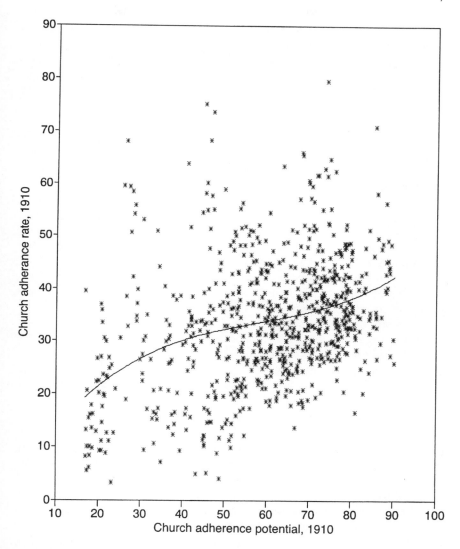

Figure 1. Relationship between church adherence rate and adherence potential

curve (indicated by the "flatter" slope in the middle of the curve) and then another high collective influence region at the upper end of the scatter (shown by the increasing slope of the line).[32]

Although the motivations of actors can only be inferred from aggregate and cross-sectional data, the pattern shown in Figure 1 is consistent with

32. See Land *et al.*, "Religious Pluralism and Church Membership", pp. 241–242.

the history of revivalism and fully anticipated by Granovetter's theory of collective influence. This history recounts the travels of revivalists through regions with low rates of church membership as they "awakened" a religious spirit in the people of these regions. The other principal destination was to revisit regions with already high rates of adherence in an effort to maintain or rekindle spiritual enthusiasm. In terms of social contagion, the theory of collective influence predicts that counties with low rates of church membership will be highly susceptible to conversion simply because their populations are "at high risk", while counties with (relatively) high rates of adherence will be vulnerable to strong imitative/conformity processes when surrounded by other counties with high adherence rates.

Example 2: vicarious violence in the American South, 1890–1919

The history of race relations in the American South during the late nineteenth and early twentieth centuries is a violent one. In addition to frequent beatings, whippings and verbal assaults, southern blacks faced the very real possibility of death at the hands of white lynch mobs. Recent scholarship has provided strong evidence that racial violence was one mechanism used by the white population to perpetuate its social, economic and political domination of southern society.[33] The lynching, these authors argue, was a form of state tolerated terrorism aimed at the black community to preserve white hegemony and maintain the caste boundary. That lynchings were tolerated by the state and sometimes even sanctioned is suggested by the extremely low probability of arrest, prosecution and conviction of mob members – despite the fact that they were often well known to authorities.

The terroristic function of lynchings, coupled with relatively efficient avenues of communication regarding lynchings that had occurred, raise the interesting possibility that incidents of white-on-black violence across regions of the South were not independent of one another. Virtually all of the evidence for spatial processes has demonstrated – as did our first example – that a characteristic or event in one location is made *more likely* by the same characteristic or event in another location. As we have pointed out, however, positive diffusion is not the only type of spatial process that could have been operating. Indeed, the spatial-effects regressions of Tolnay *et al.* show that a lynching incident in one county actually *decreased the*

---

33. See for example, Edward L. Ayers, *Vengeance and Justice: Crime and Punishment in the 19th-Century American South* (New York, 1984); Beck and Tolnay, "The Killing Fields of the Deep South", pp. 526–539; W. Fitzhugh Brundage, *Lynching in the New South: Georgia and Virginia, 1880–1930* (Urbana, 1993); Jay Corzine, Lin Corzine and James Creech, "The Tenant Labor Market and Lynching in the South: A Test of Split Labor Market Theory", *Sociological Inquiry*, 58 (1988), pp. 261–278; Herbert Shapiro, *White Violence and Black Response: From Reconstruction to Montgomery* (Amherst, 1988); Tolnay and Beck, "Racial Violence and Black Migration in the South", pp. 103–116; Tolnay and Beck, *A Festival of Violence*.

likelihood of an incident in nearby counties – net of other factors related to the frequency of lynching. There are two primary processes through which "negative spatial effects" may have operated, both of which assume the use of lynchings as a form of terroristic social control over southern blacks. The first emphasizes the reactions of whites; the second focuses on the responses of the African-American community.

It is clear from the way that lynchings were conducted that one of their important terroristic functions was to send a "message" to the black community. That message was to warn blacks not to expect more from southern society than whites were willing to give. Based on these efforts to publicize lynchings, one must conclude that southern whites believed strongly in the general deterrent effect of lynchings. That is, by punishing a single offender, they believed that they could discourage similar offenses by others. While many southern whites agreed that lynchings could be useful for keeping local African-Americans in their place, perhaps the same effect was accomplished when lynchings occurred elsewhere, especially in neighboring areas. Other things being equal, if local blacks made a special effort to avoid antagonizing the white community – in response to a nearby lynching – then the likelihood of a lynching in their own community may have been attenuated.[34] Even if nearby lynchings had little impact on the behavior of local blacks, the motivation for mob action may have been reduced *if whites were convinced of the deterrent effect of lynchings*. An even more sinister, and less utilitarian, possibility is that lynchings in other areas satisfied a certain "bloodlust" among local whites, thereby reducing their urge to lynch.

Unlike the more common "positive contagion/diffusion effect" illustrated by our previous empirical example, a "negative spillover effect" for lynching describes a process whereby an incident in one location is made *less likely* by an incident occurring in a neighboring location. The result of such a process would be a *negative* correlation in the frequency of lynchings across nearby counties suggesting a "satisfied" white population, an intimidated black population, or both causal mechanisms.

Data and variables

Information for lynching incidents is drawn from a new inventory of southern lynchings in which each event was verified through stories carried in contemporary southern newspapers.[35] The number of lynching *incidents* that

34. This speculation is not meant to imply that all southern blacks cowered in response to violent threats from the white community. There were many instances in which blacks offered strong resistance to lynch mobs (cf. W. Fitzhugh Brundage, "The Darien 'Insurrection' of 1899: Black Protest During the Nadir of Race Relations", *Georgia Historical Quarterly*, 74 (1990), pp. 234–253; Shapiro, *White Violence and Black Response*, though the result of such resistance was often intensified bloodshed.

35. For additional information about this lynching inventory and how it was constructed, see Tolnay and Beck, *A Festival of Violence*.

claimed at least one black victim is used because the type of spatial processes described above were more likely to be triggered by the mere occurrence of lynching events, rather than the number of *victims* claimed in each event, or the *rate* of victimization. Incidents are further restricted to those that were conducted by a white mob. Lynching incidents are aggregated to a county-level for ten southern states and, like the Land *et al.* study, county groups are created when a county's boundaries changed during a decade.

Separate spatial-effects models are estimated for three time periods during the "lynching era": 1895–1899, 1905–1909 and 1915–1919.[36] The second half of each of three decades (1890–1899, 1900–1909 and 1910–1919) is analyzed in order to allow for the inclusion of *lagged* effects in the models. The spatial-effects term in this analysis, therefore, refers to lynching incidents that occurred during the previous five-year period – for example, incidents in 1890–1894 are used to construct the spatial-effects term for lynchings in 1895–1899. The other explanatory variables can be grouped into four different categories: demographic, socioeconomic and cultural, lynching history, and geographic.[37]

The evidence of deterrence

As in our previous example, Tolnay *et al.* employ the two-stage procedure we described. The representation of distance in a weight matrix, however, has many possibilities. Tolnay *et al.* use a cubic transformation of distance (measured in miles) to construct their measure of *lynching exposure* because auxiliary analyses showed this closely matched an adjacency matrix in which a 30-mile radius from county centers formed the adjacency criterion, but with a smoother decay function.[38] Table 2 presents the findings obtained from estimation of the second-stage regression. Two models are reported for each decade. Model 1 is a bivariate equation that includes only *lynching exposure*, the spatial-effects term, as a predictor. Model 2 is the full equation,

36. This aggregation resulted in 783, 779 and 770 counties/county clusters for 1895–1899, 1905–1909 and 1915–1919, respectively from the ten states of Alabama, Arkansas, Florida, Georgia, Kentucky, Louisiana, Mississippi, North Carolina, South Carolina and Tennessee.
37. The relative size of the black population within each county, measured as *percentage black* and *percentage black squared*, represents the demographic controls. Two direct measures of the socioeconomic and cultural characteristics of counties, the *proportion of white farmers who were tenants* (again, both *linear* and *squared* terms are included) and the *proportion of 'improved acres' in the county that was planted in cotton* are also controlled. Cross-county variation in the general reliance on lethal punishment is represented by the *number of lynching incidents with white victims during the previous five years* and the *number of lynching incidents with black victims during the previous five years*. Finally, the *geographic location of counties*, and the selectivity this may represent, is also incorporated into the statistical controls through a set of dummy variables measuring proximity to border states. For details on the data used to construct these independent variables, see Tolnay *et al.*, "Vicarious Violence", pp. 802–804.
38. See *ibid.*, pp. 801–802.

Table 2. *Second-stage least squares coefficients: number of lynching incidents on lynching exposure and selected independent variables for US counties, 1895–1899, 1905–1909, 1915–1919 (standard errors in parentheses)*

| | 1895–1899 | | 1905–1909 | | 1915–1919 | |
	Model 1	Model 2	Model 1	Model 2	Model 1	Model 2
Spatial-effects term						
Lynching exposure	.333	-.983**	.458	−2.406***	1.728***	−.768*
	(.349)	(.437)	(.435)	(.580)	(.325)	(.449)
Demographic controls						
% Black		.095***		.115***		.122***
		(.026)		(.023)		(.016)
% Black^2		−.0009***		−.0008***		−.001***
		(.0003)		(.0002)		(.0002)
Socioeconomic and cultural controls						
% White tenants		.060**		−.095***		−.028
		(.029)		(.024)		(.023)
% White tenants^2		−.001**		.001***		.0003
		(.0005)		(.0003)		(.0003)
Cotton dominance		.024***		.044***		.026**
		(.008)		(.011)		(.011)
Lynching history controls						
Prior black lynchings		−1.519		−3.057**		−1.083
		(1.060)		(1.507)		(.837)
Prior white lynchings		.257		.992***		1.716***
		(.278)		(.335)		(.542)
Geographic controls						
Borders north		.070		.000^a		1.173*
		(.516)		(.470)		(.628)
Borders south		−.426		.067		.590
		(.343)		(.344)		(.382)
Scale	1.041	.985	.955	.853	.901	.813
Intercept	−1.162***	−3.126***	−1.501***	−1.786***	−1.803***	−4.104***
	(.112)	(.502)	(.116)	(.445)	(.096)	(.508)
Pseudo R^2	.001	.115	.001	.214	.029	.217

Notes:
^{a}Coefficient and standard error have been divided by 100,000 to adjust the scale.
*p < .10   ** p < .05   *** p < .01.

with all predictor variables. This presentation format is used so that the impact of the control variables on the effect of *lynching exposure* can be assessed. Our primary interest in Model 2 is in the direction and strength of the effect of *lynching exposure*.

Looking first at Model 1, for all three decades we find that *lynching exposure* has a *positive* bivariate effect on the observed number of *lynching*

incidents – for the 1915–1919 period the coefficient attains statistical significance. Thus the results for Model 1 would lead us to believe that lynchings
were either insensitive to events in other areas, or *more* frequent in counties
that were surrounded by other counties that had a large number of incidents. However, such a conclusion would be premature. As mentioned earlier, the "clustering" of high lynching counties in the same general area may
have been due to shared social, economic or cultural characteristics that
created an atmosphere conducive to the lynching of blacks, rather than the
operation of a spatial process distributing *lynching incidents* (independent of
these social, economic and cultural characteristics). The primary purpose of
the control variables added in Model 2 is to take into consideration those
potentially shared characteristics, thereby isolating spatial process as an independent phenomenon.

Indeed, the findings obtained from Model 2 are substantially different
from those observed for Model 1. In all three decades the coefficient for
lynching exposure reverses sign, and becomes significantly *negative* (at least
at the $p < .1$ level). Net of all other variables in the model, the spatial-effects
terms in Table 2 provide strong support for a "deterrence" process. That is,
more intensive lynching activity in surrounding areas actually *decreased* the
frequency of *lynching incidents* in these ten southern states.

"LOCALIZING" HISTORY: COUNTY-SPECIFIC
PREDICTORS OF LYNCHING

The spatial-effects model is an *interaction model*. The presence of the spatial-
effects term, *lynching exposure*, implies that the effects of the independent
variables are county-specific. The single estimates reported in Table 2 summarize these effects, but they may be quite misleading for any given county.
A more accurate representation, one that truly "localizes" the spatial process,
is given by unit-specific plots of effects. Figure 2 plots the county-specific
effect of *cotton dominance* (one of the social or economic conditions that is
related to the frequency of lynching in southern counties) using Model 2
from the 1895–1899 regression in Table 2 as our example.

The effect of *cotton dominance on lynching incidents* in this model is 0.024,
indicating that a greater reliance on cotton agriculture *increases* the likelihood of lynchings. This is consistent with several intersecting hypotheses
linking cotton agriculture to lynchings, including a racist ideology inherited
from slavery, demand for labor control over the heavily African-American
labor force, and economic competition between African Americans and poor
whites.[39] The horizontal pattern in Figure 2 shows that indeed most counties
are at or near this estimated effect, but in a spatial-effects model the effect
of *cotton dominance* on *lynching incidents* is conditioned by neighboring

39. See, for example, Tolnay and Beck, *A Festival of Violence*, ch. 5.

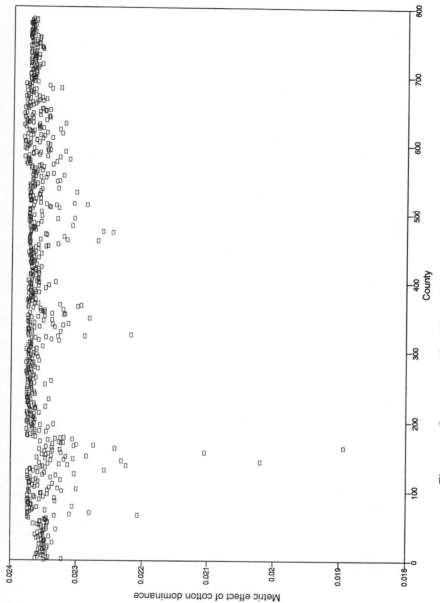

Figure 2. County-specific effects of cotton dominance, 1895–1899

counties' *lynching incidents*. Indeed, some of the counties' *cotton dominance* effects are substantially lower than 0.024 and can be seen in Figure 2 to fall away from this line. The three most extreme departures from the horizontal pattern are Marion, Clay and Alachua/Gilchrist counties in Florida. In these counties, the effect of *cotton dominance* has much less of an impact on lynchings than the coefficient in Table 2 would indicate.

Of course, a thorough understanding of the reasons behind the weakened effect in these Florida counties would require more extensive investigation, but components of the spatial-effects model do suggest some potentially fruitful avenues to pursue. In particular, three conditions probably came together to produce this departure from the norm: (1) these three counties formed a distinct spatial cluster (at the turn of the century) in that they were closer to each other than to any other counties; (2) only one lynching occurred in this cluster of counties between 1895–1899; but (3) they are situated in an area of (north-central) Florida in which almost all of the lynchings in that state occurred. Apparently this *lynching exposure* overwhelmed the typical effect of *cotton dominance* in these counties because their location concentrated the spatial effect of high *lynching incidents* to their west. Hence, the cultural and economic explanations of lynchings cited above do not apply equally well to all counties and the spatial-effects model has "localized" our social history in a very important way.

CONCLUDING REMARKS

Social historians often study phenomena that take place in geographical space and current theorizing has put forth the objective of "localizing" social processes. There is a wide range of historical phenomena that allude to the operation of spatial processes. For instance, diffusion processes in social history are customarily invoked to explain the impact of population contact through disease transfer and the spread of technologies, information, attitudes, beliefs and behaviors. Historians have amassed ample theoretical and empirical literatures on the spread of epidemic disease in "virgin populations" and considerable effort has gone into tracking the geography of epidemics in Native American populations following European contact. More recent efforts have emphasized the spread of ideas and behaviors. The European fertility decline in the nineteenth century, the diffusion of religious group/church membership across the United States in the "Great Awakenings" of the eighteenth and nineteenth centuries and in the evangelical Protestantism movements in this century, and the rise in violent crime in the second half of the twentieth century have all been regarded as contagious social processes, yet "space" rarely enters historical discourse *explicitly* as an analytic construct. Spatial-effects models do exactly this.

In this paper we have reviewed the common conditions under which spatial dependence arises, explained a two-stage procedure through which spatial dependence can be detected and removed, offered simple visual displays of the spatial process and the unit-specific effects of independent variables in the presence of spatial effects, and offered two illustrations of spatial processes in historical research. These examples were selected because they summarize the intersection of spatial dynamics with direction of influence. In both examples, spatial processes are inferred, but their verification requires data beyond those available for these studies. Much greater detail (most important of which is the *timing* of events) about specific circumstances is required to make such a determination. If this auxiliary information is available, then the "event-structure analysis" described by Griffin in this volume is possibly a more appropriate methodology for this challenge than is the cross-sectional analysis explicated in this paper.[40] However, additional evidence often is not available. In these circumstances it is reasonable to use the methods described in this essay to investigate the possibility that events occurring in different geographic areas are linked by more than mere coincidence, or by the fact that the locations share social conditions that help to determine the occurrence of those same events.

ANNOTATED BIBLIOGRAPHY

The development of the two-stage estimation for spatial models

The two-stage estimation method alluded to in this paper was developed (independently) by Luc Anselin and Kenneth Land. Their work is responsible for broadly expanding the application of spatial-effects models in the social sciences. The following publications give the technical details on model estimation:

Anselin, Luc, *Spatial Econometrics: Methods and Models* (Boston, 1988).

Land, Kenneth C. and Glenn Deane, "On the Estimation of Regression Models with Spatial Effects Terms for Large Samples: A Two-Stage Least Squares Approach", *Sociological Methodology* (Washington, DC, 1992), pp. 221–248.

Spatial-effects models applied in historical sociology/social history

To our knowledge, the following articles are the only historical studies to date using spatial-effects models:

Blau, Judith R., Kenneth C. Land and Kent Redding, "The Expansion of Religious Affiliation: An Explanation of the Growth of Church Participation in the United States, 1850–1930", *Social Science Research*, 21 (1992), pp. 329–352.

40. See also Larry J. Griffin, "Narrative, Event-Structure Analysis, and Causal Interpretation in Historical Sociology", *American Journal of Sociology*, 98 (1993), pp. 1094–1133.

Land, Kenneth C., Glenn Deane and Judith R. Blau, "Religious Pluralism and Church Membership: A Spatial Diffusion Model", *American Sociological Review*, 56 (1992), pp. 237–249.

Tolnay, Stewart E., "The Spatial Diffusion of Fertility: A Cross-Sectional Analysis of Counties in the American South, 1940", *American Sociological Review*, 60 (1995), pp. 299–308.

Tolnay, Stewart E., Glenn Deane and E.M. Beck, "Vicarious Violence: Spatial Effects on Southern Lynchings, 1890–1919", *American Journal of Sociology*, 102 (1996), pp. 788–815.

Spatial analysis: alternatives to the two-stage method of estimation

The generation of spatial models described in this paper were formulated by Keith Ord, a geographer, in the early 1970s and introduced into sociology by Patrick Doreian. A number of economists and regional scientists continue to develop spatial models using alternative methods to the two-stage procedure we describe. Anselin's contributions, most recently in the area of "exploratory spatial data analysis", are the most notable and his SpaceStat software is the only statistical package written expressly for spatial data analysis.

Anselin, Luc, "Exploratory Spatial Data Analysis and Geographic Information Systems", in *New Tools for Spatial Analysis* (Luxembourg, 1994), pp. 45–54.

Anselin, Luc, *SpaceStat Version 2.0.*, Bruton Center for Development Studies, University of Texas at Dallas, Dallas, TX (forthcoming, 1998).

Case, Anne C., "Spatial Patterns in Household Demand", *Econometrica*, 59 (1991), pp. 953–965.

Devine, Owen J., Thomas A. Louis and M. Elizabeth Halloran, "Identifying Areas with Elevated Disease Incidence Rates Using Empirical Bayes Estimators", *Geographical Analysis*, 28 (1996), pp. 187–199.

Doreian, Patrick, "Estimating Linear Models with Spatially Distributed Data", in *Sociological Methodology* (San Francisco, 1980), pp. 359–388.

Kelejian Harry H., and Dennis P. Robinson, "A Suggested Method of Estimation for Spatial Interdependent Models with Autocorrelated Errors, and an Application to a County Expenditure Model", *Papers in Regional Science*, 72 (1993), pp. 297–312.

Ord, Keith, "Estimation Methods for Models of Spatial Interaction", *Journal of the American Statistical Association*, 70 (1975), pp. 120–126.

International Review of Social History 43 (1998), Supplement, pp. 81–104
© 1998 Internationaal Instituut voor Sociale Geschiedenis

Narrative as Data: Linguistic and Statistical Tools for the Quantitative Study of Historical Events*

Roberto Franzosi

This paper illustrates some linguistic and statistical tools that can be profitably used by historians and social historians in the study of events (such as strikes, demonstrations and other types of collective conflict). More specifically, the paper shows that "semantic grammars" provide rigorous tools for the collection of rich event narratives. Semantic grammars structure information around the "canonical form" of the language: noun phrase/verb phrase, or subject, action, object and their modifiers (e.g. time, space). The fact that semantic grammars can be easily implemented in a computer environment using relational database systems (RDBMS) makes feasible the practical application of such powerful coding schemes. The data that computer-based semantic grammars make available are richer, more flexible and more reliable than those delivered by more traditional content analysis methods. They are also very well suited for the application of new tools of data analysis such as network models. Both semantic grammars and network models are fundamentally concerned with actors and their actions, with agents and agency. As such, these linguistic and statistical tools should draw sociology closer to history, traditionally much more concerned with issues of agency. I illustrate the power of both the linguistic and statistical tools using data that I collected from some 15,000 newspaper articles on the 1919–1922 period of Italian history, a period characterized by widespread working-class mobilization (1919–1920, the "red years") and fascist counter-mobilization (1921–1922, the "black years").

INTRODUCTION

Historians have relied on narrative as both data and mode of analysis and communication. Few historians, however, have analyzed the narratives that form the basis of their empirical evidence (e.g. archival documents, police records, newspaper articles) in systematic ways through the application of content analysis techniques. Yet the use of content analysis in socio-

* Data collection for this project was supported, in part, by the National Science Foundation (grant SES–8511632). Data analysis and writing have benefited from another National Science Foundation grant (SBR–9411739). I am indebted to William Bainbridge and Andrea Kline for their help in transferring the NSF grant to the University of Oxford. I would also like to thank Larry Griffin for his comments on a previous draft and Mauro Giorgetti and PierPaolo Mudu for their help with data analysis.

historical research has proved fruitful.[1] Partly, historians' reliance on qualitative methods, but also the limitations of content analysis have made historians and social historians reluctant to "go from words to numbers" using
narrative as data for quantitative analysis.

In this paper, I illustrate a linguistic approach to collecting text data that
avoids the main shortcomings of traditional content analysis. The approach
is based on intrinsic properties of narrative text as captured by a semantic
grammar (or text grammar, or story grammar). A semantic grammar is
nothing but the simple semantic structure: Subject, Action, Object (SAO)
and respective modifiers, such as time, space, etc.[2] This approach to the
systematic use of narrative texts should be particularly appealing to historians as:

(a) it is best applicable to the study of historical events;
(b) it is squarely centered on agents and their actions;
(c) it preserves both the information and the narrative flow of the original
    text;
(d) it does not rely on theoretically defined coding categories;
(e) it yields far richer and more flexible historical records than traditional
    content analysis methods;
(f) it can be easily implemented in a computer environment through com-
    mercially available relational database systems;
(g) it allows researchers to go from words to numbers, i.e. to analyze quali-
    tative narrative data in quantitative ways; in particular, the organiz-
    ational structure of the narrative data in relational format centered on
    agents and actions mirrors the requirements of such statistical tech-
    niques as network models.

I will illustrate the power of the technique with reference to data that I
collected, on the basis of such a grammar, from some 15,000 newspaper
articles on protest events during the 1919–1922 period in Italy. I will show
that the empirical evidence that the grammar produces could not be
obtained in other ways.

A LINGUISTIC APPROACH TO CONTENT ANALYSIS: SEMANTIC GRAMMARS

In recent years, social scientists have recommended the use of linguistics to
overcome methodological (e.g. reliability) and theoretical (e.g. lack of con-

---

1. See for a review, Roberto Franzosi, "The Press as a Source of Socio-Historical Data. Issues in
the Methodology of Data Collection from Newspapers", *Historical Methods*, 20 (1987), pp. 5–16.
2. Roberto Franzosi, "From Words to Numbers: A Generalized and Linguistics-Based Coding
Procedure for Collecting Event-Data from Newspapers" in Clifford Clogg (ed.), *Sociological Methodology*, vol. 19 (Oxford, 1989), pp. 263–298; idem, "From Words to Numbers: A Set Theory
Framework for the Collection, Organization, and Analysis of Narrative Data", in Peter Marsden

sistent foundations) pitfalls inherent in traditional content analysis.[3] In particular, semantic grammars have been shown to yield richer and more flexible data records than traditional coding schemes.[4] Semantic grammars consist of a set of functionally defined (coding) categories that are compatible with a large variety of input text.[5] Semantic grammars can capture the deep meaning of a unit of text within a restricted set of linguistic categories. The following provides an example of a simplified semantic grammar specifically developed for the study of protest events:

<semantic triplet>	→	{<subject>} {<action>} [{<object>}]
<subject>	→	{<actor>} [{<actor modifiers>}]
<actor>	→	crowd, mob, students, peasants, . . .
<action>	→	{<action phrase>} [{<action modifiers>}]
<action phrase>	→	riot, assemble, protest, rally, . . .
<object>	→	{<actor>} {<inanimate object>} {<implicit targets>} {<infinitive clauses>}
<inanimate object>	→	building, road, car, bomb, . . .
<implicit target>	→	<actor>
<infinitive clauses>	→	<semantic triplet>

where: the symbol → refers to a rewrite rule (or production), i.e. it "rewrites" the element to its left in terms of the element(s) to its right; the symbol <> indicates that the element enclosed within it is a non-terminal entity, i.e. it can be further rewritten in terms of other elements; terminal entities that cannot be further rewritten appear in the grammar without the angular brackets; the symbol {} indicates that the element enclosed within it can be repeated several times; the symbol [] indicates that the element enclosed within it is optional.

According to the grammar outlined above, the semantic triplet is made up of (rewritten as) the set subject/action/object. This set provides the basic template for structuring text using a semantic grammar. It corresponds to the basic linguistic structure noun phrase/verb phrase, otherwise called the "canonical form" of the language. A <subject> is made up of one or more <actor>, such as crowd, mob, etc., with possible <actor modifiers>. The type and number of modifiers varies with the type of substantive application. In collective action research, typical <actor modifiers> might be: the <proper

---

(ed.), *Sociological Methodology*, vol. 24 (Oxford, 1994), pp. 105–136; idem, *From Words to Numbers: Narrative as Data* (Cambridge, forthcoming).

3. E.g. John Markoff *et al.*, "Toward the Integration of Content Analysis and General Methodology", in David R. Heise (ed.), *Sociological Methodology*, vol. 4 (Oxford, 1974); Franzosi, "From Words to Numbers: A Generalized and Linguistics-Based Coding Procedure".

4. *Ibid.*

5. On semantic grammars as general content analysis schemes see *ibid.*; Roberto Franzosi, "Narrative Analysis, or . . . Why (and How) Sociologists Should Be Interested in Narrative", in John Hagan (ed.), *Annual Review of Sociology*, vol. 24 (Palo Alto, 1998) and the bibliography cited there.

name of an individual>, the <number of actors>, the <type of actor> (e.g. male, female, armed, skilled), or the <organization> involved. Possible <action modifiers> could be: <negation> (e.g. do not), <type of action> (such as "general" or "wildcat" for a strike), <reason for action>, <outcome of action>, the <instrument of action> (e.g. "cannons" in military actions) or <time> and <space> of the action.

A semantic grammar not only provides a set of semantically defined categories of general applicability; it also specifies explicit relationships between categories (<actors> to <actions> and both to their respective <modifiers>). Furthermore, a grammar can specify different hierarchical levels of aggregation for the information. For example, we could aggregate semantic triplets into events and events into collective campaigns. Thus, a semantic grammar can organize text in both hierarchical and relational form.

To understand how a linguistic approach to content analysis works let's take one of the events described by French historian Roland Mousnier in his *Peasant Uprisings in Seventeenth-Century France, Russia, and China*[6] and code it within the categories of a semantic grammar.

At Bordeaux in May and June, 1635, a gabelle imposed on taverns and on wine set off a revolt of tavern keepers and makers of casks which drew in many craftsmen and day-laborers, with the complicity of the majority of the bourgeois, a large number of "persons of condition," and officials of the parlement, who "regarded these rebels as their liberators." The rebels "wanted to get control of Saint Julien's Gate [. . .] and let in the peasants of the surrounding district, to help them. This was being loudly demanded by the peasants, who wanted to share in the plunder of the town, which they thought they had at their mercy." This was at any rate the motive ascribed to them by the secretary to the duc d'Épernon, who wrote these lines; but among these peasants there were, along with gardeners and market gardeners, also vinegrowers and *laboureurs*, very seriously affected by the indirect taxes. A certain number of them managed to get into the town and take part in the revolt. The duc d'Épernon, governor of Guyenne, was unable to secure the help of the town militia or that of most of the neighboring gentry, nor was he able to raise soldiers in the usual way from his lands, among his own peasants, who hid themselves. He was reduced to a few gentlemen, a few "*honnêtes bourgeois*," and, in the town, to a few of his former soldiers, with whose aid he either overcame the rebels or persuaded them to yield. Hardly had they been more or less quieted when "the madness extended to the peasants of the countryside. These, having, during one of the riots, managed to plunder some houses in the town, withdrew with the loot to their villages, and their neighbours were soon stirred up by their bad example to engage in plundering [. . .] In a moment, all the villagers dropped their ploughs and took up arms instead: after robbing the houses in the countryside they gathered in great numbers in all the suburbs and strove to enter the town itself. The poor of the town wanted them to enter and tried to open a way for them [. . .]" They assembled in the suburb of Saint-Surin, where they burned

6. Roland Mousnier, *Peasant Uprisings in Seventeenth-Century France, Russia, and China* (New York, 1972), pp. 45–46.

several houses. The duc d'Épernon mounted his horse and set forth at the head of forty or fifty gentlemen of his guard. This time he secured the support of a few companies of the town militia. The peasants scattered. The cavalry chased them and killed forty or fifty. "The rest of the peasants, who had been waiting to see whether these would succeed or not, behaved themselves properly that year [. . .]" The king then granted an amnesty.

Appendix A gives Mousnier's text coded within the semantic categories of the grammar, with events and semantic triplets chronologically ordered. As one can see, a semantic grammar provides a tight organizational structure for much of the information available in the original narrative. Only one question: why bother? What is the point of organizing text within the framework of a semantic grammar? What do we gain from that effort? After all, as far as we know, Mousnier did not rely on semantic grammars to catalogue and organize his narratives.

No doubt it is possible to tell masterful historical stories without story grammars and computers. But the more complex a story, the more difficult it is to keep the threads together. Consider the case where researchers are confronted not just with one event narrative, but with hundreds, perhaps thousands of such narratives. Clearly, the scale of those numbers make it imperative for researchers to find more systematic ways of cataloguing and retrieving the information contained in the narratives. It is out of that work that hopefully will come the evidence on patterns of historical behavior and of interactions among actors, on changes in routines and reasons. It is out of that work, in other words, that will come a shift of focus from the event to the conjuncture, from the single event to patterns of events.[7]

A grammar helps us in taking the first step in that direction (by sorting out and cataloguing information in appropriate ways), but only the first step. Because, surely, once we have all that information on thousands of events sorted out along the categories of a semantic grammar, the question remains: what are we going to do with it? To do something with "it" we need at least two things. First, we need to be able to store the information in the computer. Otherwise, we might as well keep the narrative in its original form without the paraphernalia of all those coding labels. Second, we need a way to relate coding categories to each other, for example actors to actions or both actors and actions to their characteristics, in order to trace meaningful patterns of interaction. Fortunately, the two things are closely interrelated. The logic or set theoretical underpinnings of a semantic grammar allow us to express in a formal mathematical notation the relationship between the coding categories of the grammar. Those same mathematical principles serve as the foundation of powerful organizational data models for computer storage and retrieval, namely relational database management systems (RDBMS).[8]

---

7. Fernand Braudel, *On History* (Chicago, 1980), pp. 25–54, 64–82.
8. Franzosi, "From Words to Numbers: A Set Theory Framework".

In summary, a linguistic approach to content analysis yields richer and more flexible text data than traditional coding schemes.[9] First, coding under a semantic grammar preserves much of the original text input (if not syntactically, at least semantically). Second, all factual elements of discourse find an appropriate organizing label. Third, the various parts of discourse are interconnected in complex ways. Fourth, output coded under a semantic grammar has face validity: it must make sense to any competent reader of the language. This characteristic greatly increases data quality. Fifth, a semantic grammar provides a more natural way of organizing text than traditional coding schemes. Last but not least, a semantic approach to content analysis provides a coding scheme that is invariant across a large class of texts of particular interests to historians (namely, narrative texts). This scheme is deeply rooted in a body of linguistic theoretical knowledge, rather than the empirical *ad hoc* approach of much traditional content analysis. Finally, semantic grammars can be easily implemented in a computer environment via powerful RDBMS commercially available for both mainframe and PC platforms. It is the implementation of semantic grammars in a computer environment that makes their use practical, despite the complexity of their design. For all these reasons, whenever applicable, semantic grammars can achieve quality without sacrificing quantity.

FROM WORDS TO NUMBERS: THE LINCHPIN

No doubt having narrative information in a computer-based relational structure allows investigators to store and extract rich narrative information in general ways (e.g. asking which kind of actions peasants were more likely to engage in when they protested in seventeenth-century France). But the question remains: what are we going to do with that information? The answer to that question depends upon the ability to manipulate quantitatively the qualitative information available in a relational database.

I have shown[10] that through counting of information in the different categories of the grammar one can easily construct variables and estimate statistical models of the type $y = \alpha_0 + \beta_1 X_1 + \beta_2 X_2 + \ldots + \beta_k X_k + \varepsilon$, *despite the fact* that the underlying data are basically words. The ability to manipulate information statistically gives researchers greater power to investigate relationships, to bring out patterns, to tease out structures that lie behind the surface of the myriad of historical facts. Historians, however (and an increasing number of social scientists), may not feel at ease with a

9. On these issues, see Roberto Franzosi, "Strategies for the Prevention, Detection and Correction of Measurement Error in Data Collected from Textual Sources", *Sociological Methods and Research*, 18 (1989–1990), pp. 442–471; idem, "Computer-Assisted Coding of Textual Data: An Application to Semantic Text Grammars", *Sociological Methods and Research*, 19 (1990–1991), pp. 224–256.
10. Franzosi, "From Words to Numbers: A Set Theory Framework"; see also idem, *From Words to Numbers*.

representation of social reality based on variables rather than social actors. Indeed, where are the actors gone in the representation $y = f(X_1, X_2, \ldots, X_k)$? Where is agency? *These* are the fundamental concerns of historians. In Elton's words: "Despite attempts to deny this, it [quantitative history] can effectively operate only by suppressing the individual by reducing its subject matter to a collectivity of human data in which the facts of humanity have real difficulty in surviving."[11]

There is another way to go "from words to numbers", however, that these historians and social scientists may find more appealing.[12] Again, a set theoretical framework provides the fine thread that goes from words to numbers. Consider the set of skeleton semantic triplets, SAO (without modifiers), that a project of data collection on historical events will yield. This set T of size T ($T = t_1, t_2, t_3, \ldots t_T$) will contain a set of subjects S of size S (with $S = s_1, s_2, s_3, \ldots, s_S$), a set of actions A of size A (with $A = a_1, a_2, a_3, \ldots, a_A$), and a set of objects O of size O (with $O = o_1, o_2, o_3, \ldots, o_O$). While the set of subjects S is made up exclusively of social actors, the set of objects O contains both social actors and inanimate objects (e.g. <subject> peasants <action> plunder <object> *houses*; <subject> poor <action> burn <object> *houses*). Let us now select a subset O_1 from the set of objects O that will include only those objects that are social actors; then, let us join the set S of subjects and the subset O_1 of objects, to obtain the set of actors N of size N (with $N = n_1, n_2, n_3, \ldots, n_N$). Some twenty-four actors appear in Mousnier's description of the events that took place in Bordeaux in 1635. Thus, N has size 24, with N = authorities, tavern keepers, makers of casks, craftsmen, day-laborers, bourgeois, persons of condition, officials of the *parlement*, rebels, peasants, gardeners, market gardeners, vine-growers, *laboureurs*, governor, town militia, gentry, gentlemen, *honnêtes bourgeois*, soldiers, villagers, the poor, cavalry, king.[13]

Similarly, thirty-one distinct actions appear in Mousnier's account. The set of actions A is thus of size 31 with A = are tacit accomplice, approve, assemble, burn, behave properly, chase, control, demand, enter, get into, gather, grant an amnesty, help, impose *gabelle*, join revolt, kill, let into, open a way, overcome, persuade, plunder, rebel, revolt, rob, scatter, strive, take part in revolt, take up arms, try, yield, want.

In the SAO representation, the action basically operates as a relation between actors – a relation which is both dichotomous and directional: any

11. G.R. Elton, "Two Kinds of History", in Robert William Fogel and G.R. Elton, *Which Road to the Past? Two Views of History* (New Haven, 1983), pp. 71–121, 118–119.

12. For an excellent introduction to network analysis, see Stanley Wasserman and Katherine Faust, *Social Network Analysis. Methods and Applications* (Cambridge, 1994), chs 3 and 4.

13. Many elements in N simply provide alternative descriptions of the same social actors. For example, the word "rebels" is first used in the narrative to encompass tavern keepers, makers of casks, craftsmen, day-laborers if not also bourgeois, persons of condition and officials of the *parlement*; similarly, villagers may include peasants, laborers, vinegrowers, etc.

member of the set of actors N, n_i (where $n_i \in N$) either relates to another member n_j or does not; furthermore, whether an actor occupies the role of subject or object makes a difference (consider the triplets: "cavalry kills peasants" versus "peasants kill cavalry"). Not all social actors present in the database will relate to all other actors. If a tie is present between n_i and n_j, then we say that the ordered pair $<n_i, n_j>$ belongs to a special collection of pairs L. L, in other words, represents the set of triplets that contain a (human) object. As we have seen, not all triplets do (e.g. <subject> peasants <action> behave themselves properly).[14] If an ordered pair $<n_i, n_j>$ is in L, then the first actor in the pair relates to the second on the relation under consideration; we can write $n_i \, n_j$.[15] Each relation has a corresponding set of arcs, L_r, containing L_r ordered pairs of actors as elements (the subscript r ranges from 1 to R, the total number of aggregated relations).

The trouble is that a large-scale data collection project is likely to yield hundreds, perhaps thousands, of different actions/relations, too many for easy manipulation. One could reduce the number of distinct actions, (1) by eliminating synomous expressions (e.g. "join" and "take part in"; "plunder" and "engage in plundering"; "rebel", "revolt"); (2) by aggregating the distinct actions in broader spheres of actions, such as "protest", "violence", "communication", "movement", "facilitation", "authority". Four basic spheres of action account for almost all basic actions found in Mousnier's narrative: *protest* (assemble, gather, rebel, revolt, join revolt, take part in revolt, take up arms), *violence* (burn, chase, kill, overcome, plunder, rob, scatter), *movement* (enter, get into, gather, let into, open a way, scatter), *facilitation* (are tacit accomplice, approve, grant an amnesty, help, let into).[16] If we exclude the

14. It is in connection with a network representation of a story grammar that the limits of a story grammar start becoming apparent. A story grammar captures in its structure the elements of a syntactically well-formed narrative. "Tavern keepers and makers of casks revolt" is certainly a syntactically properly formed clause. Like all intransitive verbs, the verb "revolt" does not necessarily require an object. Yet tavern keepers and makers of casks do revolt *against somebody*, namely against those who imposed the *gabelle* on taverns and wine (presumably, state authorities). When we start analyzing networks of social interactions, dropping the triplet "tavern keepers and cask makers revolt" from analysis because it contains no *explicit* object would bias the network. Thus, when using narratives as mirrors of social reality, a semantic grammar must capture not only the narrative elements explicitly present in the text but also those semantically implied by the narrative. Although it is possible to modify the rewrite rule for the <object> in the following way: <object> <explicit object> <implicit object> to correct for the problem, there are further problems with a story grammar that may ultimately require investigators to use different linguistic tools (e.g. semantic roles; see Franzosi, *From Words to Numbers*. In the analyses that follow I have used triplets with implied objects.

15. The arrow does not refer to the linguists' rewrite rule but to the statisticians' directed relation from n_i to n_j.

16. It is probably impossible to classify verbs into mutually exclusive categories. Some verbs belong to different spheres of action ("fuzzy meaning"; see Franzosi, *From Words to Numbers*). "Assemble" or "gather" are both actions of "protest" and "movement". "Scatter" and "chase" are both actions of "violence" and "movement".

Table 1. *Relations of protest, violence and facilitation from Mousnier's narrative*

L_1 Relation$_1$1 Protest	L_2 Relation$_2$ Violence	L_3 Relation$_3$ Facilitation
\<tavern keepers, authorities\>	\<peasants, town houses\>	\<bourgeois, rebels\>
\<makers of casks, authorities\>	\<governor, rebels\>	\<persons of condition, rebels\>
\<craftsmen, authorities\>	\<villagers, country houses\>	\<officials of the *parlement*, rebels\>
\<day-laborers, authorities\>	\<villagers, suburb houses\>	\<bourgeois, rebels\>
\<gardeners, authorities\>	\<governor, peasants\>	\<persons of condition, rebels\>
\<gardeners, authorities\>	\<gentlemen, peasants\>	\<officials of the *parlement*, rebels\>
\<market gardeners, authorities\>	\<town militia, peasants\>	\<rebels, peasants\>
\<vinegrowers, authorities\>	\<cavalry, peasants\>	\<gentlemen, governor\>
\<*laboureurs*, authorities\>	\<cavalry, peasants\>	\<*honnêtes bourgeois*, governor\>
\<villagers, authorities\>		\<soldiers, governor\>
\<villagers, authorities\>		\<poor, villagers\>
		\<king, rebels\>

sphere of action of movement which does not include social actors as objects, we can bring together in three sets of ordered pairs, L, the subject and object of all the triplets having actions that belong to the spheres of protest, violence, and facilitation and objects that are social actors (see Table 1).

The sets L_1, L_2, L_3 of all ordered pairs of actors and their relations on the spheres of action of protest, violence and solidarity provide the basic information on the networks of social interactions in 1635 Bordeaux. But the longer the lists, the more difficult it would be to grasp the patterns of interactions. A graphic representation of the information in the three sets L_1, L_2, L_3 would provide a better alternative. The elements, or ordered pairs of relating actors, in L_1, L_2 and L_3 can be represented graphically by drawing a line from the first actor in the element to the second. In this representation, each actor is also known as *node*, and each directed line is known as *arc*. A given set of actors and their corresponding arcs is called *directed graph* and can be visually represented as a diagram where nodes are points in a two-dimensional space and arcs are directed arrows between points.

A large number of relations implies a large number of directed graphs – one graph per relation. But a large number of actors may imply graphs with poor readability – too many nodes, with too many arcs cluttering the graph. Again, aggregation may be required in order to reduce the number of actors. Thus, such actors as makers of casks, craftsmen, day-laborers (also referred

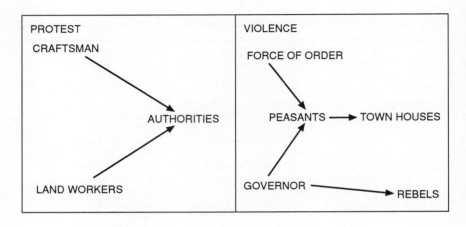

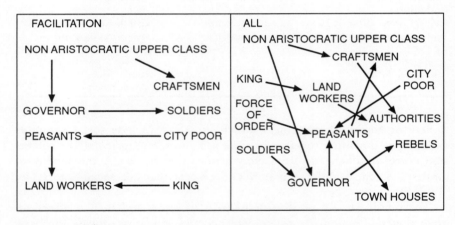

Figure 1. Network graphs of the social actors involved in Mousnier's narrative for selected spheres of action

to in the text as rebels) could all be classified as craftsmen; peasants, villagers, vinegrowers, gardeners, market gardeners, and *laboureurs* could be grouped together as agricultural workers; bourgeois, persons of condition, officials of the *parlement* and gentlemen as non-aristocratic upper class; cavalry, town militia and soldiers as forces of order. With the actors and actions properly aggregated, we can then place the arcs of the directed graphs on several figures (one for each relation), or on a single figure containing points representing the actors and arcs or lines for all relations, simultaneously (a *multivariate directed graph*). For Mousnier's data, this would yield the graphs of Figure 1.

The graph provides a clear picture of the social relations of seventeenth-century France and of the pattern of class alliances, of the coming together of town and country, of sections of the upper classes and of the lower classes against an encroaching state. Yet does one really need to enroll the help of linguistics, set theory and network analysis to get that picture? No doubt an old-fashioned but much simpler reading of Mousnier's passage would do. But would that still do if you have hundreds or thousands of passages of this kind?

TOY EXAMPLES AND REAL DATA: THE TEST OF LARGE DATA SETS

In this section, I illustrate the results of a large historical project, based on data collected from some 15,000 newspaper articles using a semantic grammar on one of Italy's most troublesome periods: the 1919–1922 period. In this span of just four years, we go from the widespread labor mobilization of 1919 and 1920 leading up to the factory occupation movement of September 1920 (the *red years*), to the reaction of 1921 with its increasing levels of political violence and ending with the fascist take-over of power by Mussolini in the fall of 1922 (the *black years*). The plots of Figure 2 of the numbers of strikers and hours lost between 1879, when reliable strike data first became available, and 1922 leave no doubt about the uniqueness of the immediate post-war years.

Figure 3, based on monthly strike data, gives the tempo of mobilization during the red years, with peaks centered around May-July 1919 and January-June 1920. Then, in the fall of 1920 silence fell upon the Italian working class, with one last quick and sudden flurry of protest in June 1922.

What explains the temporal pattern of workers' mobilization during the *red years*? Did workers' mobilization abate because they obtained what they were after? Or was such an impressive movement harshly repressed? As we start asking questions, ever more come to mind. What was the movement all about? Who was involved? What were their actions?

We will search in vain for an answer to those questions on the basis of official strike statistics. Figures 2–4 go as far as those statistics take us. To find an answer to those questions we need to turn elsewhere. The methodological development illustrated in this paper finds its roots in the limitations of official strike statistics and, more generally, in the limitations of event counts in the quantitative study of historical processes.

Data collection for my 1919–1922 project was based on the Socialist newspaper *Il Lavoro*, published in Genoa. According to comparative analyses of some ninety newspapers published in Italy at the time, *Il Lavoro* (together with another socialist paper, *Avanti!*) provides by far the largest number of articles on social and industrial conflict and violence. The data in Table 2 on the frequency distribution of articles, disputes, triplets, actors and actions present in the database give a sense of the scale of the project.

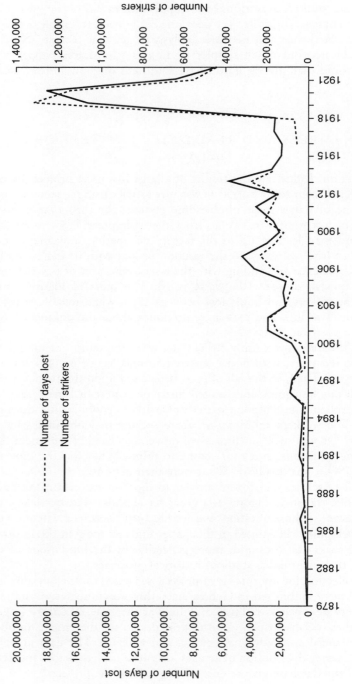

Figure 2. Yearly plots of the numbers of strikers and days lost (1879–1922)

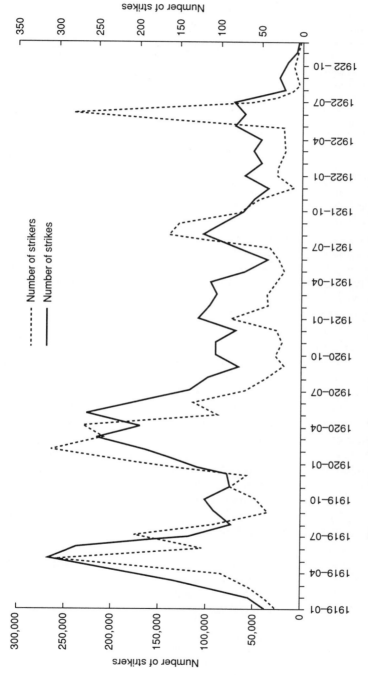

Figure 3. Monthly plots of the numbers of strikes and strikers (1919–1922)

Table 2. *Frequency distribution of articles, disputes, triplets, actors and actions in the database*

	1919	1920	1921	1922	Total
Number of articles	4,213	4,329	3,715	2,889	15,146
Number of disputes	597	622	1,132	926	3,277
Number of triplets	5,511	5,078	2,961	3,195	16,745
Number of *distinct* actors	498	412	355	367	1,052
Number of *distinct* actions	1,145	757	682	538	2,220

I have shown elsewhere[17] that even simple exploratory analyses of the relational properties of these data, of "who does what and why", can tell us a great deal about the 1919–1922 period in Italy. But the graphical represenation of the network of social relations may tell us even more. For the sake of simplicity and for the purpose of illustration, I will focus here on the network graphs around the spheres of action of conflict and violence. The network graphs for the sphere of action of *conflict* (Figure 4) give a dramatic picture of the shift in the network of social relations from the "red years" to the "black years", with a great deal of conflict in the economic arena during 1919 and 1920, as evidenced by the thickness of the line between workers and employers. In 1921, however, a distinct political arena of conflict emerges ("network cluster"), involving the fascists against the socialists and, especially, the unions. This confirms the historians' accounts on early fascist tactics, aimed at smashing both the political and economic organizations of the working class. In fact, the total amount of political conflict borne out by the network graphs is grossly underestimated because most actions performed by the fascists are classified under *violence* (next network graph). Even the revival of conflict in the economic arena hides the basic fact that the nature of conflict shifted from offensive to defensive in the four-year period. Furthermore, while in the early years the total number of actions of conflict that workers carried out against employers is roughly equal to that of employers against workers (as represented by the double-pointed arrow between employers and workers in the network graphs for 1919 and 1920), in 1921 the employers were on the offensive (as represented by the thicker line going from employers to workers).

The graphs for *violence* (Figure 5) clearly bring home the point that things changed drastically between 1919–1920 and 1921–1922. The graphs for 1919, 1920 and 1921 all show a "star" shape, with one actor at the center of the network of interactions, a hub for relations where actors have no links to one another, except with the star. But, interestingly enough, while in 1919 and 1920

17. Roberto Franzosi, "Mobilization and Counter-Mobilization Processes: From the Red Years (1919–20) to the Black Years (1921–22) in Italy. A New Methodological Approach to the Study of Narrative Data", in John Mohr and Roberto Franzosi (eds), *New Directions in Formalization and Historical Analysis*, special issue of *Theory and Society*, 26 (1997), pp. 2–3.

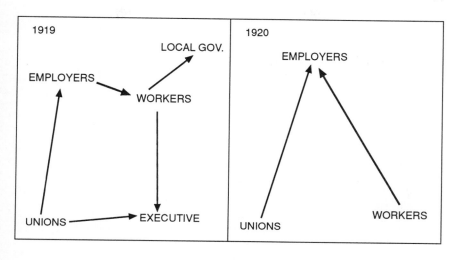

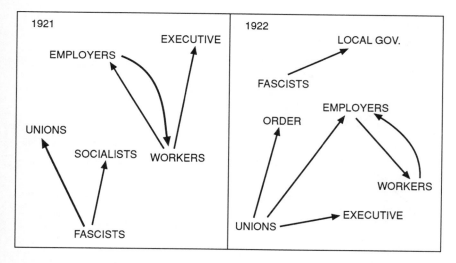

Figure 4. Network graphs of the social actors involved for the sphere of action on *conflict* (1919–1922)

the police and the army ("order") occupy the center of the star, in later years the "fascists" take that position. The graphs also bring home another point, namely that most violence is actually performed by the police and the army, as a number of studies on protest movements and collective action have long underscored.[18] The graph for 1919 highlights an important actor – the petty

18. E.g. Charles Tilly, "State-Incited Violence, 1900–1999", *Political Power and Social Theory*, 9 (1995), pp. 161–225.

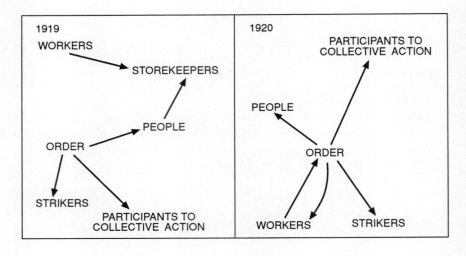

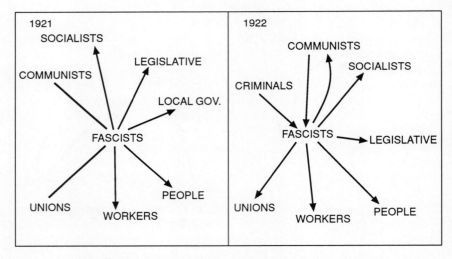

Figure 5. Network graphs of the social actors involved for the sphere of action of *violence* (1919–1922)

bourgeoisie (namely, shopkeepers) – the target of people's and workers' violence, particularly during the intense period of mobilization for the *caroviveri*. It is not surprising that the petty bourgeoisie embraced fascism a year later!

The double arrow between communists and fascists in the network graph for 1922 indicates that the communists were not mere recipients of fascist violence. They acted as agents in many violent actions against the fascists. That finding is not surprising. The Communist Party was born out of the

controversy between the reformist and the revolutionary wing of the Socialist Party after the failure of the 1920 factory occupation movement. From
the beginning, the communists took the fascists head on, responding with
violence to violence, and forming such organizations as the *arditi del popolo*
to counter the fascists' *arditi d'Italia*.

I could continue with this exercise, faithfully describing the network
graphs for different spheres of action (relations), each new graph adding
more or less detail to, shedding a dimmer or brighter light on basically the
same picture of a drastic change in the number and type of actors involved
and in the forms of their interactions from the "red" to the "black" years.
From a methodological viewpoint, the combination of a linguistic approach
to content analysis (semantic grammars) and of network models applied to
the qualitative data collected from narratives has thus proved to be a powerful tool of socio-historical research. From a substantive viewpoint, historians
are likely to take issue with the validity of my account (what conclusions
can one reach on the basis of one newspaper only, and a socialist paper at
that?); but they are also likely to sympathize with the shift of focus in
statistical representations from variables to actors and social action. Sociology, as well, has seen a resurgence of interest in issues of agency.[19] Sociologists, however, will generally find the descriptive nature of the network
graphs not to their taste. How can one test hypotheses on the basis of
descriptive work? Indeed, the network graphs on the sphere of actions of
conflict and violence presented here are not well suited to address empirically either the theoretical concerns of such theories of mobilization processes as resource mobilization, political opportunity structure and frame
alignment,[20] or, for that matter, hypotheses drawn from broad theories of
fascism based on class alliances.[21] Notwithstanding, the network evidence
does highlight specific spheres of conflict (in the economic, social and political arenas with specific sets of actors involved), specific points of tension in
the social structure (from the obvious ones, such as workers and unions
versus employers, to the less obvious ones, such as working-class women
versus storekeepers). The identification of those points of tension and of

19. E.g. Mustafa Emirbayer and Jeff Goodwin, "Network Analysis, Culture, and the Problem of
Agency", *American Journal of Sociology*, 99 (1994), pp. 1411–1454.
20. For an introduction, see McAdam *et al.*, *Comparative Perspectives on Social Movements*.
21. For example, Barrington Moore saw fascism as the political regime that results from the
alliance of the landed upper class, the state and the industrial bourgeoisie (Barrington Moore,
Social Origins of Dictatorship and Democracy (Boston, 1966), p. 436). Contrary to this view, for
Salvatorelli, "Fascism represents the class struggle of the petty bourgeoisie, wedged between capital
and proletariat": cited in Renzo DeFelice, *Le interpretazioni del Fascismo* (Bari, 1995 [1969]), p.
186. Seymour Martin Lipset echoed that view, decades later: "Fascism is basically a middle-class
movement representing a protest against both capitalism *and* socialism, big business *and* big
unions": Seymour Martin Lipset, *Political Man. The Social Bases of Politics* (Baltimore, 1981 [1959]),
p. 131; emphasis in the original.

those arenas of conflict does reveal that certain types of alliances among social actors may be more likely than others.[22]

CONCLUSIONS

The study of conflict has typically been based on event counts.[23] When I first conceived of a project on the 1919–1922 years, one thing was clear to me: to make any inroads in the understanding of those conflict-ridden years and the rise of Italian fascism I would have to abandon official strike statistics (and event counts, more generally). Those data have the advantage of being readily available; but the poverty of their information is such that nothing could be said, on the basis of those data, on what employers, the state or other social groups do during periods of high mobilization. The danger of using official strike counts is to produce a one-sided and distorted view of social conflict where only one of the social actors involved (workers) acts. Yet, if "it takes two to tango", it takes at least two to fight.[24] Paradoxically, even for workers, reliance on strike counts would produce a distorted picture of working-class strategies. After all, strikes are but one form of protest tactic within wider repertoires.

Driven by this quest for a richer source of event data, I focused on the narratives of police reports and newspaper articles. I then set out on the task of developing an approach to content analysis where coding scheme design would not be dependent upon the investigator's theoretical or substantive interests *but on the inherent linguistic properties of the text itself.* The end result of that quest was a "semantic grammar", the simple linguistic structure subject-action-object and their respective modifiers (e.g. time, space, demands of action, or number, type and organization of subjects and objects).

To some extent, a semantic grammar reflects intrinsic properties of narrative text, rather than the investigator's theoretical approach. After all, narrative texts, at their core, are characterized by actors performing some actions.[25] Furthermore, despite the complexity of semantic grammars as coding schemes, their mathematical underpinnings in set theory make them easily implementable in a computer environment using relational database systems. Finally, in the process of coding text, of extracting information from narrative accounts, of going from words to numbers, semantic gram-

---

22. Another approach to the analysis of social networks (the sociometric approach) is likely to appeal to the structural concerns of social scientists. Indeed, the blockmodels that this approach yields have enjoyed increasing popularity (see the review and critique of recent work in Emirbayer and Goodwin, "Network Analysis").

23. E.g. counts of strikes, see Roberto Franzosi, *The Puzzle of Strikes. Class and State Strategies in Postwar Italy* (Cambridge, 1995).

24. On these issues, see *ibid.*

25. See Franzosi, "Narrative Analysis, or . . .".

mars retain more of the rich texture of the original narrative than traditional content analysis techniques.

The SAO structure is not only invariant across purely narrative clauses but because of its relational properties, it also allows researchers to analyze the linguistic content of its categories with the help of statistics. In particular, the data that semantic grammars deliver are very well suited for the application of new tools of data analysis such as network models. Both semantic grammars and network models are fundamentally concerned with actors and their actions, with agents and agency. As such, these methodological tools should draw sociology closer to history, traditionally much more concerned with issues of agency. There may be a variety of ways of going from words to numbers, of analyzing qualitative data with quantitative tools. In this paper I have illustrated one thin thread that runs from words to numbers, from story grammars to network models via a common representation in set theory.

On the basis of a semantic grammar implemented in a computer environment, I coded information from some 15,000 newspaper articles on the 1919–1922 period in Italy. Even the handful of empirical analyses of the data presented in this paper as an illustration of the technique bear witness to the power of the technique. The application of network models to narrative data brings out clear historical patterns in the data, such as the stark shift from working-class mobilization in 1919–1920 to counter-mobilization in 1921–1922. No other available data could have brought out those same patterns to the extent that this technique has. Available official strike statistics, for instance, with their crude counts of just one type of event (strikes) would not have allowed us to tease out the broader repertoire of working-class actions or the variety of actors, with their specific claims and forms of actions, involved during the phase of mobilization (e.g. students, women, war veterans). Even less so would they have allowed us to map the counter-mobilization process, the quick spread of fascist violence. Official strike statistics simply do not provide information on those issues. Neither would qualitative historical studies greatly help. The growing number of city or regional monographs on the rise of fascism certainly helps to bring out the much needed detail of local situations. But it is hard to get a sense of patterns from these studies.

And yet, expressions that abound throughout my paper – "a semantic grammar preserves much of the original text input"; "semantic grammars can achieve quality without sacrificing quantity"; "coding scheme design would not be dependent upon the investigator's theoretical or substantive interests *but on the inherent linguistic properties of the text itself*" – overlook the many obstacles and problems one finds along the way in going "from words to numbers", even when using semantic grammars. Indeed, for all their power, these new tools for the collection and analysis of narrative data do have their shortcomings.[26]

26. For an in-depth treatment of these issues, see Franzosi, *From Words to Numbers.*

A purely semantic and structural analysis of narrative misses out a great deal of information contained in a text.[27] Semantic grammars do not eliminate the "role of the reader", i.e. the role of the coder in the interpretation of text. Narrative texts are hardly ever made up of purely narrative clauses only. Narrative and non-narrative clauses typically mix in a narrative text. Coding of non-narrative clauses within the framework of the grammar will pose serious problems to the coders. Even purely narrative clauses may not necessarily conform to the simple template subject-action-object of the grammar.[28] The greater the difference between the surface representation of these clauses and the deep structural representation of the grammar, the greater the interpretative role of the coder, in trying to squeeze one into the other (the simplest case being the linguistic operations required to convert passive forms to active). And semantic grammars have nothing to offer to ease the problem of aggregation. Once investigators have coded thousands of individual actions, how do they classify them, how do they aggregate them for analysis?[29]

Reliance on narratives and semantic grammars may also tend to focus scholarly attention on particularly transformative events (such as the "red years" or the "black years") and on descriptive modes of explanation. The costs of data collection on longer sample periods are responsible for the first drawback; and the very richness of the available information on "who did what" for the second. Paradoxically, the event data delivered by a semantic grammar from newspaper sources are both too rich and not rich enough. Alas, there may be no escape from a multiple-evidence, multiple-method approach to the solution of puzzles of historical nature.

APPENDIX A. MOUSNIER'S PASSAGE CODED WITHIN THE CATEGORIES OF A SEMANTIC GRAMMAR

<subject> authorities (<comment> agent inferred) <action> impose gabelle (<space> Bordeaux <time> May 1635 <time> June 1635) <object> taverns <object> wine <implicit target> tavern keepers <implicit target> makers of casks <implicit target> vinegrowers
<subject> tavern keepers <subject> makers of casks <action> revolt <implicit target> authorities
<subject> craftsmen (<number> many) <subject> day-laborers (<number> many) <action> join revolt <object> rebels <implicit target> authorities
<subject> bourgeois (<number> majority) <subject> persons of condition

27. E.g. the examples discussed in Franzosi, "Narrative Analysis, or . . .", or Larry Griffin, "Narrative, Event-Structure Analysis, and Causal Interpretation in Historical Sociology", *American Journal of Sociology*, 98 (1993), pp. 1094–1133.
28. On these issues, see Franzosi, "Narrative Analysis, or . . .".
29. For a brilliant critique see Aaron V. Cicourel, *Method and Measurement in Sociology* (New York, 1964), pp. 7–38; see also Griffin, "Narrative, Event-Structure Analysis, and Causal Interpretation".

(<number> a large number) <subject> officials of the *parlement* <action> are tacit accomplice of <object> rebels <implicit target> authorities

<subject> bourgeois (<number> majority) <subject> persons of condition (<number> a large number) <subject> officials of the *parlement* <action> approve (<comment> regarded as their liberators) <object> rebels

<subject> rebels <action> want <object> infinitive clause

<subject> rebels <action> to control <object> city gate (<proper name> Saint Julien)

<subject> rebels <action> want <object> infinitive clause

<subject> rebels <action> to let into (<space> the city) <object> peasants (<space> surrounding district)

(<triplet relation> so that) <subject> peasants <action> help <object> rebels

<subject> peasants <action> demand (<type> loudly) <object> infinitive clause

<subject> peasants <action> to enter (<space> city <reason> share in the plunder of the town (<comment> motive ascribed to the peasants by the secretary to the duc d'Épernon, who wrote these lines))

<subject> gardeners (<number> a certain number of) <subject> market gardeners (<number> a certain number of) <subject> vinegrowers (<number> a certain number of) <subject> *laboureurs* (<number> a certain number of) (<comment> very seriously affected by the indirect taxes) <action> get into (<space> the town) <action> take part in the revolt <implicit target> authorities

<subject> peasants <action> plunder <object> houses (<number> some <space> in the town)

<subject> town militia <subject> gentry (<space> neighboring <number> most) <action> do not help <object> governor (<space> Guyenne <proper name> duc d'Épernon)

<subject> gentlemen (<number> few) <subject> *honnêtes bourgeois* (<number> few) <subject> soldiers (<space> town <number> few) <action> help <object> governor (<space> Guyenne <proper name> duc d'Épernon)

<subject> governor (<space> Guyenne <proper name> duc d'Épernon) <action> overcomes <object> rebels

<subject> governor (<space> Guyenne <proper name> duc d'Épernon) <action> persuades <object> peasants <object> infinitive clause

<subject> peasants <action> to yield

<subject> villagers (<number> all) <action> take up arms (<space> countryside) <implicit target> authorities

<subject> villagers (<number> all) <action> rob <object> houses (<space> in the countryside)

<subject> villagers (<number> in great numbers) <action> gather (<space> in all the suburbs) <implicit target> authorities

<subject> villagers (<number> in great numbers) <action> strive <object> infinitive clause

\<subject\> villagers \<action\> to enter (\<space\> town)
\<subject\> poor (\<space\> town) \<action\> want \<object\> infinitive clause
\<subject\> villagers \<action\> to enter (\<space\> town)
\<subject\> poor (\<space\> town) \<action\> try \<object\> infinitive clause
\<subject\> poor (\<space\> town) \<action\> to open a way \<object\> villagers
\<subject\> villagers \<action\> assemble (\<space\> in the suburb of Saint-Surin)
\<implicit target\> authorities
\<subject\> villagers \<action\> burn \<object\> houses (\<number\> several
\<space\> in the suburb of Saint-Surin)
\<subject\> governor (\<space\> Guyenne \<proper name\> duc d'Épernon)
\<subject\> gentlemen of his guard (\<number\> forty or fifty) \<subject\> town
militia (\<number\> few companies) \<action\> scatter \<object\> peasants
\<subject\> cavalry \<action\> chase \<object\> peasants
\<subject\> cavalry \<action\> kill \<object\> peasants (\<number\> forty or fifty)
\<subject\> peasants (\<number\> all other) \<action\> behave themselves properly (\<duration\> that year)
\<subject\> king \<action\> grant an amnesty \<object\> rebels.

ANNOTATED BIBLIOGRAPHY

Braudel, Fernand, *On History* (Chicago, 1980).
A collection of essays of reflections upon history by one of the great historians of the twentieth century.
Cicourel, Aaron V., *Method and Measurement in Sociology* (New York, 1964).
A truly insightful book. The chapter on "Measurement and Mathematics" is brilliant. I would make it required reading in any graduate training.
DeFelice, Renzo, *Le interpretazioni del Fascismo* (Bari, 1995; 1st pub. 1969).
An overview of various interpretations of fascism. Social science models do not fare well in the eyes of this great historian of Italian fascism.
Elton, G.R., "Two Kinds of History", in Robert William Fogel and G.R. Elton, *Which Road to the Past? Two Views of History* (New Haven, 1983), pp. 71–121.
A debate between two great historians – G.R. Elton, a traditional, narrative historian, and Robert Fogel, the "cliometrician". A "must" for any one interested in the terms of the debate between narrative history and "scientific" history.
Emirbayer, Mustafa and Jeff Goodwin, "Network Analysis, Culture, and the Problem of Agency", *American Journal of Sociology*, 99, 6 (1994), pp. 1411–1454.
An investigation into the recent explosion of network models and into the relationship between network models and agency.
Franzosi, Roberto, "The Press as a Source of Socio-Historical Data: Issues in the Methodology of Data Collection from Newspapers", *Historical Methods*, 20, 1 (1987), pp. 5–16.

An investigation into the validity of newspapers as sources of socio-historical data and a discussion of coding scheme design for the collection of those data.

Franzosi, Roberto, "From Words to Numbers: A Generalized and Linguistics-Based Coding Procedure for Collecting Event-Data from Newspapers", in Clifford Clogg (ed.), *Sociological Methodology*, vol. 19 (Oxford, 1989), pp. 263–298.
The first step in the author's journey "from words to numbers". Traces the background of semantic grammars and develops a grammar most appropriate for the study of conflict events.

Franzosi, Roberto, "Strategies for the Prevention, Detection and Correction of Measurement Error in Data Collected from Textual Sources", *Sociological Methods and Research*, 18, 4 (1990), pp. 442–471.
An investigation into the possible sources of errors when coding narrative data with the help of a computer-based semantic grammar.

Franzosi, Roberto, "Computer-Assisted Coding of Textual Data: An Application to Semantic Text Grammars", *Sociological Methods and Research*, 19, 2 (1990), pp. 224–256.
The author highlights the characteristics that a software for the collection of narrative data on the basis of a grammar should have.

Franzosi, Roberto, "From Words to Numbers: A Set Theory Framework for the Collection, Organization, and Analysis of Narrative Data", in Peter Marsden (ed.), *Sociological Methodology*, vol. 24 (Oxford, 1994), pp. 105–136.
The final step in going "from words to numbers". And set theory provides the link.

Franzosi, Roberto, *The Puzzle of Strikes. Class and State Strategies in Postwar Italy* (Cambridge, 1995).
An attempt to solve the puzzle of Italian strikes in light of economic, institutional, organizational and political factors. Brings in a great deal of both quantitative and qualitative evidence. A scathing critique of mindless quantitative approaches to historical processes through "doing it".

Franzosi, Roberto, "Mobilization and Counter-Mobilization Processes: From the Red Years (1919–20) to the Black Years (1921–22) in Italy. A New Methodological Approach to the Study of Narrative Data", in John Mohr and Roberto Franzosi (eds), *New Directions in Formalization and Historical Analysis*, a special issue of *Theory and Society*, 26, 2–3 (1997).
The first substantive results of the author's long journey "from words to numbers".

Franzosi, Roberto, "Narrative Analysis, or . . . Why (and How) Sociologists Should Be Interested in Narrative", in John Hagan (ed.), *Annual Review of Sociology*, vol. 24 (Palo Alto, 1998).
An analysis of narrative focused on the linguists' contribution but with an eye to the sociologist. A very provocative piece.

Franzosi, Roberto, *From Words to Numbers: Narrative as Data* (Cambridge, forthcoming).
A long journey across time and a number of disciplines as the author tackles the problem of narrative as a source of data for quantitative analysis. An investigation into the methodological, epistemological and ontological aspects of this enterprise with much breaking of academic canons.

Griffin, Larry, "Narrative, Event-Structure Analysis, and Causal Interpretation in Historical Sociology", *American Journal of Sociology*, 98, 5 (1993), pp. 1094–1133.
A very detailed and careful investigation in the structure of a short narrative on the basis of structural properties of narrative and using ETHNO as an aid.

Lipset, Seymour Martin. *Political Man. The Social Bases of Politics* (Baltimore, 1981; 1st pub. 1959).
A classic that deals with many aspects of politics, including fascism.

Markoff, John, *The Abolition of Feudalism: Peasants, Lords, and Legislators in the French Revolution* (University Park, PA, 1996).
Twenty years in the making, this is a book that was well worth waiting for. Approaches issues of historical explanations with an incredible wealth of historical evidence (including content analysis of the *Cahiers de doleances*). Well done!

Markoff, John, Gilbert Shapiro and Sasha Weitman, "Toward the Integration of Content Analysis and General Methodology", in David R. Heise (ed.), *Sociological Methodology* (Oxford, 1974), pp. 1–58.
A plea for a linguistic approach to content analysis that delivers more than previous pleas and less than hoped for.

McAdam, Doug, John D. McCarthy and Mayer N. Zald (eds), *Comparative Perspectives on Social Movements* (Cambridge, 1996).
The latest reader in a "growth industry".

Moore, Barrington, *Social Origins of Dictatorship and Democracy* (Boston, 1966).
Many argue that modern historical sociology started from here.

Mousnier, Roland, *Peasant Uprisings in Seventeenth-Century France, Russia, and China* (New York, 1972).
A narrative account by a French historian of the peasants' rebellions of the seventeenth century.

Tilly, Charles, "State-Incited Violence, 1900–1999", *Political Power and Social Theory*, 9 (1995), pp. 161–225.
There are some advantages in having monopoly control over the means of violence. Not surprisingly, it is the state that is the most violent social actor.

Wasserman, Stanley and Katherine Faust, *Social Network Analysis. Methods and Applications* (Cambridge, 1994).
A clear and thorough exposition of network models. Successive chapters get progressively more difficult without mathematics.

International Review of Social History 43 (1998), Supplement, pp. 105–124
© 1998 Internationaal Instituut voor Sociale Geschiedenis

The Logic of Qualitative Comparative Analysis

CHARLES C. RAGIN

INTRODUCTION

Social scientists often face a fundamental dilemma when they conduct social research. On the one hand, they may emphasize the *complexity* of social phenomena – a common strategy in ethnographic, historical and macro-social research – and offer in-depth case studies sensitive to the specificity of the things they study. On the other hand, they may make broad, homogenizing assumptions about cases, and document *generalities* – patterns that hold across many instances. Research strategies that focus on complexity are often labeled "qualitative", "case-oriented", "small-N", or "intensive". Those that focus on generality are often labeled "quantitative", "variable-oriented", "large-N", or "extensive". While the contrasts between these two types of social research are substantial, it is easy to exaggerate their differences and to caricature the two approaches, for example, portraying quantitative work on general patterns as scientific but sterile and oppressive, and qualitative research on small Ns as rich and emancipatory but journalistic. It is important to avoid these caricatures because the contrasts between these two general approaches provide important leads both for finding a middle path between them and for resolving basic methodological issues in social science.

Social scientists who study cases in an in-depth manner often see empirical generalizations simply as a means to another end – the interpretive understanding of cases. In this view, a fundamental goal of social science is to interpret significant features of the social world and thereby advance our collective understanding of how existing social arrangements came about and why we live the way we do. The rough general patterns that social scientists may be able to identify simply aid the understanding of specific cases; they are not viewed as predictive. Besides, the task of interpreting and then representing socially significant phenomena (or the task of making selected social phenomena significant by representing them) is a much more immediate and tangible goal. In this view, empirical generalizations and social science theory are important – to the extent that they aid the goal of interpretive understanding.

By contrast, those who study patterns across many cases with an eye toward formulating social scientific generalizations believe that the fundamental goal of social science is to advance general, explanatory theories that address wide expanses of the social terrain. In this view, there is a great deal of order and repetition in social life. Social scientists should uncover general patterns, refine their theories, and use this abstract knowledge to advance the common good. Thus systematic theory is seen as the centerpiece of good social science. All social research should be both theoretically driven and relevant.

This bifurcation of social scientists with respect to the issue of generalization is evident in their published work. The examination of almost any social scientific subdiscipline reveals that there is a sharp divide separating those who do small-N, qualitative studies from those who do large-N, quantitative studies. In comparative sociology and comparative politics, for example, a frequency distribution showing the number of studies with different size Ns reveals a clear U-shaped pattern. At the small-N end of the horizontal axis there are many studies, just as there are at the large-N end of this axis. But in the middle the relative number of studies is very low. There are very few comparativists who conduct studies of 10 or 20 countries, but many who study 1 or 2 or 75 (i.e. enough to permit the use of conventional quantitative methods).

While easy to explain, there is no simple way to justify this U-shaped pattern. It is true that social scientists value both kinds of knowledge – in-depth knowledge of cases and broad statements about patterns that hold across many cases. It is also true that these two forms of knowledge are very different. But in-depth knowledge of cases is often dependent on knowledge of patterns that hold across many cases, and vice versa. Case-oriented researchers, for example, often cite general patterns that they themselves have not documented to explain case-specific phenomena (e.g. citing the "well-known" tendency for peasants to be highly risk averse to explain the failure of an agricultural diversification program). If these general patterns turn out to be without empirical support, then the case-specific argument is suspect (e.g. political corruption, ignored by the researcher, may have stymied the diversification project). Likewise, it is very difficult to explain broad patterns across many cases without reference to case-level processes.[1] Variable-oriented researchers regularly cite unobserved case-level mechanisms to explain the cross-case patterns they document. If these mechanisms cannot be observed at the case level, then the variable-oriented conclusions are suspect.

Consider also the fact that a deep complementary relationship between case-oriented and variable-oriented research augments their mutual dependence. With variable-oriented techniques, for example, it is very difficult to address questions about actors' motives and subjectivities or to observe event sequences and causal processes.[2] Case-oriented methods, by contrast, excel in these areas. With case-oriented techniques, however, it is difficult to gain

---

1. Andrew Abbott, "What Do Cases Do?", in Charles C. Ragin and Howard S. Becker (eds), *What Is a Case?* (Cambridge, 1992), pp. 53–82.
2. Dietrich Rueschemeyer and John D. Stephens, "Comparing Historical Sequences: A Powerful Tool for Causal Analysis", *Comparative Social Research*, XVI (1997), pp. 55–72.

confidence that inferences are well grounded or that findings are general in any way. These are central strengths of the variable-oriented approach.[3]

The complementarity and mutual dependence of these two types of social research undermines the idea that there can be a convenient division of labor between social scientists who study general patterns and those who interpret significant or important cases. As much as they might want to, the two types of social research simply cannot ignore each other. Perhaps this mutual dependence, combined with an unhealthy measure of mutual suspicion, explains the periodic eruption of "holy wars" in academic journals, departments and other arenas. While it seems unlikely that the boundary separating these two general strategies will ever disappear, it is clear that their tendency toward mutual isolation is unhealthy.

The best way to bridge these two approaches and end the mutual suspicion is to find some middle ground where the concerns of both approaches can be addressed. This middle ground obviously involves compromises on both sides, but it should provide a way to address the practical differences between the two approaches, especially their different approaches to the process of constructing representations of social phenomena from empirical evidence. Finding this middle ground at the same time solves basic methodological issues in social research, for example: must social scientists choose between generality and complexity, between research that is broad but shallow and research that is narrow but deep? Can they have both in the same study – in the same analytic breath?

In the remainder of this paper, I sketch a middle path between complexity and generality. This middle path emphasizes the use of a configurational approach to cases in the analysis of cross-case patterns, and thus retains some of the holism of the case study approach in the analysis of cross-case patterns.[4] Specifically, I describe a technique called "Qualitative Comparative Analysis" (QCA), originally designed as a formalization of the logic of the comparative case-oriented approach.[5] In a nutshell, QCA provides analytic tools for conducting holistic comparisons of cases as configurations and for elucidating their patterned similarities and differences. This approach to cross-case research, based on a configurational understanding of social phenomena, is the foundation of what I call "diversity-oriented

3. Stanley Lieberson, "Causal Analysis and Comparative Research: What Can We Learn from Studies Based on a Small Number of Cases?", in Hans-Peter Blossfeld and Gerald Prein (eds), *Rational Choice Theory and Large-Scale Data Analysis* (Westview, 1998), pp. 129–145.
4. The rationale for this approach is presented in Charles Ragin, *The Comparative Method: Moving Beyond Qualitative and Quantitative Strategies* (Berkeley, 1987), pp. 121–123, 164–171.
5. Kriss Drass and Charles Ragin, *Qualitative Comparative Analysis* (Evanston, 1992). QCA is a DOS program distributed by the Institute for Policy Research, Northwestern University. For the full address see the Annotated Bibliography.

research", which is distinct from case-oriented and variable-oriented research.[6]

Most of the discussion is devoted to describing the application of QCA to dichotomous social data on the memberships of cases in categories and sets. In contrast to statistical methodology, which is based on linear algebra, QCA is based on Boolean algebra, the algebra of logic and sets. QCA treats social scientific categories as sets and views cases in terms of their multiple memberships. In Boolean algebra a case is either "in" or "out" of a set; that is, memberships in sets are "crisp".[7] Each case is viewed as a member of multiple sets, and membership *combinations* are compared and contrasted to identify decisive patterns of similarity and difference, which, in turn, provide the basis for constructing causal arguments. With QCA it is possible to view cases as configurations, examine causal complexity (defined as patterns of multiple conjunctural causation – where no single cause may be either necessary or sufficient), and identify types of cases based on the different patterns of causal conditions they exhibit. Thus social scientists can free themselves from some of the restrictive, homogenizing assumptions of variable-oriented social science without giving up the possibility of formulating statements about broad, cross-case patterns.

WORKING WITH CASES AS CONFIGURATIONS

In QCA, cases are examined in terms of their multiple memberships in sets, viewed as configurations. This interest in how different aspects or features combine in each case is consistent with an emphasis on understanding aspects of cases in the context of the wholes they form. For example, having many small- to medium-sized political parties ("fractionalization") signifies different things about a country's political stability, depending on the nature of its electoral system, its social diversity, the age of its political institutions, and so on. Another example: having many debts can signal different things about a person's financial situation, depending on his or her other attributes – age, income, employment status, assets, and so on. By looking at combinations of aspects, it is possible to get a sense of a case as a whole, especially how its different aspects fit together. This emphasis on how characteristics combine contrasts sharply with the tendency of the variable-oriented approach to view aspects of cases as analytically independent features.

In every social scientific investigation, the selection of cases and attributes to study is dependent on the substantive and theoretical interests of the researcher and his or her intended audiences. Sometimes a research literature

6. I contrast diversity-oriented research with case-oriented and variable-oriented research in my forthcoming book, *Fuzzy-Set Social Science* (Chicago, 1999).
7. In *ibid.*, I show how to work with grades of memberships in sets, using fuzzy algebra.

is especially well developed, and the selection of cases and attributes is relatively unproblematic. In other situations, however, the researcher can formulate a worthwhile selection of attributes only through in-depth analysis of cases. Sometimes it is necessary to constitute relevant cases and their key aspects through a systematic dialogue of ideas and evidence. Researchers progressively refine their understanding of relevant cases and their key aspects as they sharpen the concepts appropriate for studying them.[8]

Often the selection of aspects is shaped by the nature of the outcome to be investigated and the researcher's understanding of the causal conditions relevant to this outcome. The selection of causal conditions is usually quite broad because the concern is to identify not only the factors that seem connected to the outcome as proximate causes, but also the conditions that provide the contexts for the operation of these factors. A fractionalized party system, for example, could be a proximate cause of political breakdown in some situations; in others, it might be irrelevant and could even contribute to long-term political stability. Thus it is important to consider the contexts and conditions that enable and disable causal connections. This concern for how context structures causal connections is one of the key features of the configurational approach.

Once a set of relevant aspects has been identified, the researcher constructs a table listing the different logically possible combinations of attributes ("configurations") along with the cases that conform to each configuration. This table can be seen as a "property space"; each location within a property space, in turn, can be seen, potentially at least, as a different kind or type of case.[9] In QCA, attributes are represented with presence/absence dichotomies, with 0 indicating absence (the case is not in the set in question), and 1 indicating presence (the case is in the set in question). Multichotomies (e.g. race/ethnicity at the individual level) are represented with sets of dichotomies, which can be arranged in a variety of ways, depending on the interests of the investigator.

By examining the cases that conform to each configuration, represented as a row of the table, it is possible for the investigator to evaluate attributes he has identified. The researcher asks for each configuration: do these cases go together? Are they comparable instances, in the context of this investigation? Thus the configurational understanding of cases problematizes the comparability of cases at the level of the configuration, not simply at the more global level of the population.

Consider, for example, Table 1, which shows different configurations of conditions relevant to ethnic political mobilization among territorially-based

8. Charles Ragin, "Turning the Tables: How Case-Oriented Research Challenges Variable-Oriented Research", *Comparative Social Research*, XVI (1997), pp. 27–42.
9. Paul F. Lazarsfeld, "Some Remarks on the Typological Procedures in Social Research", *Zeitschrift für Sozialforschung*, VI (1937), pp. 119–139.

linguistic minorities in Western Europe. Four attributes define the property space: (1) whether the minority is large or small, (2) whether the minority has a weak or strong linguistic base, (3) whether the minority region is richer or poorer than the core region of the host country, and (4) whether the minority region is growing or declining.[10] There are sixteen logically possible combinations ("configurations") of these four presence/absence dichotomies, and thus sixteen "kinds" of cases. For notational convenience in the discussion that follows, the presence of an attribute is denoted by the name of the attribute; the absence of the attribute (negation) is denoted with the "~" symbol preceding the attribute name. Thus, *large* indicates that the linguistic minority is large in size, while ~*large* indicates that it is small; *fluent* indicates good linguistic ability; ~*fluent* indicates poor linguistic ability; *wealthy* indicates that the minority region is wealthier than the core region; ~*wealthy* indicates that it is poorer than the core region; *growing* indicates that the region is growing; ~*growing* indicates that it is not growing.

Table 1 also shows the cases conforming to each logically possible combination of these four dichotomies. By evaluating the comparability of the cases conforming to each configuration, the researcher can make a preliminary assessment of the adequacy of the aspects selected for investigation. For example, the first configuration (~*large**~*fluent**~*wealthy**~*growing* – asterisks are used to indicate combinations of characteristics) brings together Lapps in Finland, Lapps in Sweden, Lapps in Norway, Torne Valley Finns in Sweden, Albanians in Italy and Greeks in Italy. Viewing these six cases together, the researcher asks whether or not it is reasonable to group these as similar cases in a study of the political mobilization of territorially-based linguistic minorities in Western Europe. If not, then additional attributes should be added to the list of relevant causal conditions, or perhaps the researcher should substitute different attributes for some of the existing attributes. For example, the investigator may believe that the four minorities in Scandinavia differ in some causally decisive way from the two minorities in Italy. If so, the causal condition that distinguishes these two groups should be added to the table. The cases conforming to each location in the property space should be evaluated in this manner.

When researchers view their evidence in terms of logically possible combinations of conditions and the cases conforming to each configuration, as in Table 1, they also evaluate the cases in each row to see if they display the same outcome, or at least roughly comparable outcomes. For example, a researcher might ask: are the six cases in the first row similar with respect to the ethnic political mobilization they exhibit? Each row is examined in this manner, so that the researcher can gain some confidence that a viable

10. Erik Allardt, *Implications of the Ethnic Revival in Modern, Industrialized Society* (Helsinki, 1979), pp. 52–65; Ragin, *Comparative Method*, pp. 133–149.

Table 1. *Territorially-based linguistic minorities in Western Europe*

Row	Size	Language	Wealth	Growth	Instances
1	~large	~fluent	~wealthy	~growing	Lapps, Finland Lapps, Sweden Lapps, Norway Finns, Sweden Albanians, Italy Greeks, Italy
2	~large	~fluent	~wealthy	growing	N. Frisians, Germany Danes, Germany Basques, France
3	~large	~fluent	wealthy	~growing	Ladins, Italy
4	~large	~fluent	wealthy	growing	none
5	~large	fluent	~wealthy	~growing	Magyars, Austria Croats, Austria Slovenes, Austria Greenlanders, Denmark
6	~large	fluent	~wealthy	growing	none
7*	~large	fluent	wealthy	~growing	Aalanders, Finland
8*	~large	fluent	wealthy	growing	Slovenes, Italy Valdotians, Italy
9	large	~fluent	~wealthy	~growing	Sards, Italy Galicians, Spain
10*	large	~fluent	~wealthy	growing	W. Frisians, Neth. Catalans, France Occitans, France Welsh, Great Britain Bretons, France Corsicans, France
11	large	~fluent	wealthy	~growing	none
12*	large	~fluent	wealthy	growing	Friulians, Italy Occitans, Italy Basques, Spain Catalans, Spain
13	large	fluent	~wealthy	~growing	Flemings, France
14*	large	fluent	~wealthy	growing	Walloons, Belgium
15*	large	fluent	wealthy	~growing	Swedes, Finland S. Tyroleans, Italy
16*	large	fluent	wealthy	growing	Alsatians, France Germans, Belgium Flemings, Belgium

Notes: The "~" symbol preceding an attribute name indicates negation. The "*" symbol indicates rows with strong evidence of ethnic political mobilization. Size: whether the minority is large or small. Language: whether the minority has a strong or weak linguistic ability. Wealth: whether the minority region is richer or poorer than the core region of the country. Growth: whether the minority region is growing or declining.

specification of causal conditions has been realized. Obviously, if the cases in
a row display widely divergent outcomes or if they are evenly split between
contrasting outcomes, the researcher will examine these cases closely and
reformulate his or her specification of causal conditions accordingly. This
evaluation of cases with respect to outcomes is separate from the first evaluation, just described, where the researcher asks simply whether or not the
cases grouped within each combination of attributes belong together as
comparable cases, regardless of their outcomes.

When making assessments of outcomes, it is unrealistic to expect that all
the cases in each row will be perfectly consistent with respect to the outcome
in question. It is very difficult to capture all causally relevant conditions in
broad cross-case analyses. Furthermore, mistakes can be made when
assigning cases to sets or when evaluating the evidence with respect to the
outcome in question. As an illustration of the general problem, consider the
twelfth row of Table 1. The Friulian and Occitan minorities of Italy occupy
this row, along with the Basques and Catalan minorities of Spain. But the
two minorities in Spain are more politically active than the two in Italy,
and the Basque minority is more active that the Catalan. This information
could be used to identify a fifth causal condition, perhaps specifying a condition relevant to class divisions within linguistic minorities. The researcher
might even want to reformulate the property space altogether, with a completely new set of conditions. Alternatively, the researcher might decide
simply that there is enough evidence of ethnic political activity across the
four cases in this row to justify treating them all as instances of ethnic
political mobilization. In other words, the researcher might conclude that
the discordance is not so great as to motivate any change in the specification
of conditions.

The larger point is that the examination of outcomes is a central part of
constructing a property space and generating configurations, especially when
it comes to the selection of causally relevant aspects of cases. The researcher
conducts an elaborate dialogue of ideas and evidence that leads to a progressive refinement of his or her understanding of relevant cases and to a more
nuanced elaboration of the ideas guiding the research. Again, perfect consistency in outcomes for the cases with the same combination of causal conditions is rare. As I show subsequently in this paper, it is possible to use
probabilistic criteria when evaluating the links between causal conditions
and outcomes. This tactic partially ameliorates the problem of contrary
evidence and thus allows for some discordance in outcomes within configurations.

It is important to understand that in QCA the fundamental unit of
analysis is the configuration, along with the cases conforming to each configuration. Thus Table 1 should *not* be viewed as a presentation of four
presence/absence dichotomies, but rather as a specification of sixteen qualitatively distinct conditions – that is, sixteen kinds of cases. The principle of

holism mandates allowance for the possibility that a single difference between two cases may signal a difference in kind. This thinking provides the conceptual basis for constructing and evaluating evidence in terms of logically possible combinations of causes (i.e. as configurations). Thus the table should be viewed as a property space with sixteen separate locations. Each of the sixteen configurations constitutes, potentially at least, a qualitatively distinct constellation. If 5 dichotomies had been used, there would have been 32 configurations ($2^5 = 32$); 6 dichotomies would yield 64 configurations and so on. Using dichotomies, the number of logically possible combinations is equal to 2^k, where k is the number of attributes.

The four dichotomies presented in Table 1 can be viewed not only as sixteen configurations (logically possible combinations of attributes), but also as eighty logically possible groupings. The sixteen configurations presented in Table 1 provide the elemental or foundational groupings. Additional groupings can be formed by merging configurations that share one or more attributes. For example, the last two rows of Table 1, linguistic minorities that are *large*fluent*wealthy*~growing* (the penultimate row) and those that are *large*fluent*wealthy*growing* (the last row), share three attributes and thus can be merged to form a larger grouping, namely minorities that are *large*fluent*wealthy*. In set terminology, the larger set is formed from the union of its component sets. Still larger groupings can be formed from the union of more rows, as long as the rows that are grouped contain at least one attribute in common. For example, the first eight rows display ~*large*. Merging these eight rows, yields the set of cases that have ~*large* in common – that is, all the smaller linguistic minorities.

Just as it is possible to calculate the logically possible number of combinations (2^k), it is possible to calculate the number of logically possible groupings, including the original sixteen configurations as elemental groupings. The formula is 3^k-1, where k again is the number of dichotomies. Table 2 shows the logically possible groupings of the four dichotomies presented in Table 1. Using the formula just described, there are eighty possible groupings: sixteen elemental groupings involving combinations of four attributes (the original sixteen configurations presented in Table 1); thirty-two groupings using combinations of three attributes; twenty-four groupings using two attributes, and eight groupings using one attribute.

These larger groupings are important because they are relevant to any conclusions about cross-case patterns the researcher may wish to construct from the evidence in Table 1. For example, the researcher might examine all minorities that are wealthy and growing (*wealthy*growing*) to see if they have similar levels or forms of ethnic political mobilization. The eighty groupings listed in Table 2 provide the basis for formulating *any* statement that can be made regarding cross-case patterns. As I show next, the examination of these different groupings is central to the assessment of causal

Table 2. *Groupings using four dichotomies (from Table 1)*

16 initial configuration combinations of four aspects	32 groups involving combinations of three aspects	24 groups involving combinations of two aspects	8 groups involving a single aspect
~large*~fluent*~wealthy*~growing	~large*~fluent*~wealthy	~large*~fluent	~large
~large*~fluent*~wealthy*growing	~large*~fluent*wealthy	~large*fluent	large
~large*~fluent*wealthy*~growing	~large*fluent*~wealthy	large*~fluent	~fluent
~large*~fluent*wealthy*growing	~large*fluent*wealthy	large*fluent	fluent
~large*fluent*~wealthy*~growing	large*~fluent*~wealthy	~large*~wealthy	~wealthy
~large*fluent*~wealthy*growing	large*~fluent*wealthy	~large*wealthy	wealthy
~large*fluent*wealthy*~growing	large*fluent*~wealthy	large*~wealthy	~growing
~large*fluent*wealthy*growing	large*fluent*wealthy	large*wealthy	growing
large*~fluent*~wealthy*~growing	~large*~fluent*~growing	~large*~growing	
large*~fluent*~wealthy*growing	~large*~fluent*growing	~large*growing	
large*~fluent*wealthy*~growing	~large*fluent*~growing	large*~growing	
large*~fluent*wealthy*growing	~large*fluent*growing	large*growing	
large*fluent*~wealthy*~growing	large*~fluent*~growing	~fluent*~wealthy	
large*fluent*~wealthy*growing	large*~fluent*growing	~fluent*wealthy	
large*fluent*wealthy*~growing	large*fluent*~growing	fluent*~wealthy	
large*fluent*wealthy*growing	large*fluent*growing	fluent*wealthy	
	~large*~wealthy*~growing	~fluent*~growing	
	~large*~wealthy*growing	~fluent*growing	
	~large*wealthy*~growing	fluent*~growing	
	~large*wealthy*growing	fluent*growing	
	large*~wealthy*~growing	~wealthy*~growing	
	large*~wealthy*growing	~wealthy*growing	
	large*wealthy*~growing	wealthy*~growing	
	large*wealthy*growing	wealthy*growing	
	~fluent*~wealthy*~growing		
	~fluent*~wealthy*growing		
	~fluent*wealthy*~growing		
	~fluent*wealthy*growing		
	fluent*~wealthy*~growing		
	fluent*~wealthy*growing		
	fluent*wealthy*~growing		
	fluent*wealthy*~growing		

complexity, especially the evaluation of the *sufficiency* of different combinations of causal conditions.

ANALYZING CAUSAL COMPLEXITY

Usually, social research begins with the goal of explaining some outcome. For example, a researcher might ask why some territorially-based linguistic minorities participate in politics on an ethnic basis while others do not. Table 1, for example, shows that linguistic minorities in rows 7, 8, 10, 12, 14, 15 and 16 offer strong evidence of ethnic political mobilization, while those in the other rows offer weak or no evidence of such mobilization. How should the researcher describe the key differences between these two sets of minorities? In other words, what combinations of causal conditions are linked to ethnic political mobilization?

In diversity-oriented research, investigators assume maximum causal complexity. This concern for causal complexity is best implemented by allowing for the possibility that no single causal condition may be either necessary or sufficient for the outcome in question. When no single causal condition is either necessary or sufficient, researchers anticipate finding that different *combinations* of causal conditions are sufficient for the outcome. This emphasis on causal complexity does not preclude the possibility of finding either a necessary cause or a cause that by itself is sufficient for an outcome. If researchers find that the different combinations of conditions sufficient for an outcome have one or more conditions in common, then the shared cause(s) may be considered necessary, though not sufficient, for the outcome. Researchers also may examine single causes to see if any is sufficient for the outcome.

To assess the sufficiency of a cause or causal combination, the researcher examines the cases conforming to the cause or combination and evaluates whether or not they display the outcome in question. For example, the evidence presented for row 10 of Table 1 (cases conforming to the combination *large**~*fluent**~*wealthy**growing) indicates that this causal combination may be sufficient for ethnic political mobilization because all six cases with this combination display ethnic political mobilization. Of course, the researcher must establish standards for evaluating sufficiency. Is six positive cases and no negative cases enough to establish the sufficiency of a causal combination? What about two positive cases and no negative cases, or only one positive case? In each investigation, the investigator must justify the method used to assess sufficiency, based on the nature of the evidence, previous research, the state of relevant theoretical and substantive knowledge, the intended audience for the research, and so on.

The assessment of sufficiency can take either of two general forms. It can be strict, with no allowance for discordant outcomes among the cases conforming to a causal combination, or it can be probabilistic, using

benchmark proportions. In *The Comparative Method* and in most applications of the techniques I presented in that work the assessment of the
sufficiency of causal combinations is strict: in order to be considered sufficient for an outcome, *all* the cases conforming to a particular causal combination must display the outcome in question.[11] When the number of relevant cases is small, as in most comparative research, this method is the
only one available; probabilistic assessments of sufficiency require larger
numbers.[12] Because the example developed here, ethnic political mobilization among linguistic minorities, involves a moderate number of cases (36),
I present both assessments, strict and probabilistic.

The core of the probabilistic approach to the assessment of the sufficiency
of causal combinations is to test the significance of the difference between
the observed proportion of positive instances and a benchmark proportion
specified by the investigator. The benchmark proportion can be linked to
linguistic qualifiers, such as "almost always sufficient" (.80) and "sufficient
more often than not" (.50). When the number of cases conforming to a
causal combination is modest, say 20 or fewer, researchers should use an
exact probability test; otherwise, the z test for the difference between two
proportions will suffice.[13] To conduct either test, the researcher must set a
benchmark proportion and a significance level for making the assessment.
For example, a researcher might argue that if the proportion of cases displaying the outcome in question is significantly greater than .65, with a
significance level of .05 (using a one-tailed test), then the causal combination
in question is "usually sufficient" for the outcome.

This sufficiency test is applied not only to the original sixteen configurations listed in Table 1, but also to the remaining 64 groupings listed in
columns 2 through 4 of Table 2. In essence, by applying the test to each of
the eighty groupings in Table 2, the researcher examines all logically possible
causal arguments that can be constructed from the four presence/absence
dichotomies. In each of the eighty tests of sufficiency, the observed proportion of cases displaying ethnic political mobilization is contrasted with
the benchmark proportion (.65) to see if the observed proportion is significantly greater than the benchmark. Eight of the eighty groupings pass the
sufficiency test.

11. An early list of applications of QCA is published in Charles Ragin, "Introduction to Qualitative
Comparative Analysis", in Thomas Janoski and Alexander Hicks (eds), *The Comparative Political
Economy of the Welfare State* (Cambridge, 1994), pp. 313–317. A more up-to-date list is available
from the author upon request.
12. For example, using very generous probabilistic criteria and a relatively weak sufficiency benchmark, an investigator still must have four positive instances and no negative instances for a specific
combination of conditions to be judged "sufficient more often than not": see Ragin, *Fuzzy-Set
Social Science*.
13. William Hays, *Statistics* (New York, 1981), pp. 211–214. The z test of the statistical significance
of the difference between an observed proportion and a benchmark proportion is, in effect, a
large-N approximation of the exact test of the same difference: see *ibid.*, pp. 552–553.

None of the sixteen elemental groupings (the configurations from Table 1) passes the sufficiency test. For a proportion of 1.0 to be significantly greater than .65, with a one-tailed significance level of .05, a grouping needs at least 7 cases. Because none of the sixteen configurations has this many cases (6 cases is the maximum for these combinations), none passes the sufficiency test. For 6 positive cases and no negative cases to pass a sufficiency test, either the benchmark must be lowered (e.g. to "sufficient more often than not" or .50), or the significance level must be raised (e.g. to .10 significance). Close examination of the eight groupings that pass the sufficiency test reveals that all have very high proportions: seven are 1.0; the eighth is .92. Thus, even though the benchmark proportion is relatively modest ("usually sufficient" or .65), only very high proportions with seven or more cases actually pass the test. This result follows from the use of a relatively stringent significance level for evidence of this type.

The eight groupings that pass the sufficiency test are:

1. *large*~fluent*growing*
2. *large*~wealthy*growing*
3. *large*wealthy*growing*
4. *large*wealthy*
5. *large*growing*
6. *fluent*wealthy*
7. *wealthy*growing*
8. *wealthy*

While it is possible to use the minimization algorithms presented in my book to simplify these eight groupings into a simple logical equation for ethnic mobilization, it is not necessary to do so in this example because the pattern is straightforward.[14] A logically minimal equation can be derived using the *subset rule*. Some groupings are subsets of other groupings and thus are redundant. For example, linguistic minorities that are *large*wealthy*growing* (#3) are a subset of minorities that are *large*wealthy* (#4), which in turn are a subset of minorities that are *wealthy* (#8). Thus, groupings #3 and #4 are contained within grouping #8 and thus can be eliminated. Altogether, four groupings (#3, #4, #6 and #7) are subsets of #8, and three are subsets of #5 (#1, #2 and #3). These redundant groupings can be dropped. Eliminating these groupings yields the following simplified statement of the causal conditions sufficient for ethnic political mobilization. (As noted previously, in logical statements addition indicates logical *or* – alternatives; asterisks indicate logical *and* – the combination of aspects.)

ethnic political mobilization = large*growing + wealthy

14. Ragin, *Comparative Method*, pp. 85–102.

Using a probabilistic approach to the assessment of causal sufficiency thus produces a relatively parsimonious statement of the conditions for ethnic political mobilization: linguistic minorities that are either wealthy or combine large size and growth are the ones that mobilize. Because these two terms do not contain a common condition, the results show that there is no necessary condition for ethnic political mobilization. However, being wealthy, relative to the core region of the host country, is sufficient, by itself, for such mobilization. Using this logical statement as a prediction equation yields only one incorrect assignment: Ladins of Italy are a false positive. According to the equation they should offer strong evidence of ethnic political mobilization, but using the criteria applied to all linguistic minorities, they do not. In fact, this outlying case is very complex. Ladins in Italy are a territorial minority within a territorial minority – South Tyroleans, a highly mobilized minority. While every ethnic situation is unique, some clearly are more complex than others. More than likely, the researcher would treat this case as an exception to the general patterns specified in the equation and check to see if features specific to this case were of any general relevance to other cases.

Just as the probabilistic approach to the assessment of sufficiency entails specification of benchmarks and significance levels, the alternative, "strict" approach requires a qualitative evaluation of the strength of the evidence. As already noted, if a causal combination includes any negative cases of the outcome, it fails the strict test of sufficiency. Additionally, the investigator may establish a *frequency threshold* for the number of positive instances. If a causal combination has one positive instance of the outcome and no negative instances, does the evidence support the claim that the causal combination in question is sufficient for the outcome? Is two positive instances enough? How many does it take? Again, the researcher must justify the method used to evaluate sufficiency in each investigation. In some studies, especially small-N comparative studies of large-scale macrosocial processes and events, a claim of sufficiency may be based on a single positive instance. In other studies, more positive instances may be required.

In order to enhance the potential for contrast with the probabilistic approach, with its implicit frequency threshold – in this example – of seven positive cases when there are no negative cases, the illustration of the strict approach that follows uses a relatively low frequency threshold: if a grouping has *no negative instances* of the outcome and *two or more* positive instances of the outcome, it is judged sufficient for ethnic political mobilization. Applying these criteria to the eighty groupings listed in Table 2 yields the following twenty-three that pass the sufficiency test:

1 ~large*fluent*wealthy*growing
2. large*~fluent*~wealthy*growing
3. large*~fluent*wealthy*growing

4. *large*fluent*wealthy*~growing*
5. *large*fluent*wealthy*growing*
6. *~large*fluent*wealthy*
7. *large*~fluent*wealthy*
8. *large*fluent*wealthy*
9. ~large**fluent*growing*
10. *large*~fluent*growing*
11. *large*fluent*growing*
12. *~large*wealthy*growing*
13. *large*~wealthy*growing*
14. *large*wealthy*~growing*
15. *large*wealthy*growing*
16. *~fluent*wealthy*growing*
17. *fluent*wealthy*~growing*
18. *fluent*wealthy*growing*
19. *large*wealthy*
20. *large*growing*
21. *fluent*wealthy*
22. *fluent*growing*
23. *wealthy*growing*

The subset rule described previously can be applied to this list to simplify these twenty-three causal combinations into a single logical statement. Alternatively, the minimization algorithms described in *The Comparative Method* and implemented in the computer program QCA may be used; the results are the same. Applying either technique results in the following logical statement describing the causal combinations linked to ethnic political mobilization:

ethnic political mobilization = large*growing + fluent*wealthy

In short, the results are very similar, though not identical, to those obtained using the probabilistic approach. Translated to prose, the equation states that territorially-based linguistic minorities that combine either large size and growth or a strong linguistic base and greater relative wealth are the ones that exhibit substantial ethnic political mobilization. In this equation, no single condition is either necessary or sufficient because both terms are combinations formed from different causal conditions.

While not as parsimonious as the results using the probabilistic approach, it is easy to see that the two equations differ precisely because the strict test does not allow false positives. Thus, Ladins of Italy are not included in the equation that results from the application of the strict test. They are excluded because of their weaker linguistic ability, compared with the positive cases of mobilization.

It is not productive at this point to ask "Which equation is correct?"

because correctness is not intrinsic to analytic techniques. Analytic techniques offer social scientists different ways of constructing representations of social phenomena from evidence.[15] The two equations are nothing more than alternate representations of the evidence on ethnic political mobilization using different rules. In social research, different analytic approaches almost always result in different representations. Which approach is "best" depends on the criteria applied. For example, if the criterion is "no false positives", then the strict approach is best. If the criteria are "makes abundant allowance for imperfect evidence" and "provides greater parsimony", then the probabilistic approach is best. Generally, when the number of cases is small, the first criterion may be more important; when the number is large, the second criteria may be more important.

Ultimately, the question of correctness can be addressed only through case-level analysis. For example, the investigator might take a close look at the positive instances of ethnic political mobilization where greater relative wealth seems important as a causal factor and examine whether or not linguistic ability also seems important in these cases. Additionally, the researcher could ask whether weaker linguistic ability seems to be the main factor impeding the development of strong ethnic political mobilization among Ladins in Italy. More generally, as I stress repeatedly in *The Comparative Method* and subsequent work, representations of this type, where large amounts of evidence are reduced to broad patterns summarized in an equation (or using some other shorthand), must be evaluated in every instance in terms of their utility for understanding specific cases. Broad representations are best viewed as maps or guides to help a researcher through difficult terrain. They cannot show many details, only the most important. As Charles Tilly would argue, representations of this type "discipline our thinking about [...] complex phenomena in preparation for genuine explanatory efforts" at the case level.[16]

Finally, it is also possible to use summary equations, like the equation for ethnic political mobilization, to differentiate types of cases. Essentially, a summary equation shows, in a logically shorthand manner, the different combinations of conditions linked to some outcome. These different combinations provide a basis for differentiating alternate paths to a given outcome, and cases can be classified according to the paths they travel. For illustration, consider again the results of the strict analysis:

$$ethnic\ political\ mobilization = large^*growing + fluent^*wealthy$$

In essence, the equation states that there are two sets of conditions linked to ethnic political mobilization: large size combined with growth, and

15. Charles Ragin, *Constructing Social Research* (Thousand Oaks, 1994), pp. 5–30.
16. Charles Tilly, "Means and Ends of Comparison in Macrosociology", *Comparative Social Research*, XVI (1997), p. 54.

Table 3. *Conformity of cases to causal combinations*

Minorities that are *large*growing*	Minorities that are *fluent*wealthy*	Minorities that conform to both
W. Frisians, Netherlands	Aalanders, Finland	Alsatians, France
Catalans, France	Slovenes, Italy	Germans, Belgium
Occitans, France	Valdotians, Italy	Flemings, Belgium
Welsh, Great Britain	Swedes, Finland	
Bretons, France	S. Tyroleans, Italy	
Corsicans, France		
Friulians, Italy		
Occitans, Italy		
Basques, Spain		
Catalans, Spain		
Walloons, Belgium		

linguistic strength combined with relative wealth. Table 3 shows the different linguistic minorities conforming to each combination of conditions. Note that three minorities conform to both combinations, as shown in the third column. This pattern of results indicates that both interpretive frames (shown in the first two columns) can be applied to these cases.

While far beyond the scope of this paper, a researcher might find important differences between the nature of the ethnic political mobilization present in these different sets of cases. In fact, an important way to reinforce the results would be to examine the cases to see if differences in the character or course of ethnic mobilization can be traced to differences in relevant causal conditions. In the end, the researcher might be able to differentiate types of ethnic political mobilization and assign cases to types (including mixed types) based on these results. Thus the results provide a basis for reconstituting cases as broad types.

SUMMARY: USING QCA

There are three distinct phases to the application of QCA to cross-case evidence: (1) selecting cases and constructing the property space that defines kinds of cases (configurations), (2) testing the sufficiency of causal conditions, and (3) evaluating and interpreting the results. As already noted, the summary equations that result from the application of QCA should be viewed as part of the larger dialogue of ideas and evidence.[17] The real test of any representation of evidence is how well it helps the researcher and his or her audiences understand specific cases or sets of cases. Broad representations of cross-case patterns provide maps that guide and facilitate in-depth investigation; they are not substitutes for this type of investigation. Thus

17. Ragin, *Comparative Method*, pp. 164–171.

QCA has an implicit fourth phase involving the application of the results to specific cases, but this phase is not part of QCA proper.

In many respects the first phase of QCA is the most difficult. The dimensions of the property space (i.e. relevant aspects of cases) must be clarified and refined to see if the resulting scheme sorts cases into kinds that make sense. At the same time, the researcher must study the cases initially chosen for investigation and evaluate whether or not the set as a whole has integrity. Dropping or adding cases may help the researcher refine the property space while at the same time increase the comparability of the cases in the study. Simultaneously, the researcher also examines cases conforming to each configuration defined by the property space with respect to the outcome under investigation, with an eye toward their concordance. If cases differ too greatly on the outcome, then either the property space must be reformulated, the population must be reconstituted, or both.

Once the researcher successfully stabilizes the relevant cases and the property space that sorts them into kinds, then the assessment of causal sufficiency can proceed. In this phase, the key issue is the definition of sufficiency: how should the test be structured? The answer to this question is shaped in large part by the nature of the evidence and the criteria that are most important to the investigator. Still, in most analyses, it is probably best to work with several definitions of sufficiency, and conduct tests favoring competing criteria. Once these tests are complete, algorithms implemented in the program QCA can be used to analyze and simplify the patterns.[18]

More generally, QCA offers comparative analysts a middle path between complexity and generality. With QCA it is possible to allow for causal complexity and case specificity while examining general patterns. The considerable intellectual effort that goes into the construction of a useful property space forces investigators to establish a great deal of empirical intimacy with their cases. Likewise, the procedures used to simplify evidence represented with the resulting property spaces avoid homogenizing assumptions – for example, the idea that a cause must act the same way in all cases – and thus maintain the configurational complexity of individual cases. Finally, the results of QCA provide a basis for interpreting cases, reconstructing them as types, and evaluating their different trajectories. In the end, the results of any application of QCA must be judged relative to their value as interpretive aids in the analysis of specific cases. These results also provide limited generalizations about patterns holding across empirically circumscribed sets of cases.

18. This introduction to the logic of QCA does not cover two important issues: (1) how to treat logically possible combinations of causes for which there are no empirical instances and (2) how to use theory to evaluate and enrich the results of any logical minimization. These two issues are addressed in *ibid.*, pp. 103–113, 142–147.

ANNOTATED BIBLIOGRAPHY

Abell, Peter, "Foundations for a Qualitative Comparative Method", *International Review of Social History*, 34, 1 (1989), pp. 103–109.
This long essay on *The Comparative Method* (Ragin, 1987) offers a good introduction to the use of Boolean algebra in comparative analysis and suggests some directions for extending the approach.

Amenta, Edwin, Bruce G. Carruthers and Yvonne Zylan, "A Hero for the Aged? The Townsend Movement, the Political Mediation Model, and U.S. Old-Age Policy, 1934–1950", *American Journal of Sociology*, 98, 2 (1992), pp. 308–339.
This examination of US social policy uses state-level data to test basic arguments about the Townsend movement. The qualitative comparative analysis reinforces conclusions drawn from historical and statistical analyses and shows the different paths to four movement outcomes at the state level: polity membership, concessions, co-optation and collapse.

Berg-Schlosser, Dirk and Gisèle De Meur, "Conditions of Democracy in Inter-War Europe: A Boolean Test of Major Hypotheses", *Comparative Politics*, 26, 3 (1994), pp. 253–280.
This sophisticated examination of a variety of theoretical arguments presents a wide array of Boolean analyses using qualitative data on conditions conducive to democracy. The authors construct and then simplify truth tables for each major theoretical perspective.

Drass, Kriss A. and Charles C. Ragin, *Qualitative Comparative Analysis, Version 3* (Evanston, IL, 1992).
QCA is a software package for Boolean analysis of social data. It is a DOS program distributed on a single diskette along with a brief manual. Available from: Publications Department, Institute for Policy Research, 2040 Sheridan Road, Evanston, IL 60208, USA. The charge is $25.00 to cover duplication, postage and handling. Purchasers are welcome to make copies of the program and the documentation to share with other users, as long as they do not charge a fee.

Hicks, Alexander, Joya Misra and Nah Tg Tang, "The Programmatic Emergence of the Social Security State", *American Sociological Review*, 60, 3 (1995), pp. 329–350.
Focusing on the advanced industrial societies after World War I, this nuanced examination of welfare state consolidation highlights the importance of working-class mobilization. The QCA results in this paper demonstrate the importance of theory in the treatment of logically possible combinations of causes that lack empirical instances.

Lieberson, Stanley and Eleanor O. Bell, "Children's First Names: An Empirical Study of Social Taste", *American Journal of Sociology*, 98, 3 (1992), pp. 511–554.

This paper features a truth table approach to the interpretation of complex data patterns without taking advantage of the formal methods of data reduction. The paper illustrates a concern for configurations and the use of truth tables (property spaces) to represent and analyze complexity.

Markoff, John, "A Comparative Method: Reflections on Charles Ragin's Innovations in Comparative Analysis", *Historical Methods*, 23, 4 (1990), pp. 177–181.

Another long essay on *The Comparative Method*, this discussion addresses the advances afforded by the Boolean approach and sketches its limitations. The primary limitation that Markoff addresses is the fact that the Boolean approach is a method of data analysis that requires a good prior grasp of relevant substantive and historical knowledge.

Ragin, Charles C., *The Comparative Method: Moving Beyond Qualitative and Quantitative Strategies* (Berkeley, 1987).

The sharp contrast between case-oriented and variable-oriented research strategies provides a backdrop for a systematic, in-depth presentation of Boolean methods of data analysis. A cornerstone of the discussion is the problem of multiple conjunctural causation and the difficulty of assessing this type of causation with linear, statistical models.

Ragin, Charles C., *Issues and Alternatives in Comparative Social Research* (Leiden, 1991).

A collection of essays on comparative methodology. The volume includes two applications of QCA: Larry J. Griffin, Christopher Botsko, Ana-Maria Wahl and Larry W. Isaac, "Theoretical Generality, Case Particularity: Qualitative Comparative Analysis of Trade Union Growth and Decline" and Timothy P. Wickham-Crowley, "A Qualitative Comparative Approach to Latin American Revolutions".

Ragin, Charles C., "Introduction to Qualitative Comparative Analysis", in Thomas Janoski and Alexander Hicks (eds), *The Comparative Political Economy of the Welfare State* (Cambridge, 1994), pp. 299–319.

This paper offers a brief overview of the analytic procedures central to QCA and presents a bibliography of pre-1993 applications.

Ragin, Charles C., "Using Qualitative Comparative Analysis to Study Configurations", in Udo Kelle (ed.), *Computer-Aided Qualitative Data Analysis* (London, 1995), pp. 177–189.

Two problems structure this discussion of QCA: limited diversity and contradictions. Limited diversity refers to the fact that it is rare that investigators are able to identify empirical instances of all the logically possible combinations of causal factors that are relevant to the property spaces they construct. Contradictions occur when cases with the same combination of causal conditions display discordant outcomes and the investigator is unable, for whatever reason, to resolve these contradictions.

International Review of Social History 43 (1998), Supplement, pp. 125–144
© 1998 Internationaal Instituut voor Sociale Geschiedenis

Historical Social Network Analysis*

CHARLES WETHERELL

INTRODUCTION

In the past two decades, social network analysis (SNA) has become a major analytical paradigm in sociology and now occupies a strategic place in disciplinary debates on a wide variety of issues.[1] Historians, however, have been slow to adopt the approach for at least three reasons. First, the conceptual orientation of sociologists practicing historical social network analysis (HSNA) remains unfamiliar to the majority of professional historians. Just when SNA was maturing in the late 1980s and 1990s, the interdisciplinary interest in social science theory among historians, so characteristic of the 1970s and early 1980s, began to wane. The subsequent turn toward postmodernist thinking in history left the profession increasingly uninformed about both classical and contemporary social theory.[2] Second, those quantitatively-oriented historians who might be predisposed to use SNA's specialized statistical methods constitute less than a quarter of the profession today, thus the risk of SNA finding its way into mainstream historical scholarship is low to start.[3] Third, SNA's data requirements are formidable. SNA demands evidence of social interaction among all members of a social system for a variety of behaviors, and thus necessitates a broad range of high-quality records for the place, time and activities being studied. Because historians are plagued by an incomplete historical record and imperfect understandings of past social relations, HSNA remains an inherently problematic enterprise. Yet despite conceptual, methodological and evidentiary obstacles, SNA possesses real potential for historical analysis.

This essay does three things. First, it reviews the essential tenets of SNA as a method of social analysis. Second, it provides a brief overview of the underlying historical vision guiding SNA. Third, using a concrete example from a nineteenth-century European peasant community, it illustrates how HSNA can advance our understanding of historical kinship, which remains

* The author would like to to thank Larry Griffin and Barry Wellman for comments on earlier versions, and the Academic Senate of the University of California, Riverside, for financial support.
1. Barry Wellman, "Structural Analysis: From Method and Metaphor to Theory and Substance", in B. Wellman and S.D. Berkowitz (eds), *Social Structures: A Network Approach* (New York, 1988), pp. 19–61; Mark S. Mizruchi, "Social Network Analysis: Recent Achievements and Current Controversies", *Acta Sociologica*, 37 (1994), pp. 329–343; and Mustafa Emirbayer, "Manifesto for a Relational Sociology", *American Journal of Sociology*, 103 (1997), pp. 281–317.
2. Peter Novick, *That Noble Dream: The "Objectivity Question" and the American Historical Profession* (New York, 1988), pp. 522–629.
3. John F. Reynolds, "Do Historians Count Anymore? The Status of Quantitative Methods in History, 1975–1995", *Historical Methods*, 31 (1998), pp. 141–148.

one of the more important, yet most elusive matters in contemporary social history. More than a decade ago, Charles Tilly argued that the real task of social history lay in "(1) documenting large structural changes, (2) reconstructing the experiences of ordinary people in the course of those changes, and (3) connecting the two".[4] Tilly's challenge remains as vital today as ever, and this essay shows how a network analytic approach can help to meet it.

Network analysts maintain that SNA is a distinct theoretical and methodological approach.[5] They point not only to operating precepts and assumptions about social structure and behavior, but also to the wide assortment of methods that a broad focus on social relations have forced analysts to develop. While SNA's pedigree reaches back into the 1930s and the field of sociometry, SNA matured in the late 1970s and 1980s as practitioners in sociology, social psychology and anthropology developed analytical concepts and measures to exploit new forms of data collected about economic, political and social structures of the modern world. The International Network for Social Network Analysis (INSNA), established in 1976, has served as a forum for network analysts in the social and medical sciences for more than two decades.[6] INSNA's journal, *Social Networks*, was founded in 1978 to disseminate a growing body of network research. Explicitly network analytic work also appears regularly in the two major American sociological journals, the *American Journal of Sociology* and the *American Sociological Review*. Today, SNA represents a mature, self-conscious analytical perspective, and its place in disciplinary studies of human behavior is assured.

SNA BASICS

The social network perspective consists of four basic propositions that together give coherence to the larger approach. First, actors in all social systems are viewed as "interdependent rather than independent".[7] Second, the linkages or relations among actors channel information, affection and other resources. Third, the structure of those relations or ties among actors both constrain and facilitate action. Fourth, and finally, the patterns of relations among actors define economic, political and social structure. Critics argue that SNA's excessive focus on structural relationships tends to minimize the role of individual agency, and that this represents a major weakness of the approach.[8] A case can be made, however, that SNA neither

4. Charles Tilly, "Retrieving European Lives", in Olivier Zunz (ed.), *Reliving the Past: The Worlds of Social History* (Chapel Hill, 1985), p. 31.
5. Wellman, "Structural Analysis", pp. 19–30; Stanley Wasserman and Katherine Faust, *Social Network Analysis: Methods and Applications* (New York, 1994), pp. 3–25.
6. See INSNA's website at www.heinz.cmu.edu/project/INSNA.
7. Wasserman and Faust, *Social Network Analysis*, p. 4.
8. Valerie A. Haines, "Social Network Analysis, Structuration Theory and the Holism-Individualism Debate", *Social Networks*, 10 (1988), pp. 157–182; Mustafa Emirbayer and Jeff Goodwin, "Network Analysis, Culture, and the Problem of Agency", *American Journal of Sociology*, 99

denies nor downplays human agency. Community network analysts, in particular, view human behavior as largely instrumental, and explicitly portray people acting consciously and purposefully. As the relative importance of agency and structure in human affairs remains a general problem in social theory and social history, the matter will be neither easily nor quickly resolved.[9]

SNA's basic precepts stand in sharp contrast to traditional social analysis, which normally uses differences in the attributes of individuals (wealth, age, education) to define social structure, and relies on standard descriptive (e.g. mean and standard deviation) and predictive (e.g. regression) statistics to convey central tendency and model variation. Rather than the individual person, group or institution, SNA views the ties or linkages between two or more persons, groups or institutions as the essential units of analysis. Those ties may, in turn, be ones of resource transfer (creditor-debtor), association (shared membership) or biological connection (kinship), among others. Whatever the nature of the ties, the "social network" is the amalgamation of ties among actors and the "social structure" is the pattern those ties assume. Special statistical procedures designed to formalize SNA notions about the density of ties (what proportion of all potential ties actually exits), the centrality of actors (which actor can be reached by the most people), and structural equivalence (do actors have similar patterns of ties), among others, all contribute to a unique analytical vocabulary and toolbox that further distinguishes SNA from conventional social analysis.[10]

Perhaps the most fundamental analytical division in SNA is between a whole network (WN) and an egocentric (EC) approach. The WN approach seeks to capture all essential relations or ties among actors in a social system. All members are theoretically included and all relevant ties are documented and analyzed. Analysts of modern business behavior and interlocking

(1994), pp. 1411–1454; Steven Brint, "Hidden Meanings: Cultural Content and Context in Harrison White's Structural Sociology", *Sociological Theory*, 10 (1992), pp. 194–208; Harrison C. White, "Social Grammar for Culture: Reply to Brint", *ibid.*, pp. 209–213; and idem, *Identity and Control* (Princeton, NJ, 1992).

9. As a starting point, see Anthony Giddens, *Central Problems in Social Theory* (London, 1979); and Philip Abrams, *Historical Sociology* (Ithaca, 1982).

10. Wasserman and Faust, *Social Network Analysis* contains complete explanations of most network measures, and is virtually a one-stop methodological guide. See Bonnie Erickson, "Social Networks and History: A Review Essay", *Historical Methods*, 30 (1997), pp. 149–157. Most network measures have been incorporated into the software package UCINET (Steven Borgatti, Martin Everett and Linton C. Freeman, *UCINET IV*, Analytic Technologies (Natick, MA, 1995), www.analytictech.com). Older, but still useful, guides are S.D. Berkowitz, *An Introduction to Structural Analysis* (Toronto, 1982); David Knoke and James Kuklinski, *Network Analysis* (Beverly Hills, 1982); and John Scott, *Network Analysis: A Handbook* (Newbury Park, 1992). See also Peter V. Marsden and Nan Lin (eds), *Social Structure and Network Analysis* (Beverly Hills, 1982), and Ronald S. Burt and Michael Minor (eds), *Applied Network Analysis: A Methodological Introduction* (Beverly Hills, 1983).

corporate directorates illustrate this research tradition.[11] By contrast, analysts of egocentric networks study the ties that single individuals possess and use. Research questions in this tradition focus on the nature and quality of ties, and how those relations serve to structure individual life by opening up or closing down channels of affection, support and action.[12] Some network analysts contend that the whole network approach is the more powerful of the two approaches because it presumes to capture the essence of a social system, and because the vast majority of specialized statistical techniques that analysts have developed in the past thirty years are designed for whole networks.[13]

WN methods are grounded in graph theory as a network may be portrayed easily and comprehensibly as a matrix. Rows and columns represent all actors in the social system and the contents of individual cells the existence and nature of the relationship between any two network members. Consider, for example, the small groups of individual investors who underwrote the risks of ocean-going commerce in the early modern world. A 1765 London insurance syndicate could be represented by the matrix, X,

	Smith	Parish	Herder	Willis	Cotton	Hoyle
Smith	–	1	0	0	0	0
Parish	1	–	0	0	0	1
Herder	0	0	–	0	0	1
Willis	0	0	0	–	0	1
Cotton	0	0	0	0	–	1
Hoyle	0	1	1	1	1	–

and the cell contents, X_{ij}, whether members had any previous underwriting ties or experience with each other. A one would indicate the presence of an earlier tie and a zero the absence of a tie. It is clear that the members had only modest experience with each other. Indeed, the density of the network is .33, which means that only 33 per cent of all possible ties exist.[14] Equally clear is that Hoyle had been involved previously in syndicates with four of the investors, and that he was the most connected or central member of the network.

It is from matrix representations of ties such as this that WN methods

11. Mark S. Mizruchi, *The American Corporate Network: 1904–1974* (Beverly Hills, 1982); and idem, *The Structure of Corporate Political Action: Interfirm Relations and Their Consequences* (Cambridge, MA, 1992).

12. Barry Wellman, Peter J. Carrington and Alan Hall, "Networks as Personal Communities", in Wellman and Berkowitz, *Social Structures*, pp. 130–184.

13. Wasserman and Faust, *Social Network Analysis*, pp. 17–19.

14. Density, Δ, is defined as $2L/g(g\text{-}1)$, where g is the number of actors (investors), and L is the number of ties present. As ties are bi-directional, the number of ties (L) is thus assessed on only one diagonal, i.e. L is equal to 5, not 10: *ibid.*, pp. 101–103, 164.

can extract information about patterns of ties and the structure of the social system being studied; density is but one of many measures that might be used. In this respect at least, the WN approach enjoys an advantage over the EA approach since the methods of conventional social analysis cannot be employed on a matrix conceptualized as a complete social system. At the same time, WN measures such as density can be used as attributes in an egocentric analysis. In conjunction with standard social data such as age, wealth or residence, for example, it might be that unsuccessful syndicates tended to be those composed of investors who had previous experience with each other, that is networks with high densities. Although this might seem to contradict commonsense notions that experience would be an advantage, the network notion that new information tends to flow through networks that are not dense with overlapping ties could well explain the pattern.[15] New men brought to any syndicate a collectively larger store of information that the group could use to assess better the risks of any particular voyage or trading enterprise. Thus WN and EC approaches can be employed together with real analytic gain.

Darrett B. and Anita H. Rutman's "community study" of Middlesex County, Virginia, in the seventeenth and eighteenth centuries illustrates both the demanding data requirements of the WN approach as well as the enormous payoff of using WN methods in historical research.[16] While conceptually the WN approach presumes to capture a social system completely, practically this means collecting from all available sources all possible instances of social interaction, a formidable task under the best of circumstances. The Rutmans conducted a collective biography or prosopography of more than 12,000 persons who resided in Middlesex between 1650 and 1750 long enough to be caught in the historical record. From tax, court and church records they collected information on social interactions that bound people as buyers and sellers of property, or as executors of estates, guardians of minors, witnesses at marriages and as godparents at baptisms. They used civil and ecclesiastical registers of births, marriages and deaths to reconstruct the kinship of Middlesex residents so that they could analyze what interactions were those with kin. The Rutmans' explicit network analytic approach allowed them to see change in the overlapping of kinship and friendship ties as the demographic regime improved from the seventeenth to the eighteenth centuries, to capture the geographic concentration of kinship ties within neighborhoods, and to measure the contrasting balance in local and provincial ties among the county's elite and commoners. It was network analytic

15. Mark Granovetter, "The Strength of Weak Ties: A Network Theory Revisited", in Peter Marsden and Nan Lin (eds), *Social Networks and Social Structure* (Beverly Hills, 1982), pp. 105–130.
16. Darrett B. and Anita H. Rutman, *A Place in Time: Middlesex County, Virginia, 1650–1750*, 2 vols (New York, 1984).

methods in particular that helped the Rutmans to uncover key features of the social structure of a community in the early modern world.[17]

The data requirements of the EC approach are arguably less severe than the WN approach, but nonetheless still formidable. Since EC analysts focus on the nature and quality or ties individuals possess, sources that reveal the subjective importance of social ties are often more important than those that simply document those ties. A few qualitatively revealing diaries or collections of personal correspondence can sustain an EC analysis since the object of study is to analyze the social network of an individual, never the entire social system that the WN approach seeks to comprehend. Women separated by westward migration in the nineteenth-century United States, for example, left voluminous personal accounts in diaries and letters that reveal the composition of their emotional networks and how those often spatially far-flung network members served to sustain them over time in different objective circumstances.[18] Historical accounts that document affection or social support have been used to reconstruct visions of networks in the past, but not in systematic ways characteristic of contemporary egocentric SNA.[19] Indeed, the promise of the EC approach in HSNA has yet to be realized.

Analysts in the egocentric tradition have reconceptualized contemporary personal networks as "personal communities". These analysts study individuals' ties with kin, neighbors, friends and coworkers, and how they actively use those ties in the conduct of everyday life.[20] Findings about the size,

17. There are excellent works of HSNA that employ WN methods, but these remain the product of only a handful of historical sociologists. See, for example, Peter S. Bearman, *Relations into Rhetorics: Local Elite Social Structure in Norfolk, England, 1540–1640* (New Brunswick, NJ, 1993); Bearman and Glenn Deane, "The Structure of Opportunity: Middle-Class Mobility in England, 1548–1689", *American Journal of Sociology*, 98 (1992), pp. 30–66; Bearman and Kevin D. Evertt, "The Structure of Social Protest", *Social Networks*, 15 (1993), pp. 171–200; John F. Padgett and Christopher K. Ansell, "Robust Action and the Rise of the Medici, 1400–1434", *American Journal of Sociology*, 98 (1993), pp. 1259–1319; Ansell, "Symbolic Networks: The Realignment of the French Working Class, 1887–1894", *American Journal of Sociology*, 103 (1997), pp. 359–390; Roger V. Gould, *Insurgent Identities: Class, Community, and Protest in Paris From 1848 to the Commune* (Chicago, 1995); and idem, "Patron-Client Ties, State Centralization, and the Whiskey Rebellion", *American Journal of Sociology*, 102 (1996), pp. 400–429.

18. See, for example, John Mack Farahger, *Woman and Men on the Overland Trail* (New Haven, 1979), pp. 110–143; Carroll Smith-Rosenberg, "The Female World of Love and Ritual: Relations Between Women in Nineteenth-Century America", *Signs*, 1 (1975), pp. 1–30; and Elizabeth Hampsten, *Read This Only to Yourself: The Private Writing of Midwestern Women, 1880–1910* (Bloomington, IN, 1982). Although these works represent an older strain in women's history that has given way to more postmodernist concerns about the relationship of gender to race and class, their findings remain relevant for egocentric HSNA.

19. The classic example of the egocentric approach in history remains Alan MacFarlane, *The Family Life of Ralph Josselin, A Seventeenth-Century Clergyman: An Essay in Historical Anthropology* (Cambridge, 1970).

20. The most prominent advocate of the personal community model is Barry Wellman. See Wellman and Barry Leighton, "Networks, Neighborhoods and Communities", *Urban Affairs*

composition, character and support functions of contemporary personal networks provide a point of departure for discussing the utility of the "personal community" model for HSNA.

1. *Size*: Analysts have estimated that contemporary North Americans and Western Europeans have an average of about 20 strong, active ties and 1,500 weaker ties. Active ties provide people with most of their significant affection, support and social contact. Weak ties integrate and speed the diffusion of information; strong ties, by contrast, impede diffusion as they connect people in similar social circles.[21]

2. *Composition*: Kin comprise 30 to 45 per cent of all active ties; friends, neighbors and coworkers constitute the remaining part. Most intimate kin are immediate kin, and are about equally divided between spouses, parents or adult children (depending on age) and siblings.[22]

3. *Spatial Dispersion*: Personal communities are rarely either local residential groups or spatially dispersed networks, but rather a combination of both. Critically, there is no association between frequency of contact and the strength of relationships.[23]

4. *Interconnection*: Most members of personal community networks are not connected with each other. On average, only one-third of all possible ties actually exist, thus there is little structural basis for network members to work together to provide social support.

5. *Support*: Networks provide a broad range of support, but most members provide only specialized support. Kin behave differently from friends in rendering support. Ties between parents and adult children are the strongest and most broadly supportive. Siblings are similar to friends in providing emotional support, while extended kin are the least likely of all network members to provide any support. In sum, contemporary

Quarterly, 14 (1979), pp. 363–390; Wellman, "The Community Question Re-evaluated"; Wellman *et al.*, "Networks as Personal Communities"; and Wellman, "An Egocentric Network Tale", *Social Networks*, 15 (1993), pp. 423–436. See also Claude S. Fischer, *To Dwell Among Friends: Personal Networks in Town and City* (Chicago, 1983).

21. Manfred Kochen (ed.), *The Small World* (Norwood, NJ, 1989); Mark Granovetter, "The Strength of Weak Ties", *American Journal of Sociology*, 78 (1973), pp. 1360–1380; Herbert Gans, "Comment", *ibid.*, 80 (1974), pp. 524–529; and Granovetter, "The Strength of Weak Ties" . . . Revisited".

22. Barry Wellman and Scot Wortley, "Brothers' Keepers: Situating Kinship Relations in Broader Networks of Social Support", *Sociological Perspectives*, 32 (1989), pp. 273–306; idem, "Different Strokes From Different Folks: Community Ties and Social Support", *American Journal of Sociology*, 96 (1990), pp. 558–588; Wellman, "The Place of Kinfolk in Community Networks", *Marriage and Family Review*, 15 (1990), pp. 195–228.

23. Barry Wellman, "Are Personal Communities Local? A Dumptarian Reconsideration", *Social Networks*, 18 (1996), pp. 347–354.

personal communities have distinct divisions of labor, and network members are rarely interchangeable parts.[24]

The analytical imperatives of HSNA, in general, and of the personal community model in particular, derive from what Barry Wellman calls the "community question", or what happened to community and community life in the transition from the pre-modern to the modern worlds?[25] The historical vision underlying the community question belongs to Ferdinand Tönnies, whose portrayal of the shift from *Gemeinschaft* to *Gesellschaft* was an attempt to understand the changes that attended urbanization, industrialization and bureaucratization in the Western world at the end of the nineteenth century. Tönnies argued that there was a fundamental difference between communally (*Gemeinschaft*) and contractually (*Gesellschaft*) organized societies.[26] He assumed that social, economic and political life would be fundamentally different in each. He thought that in largely rural, communally-organized societies ties would be principally with kin and neighbors, and that social relationships would be densely knit; that is, most people would be connected with each other in some way. By contrast, Tönnies asserted that social relationships in modern, urbanized, industrial society would be more sparsely knit and would be with friends and acquaintances who were neither kin nor connected with each other. In sum, in the transition to the modern world, urbanization and attending migration ruptured spatial constraints on life, and instrumental, contractual social arrangements superseded customary behavior and informal communal control.

Tönnies' view was part of a particularly nineteenth-century European debate about the transformation of society, but he bequeathed to later generations of European historians the disciplinary imperative to understand the destruction of isolated, territorial, immobile, rural communities, and the construction of new, spatially dispersed, communities of interest. Although Tönnies' vision of the traditional European world turned out to be essen-

24. Wellman and Wortley, "Brothers' Keepers"; idem, "Different Strokes From Different Folks"; and Wellman, "Which Types of Ties and Networks Give What Kinds of Social Support?", in Edward Lawler, Barry Markovsky, Cecilia Ridgeway and Henry Walker (eds), *Advances in Group Processes* (Greenwich, CT, 1992), vol. 9, pp. 207–235.

25. Barry Wellman, "The Community Question: The Intimate Networks of East Yorkers", *American Journal of Sociology*, 84 (1979), pp. 1201–1231; idem, "Studying Personal Communities", pp. 61–80; idem, "The Community Question Re-evaluated", in Michael Peter Smith (ed.), *Power, Community and the City* (New Brunswick, NJ, 1988), pp. 81–107; idem, "Structural Analysis". The following section draws upon Barry Wellman and Charles Wetherell, "Social Network Analysis of Historical Communities: Some Questions from the Present for the Past", *History of the Family*, 1 (1996), pp. 97–121, which discusses how European and American historians have approached community.

26. Ferdinand Tönnies, *Community and Organization* (London, 1955; 1st pub. 1887).

tially wrong, his legacy shaped the debate for nearly a century.[27] Work on the importance of kinship in historic Europe illustrates both the power of Tönnies' legacy and the utility of HSNA.

From the early 1960s, family historians addressed Tönnies' assertion that modernization destroyed kinship as the social glue of the traditional world. They initially constructed a vision of a diminution of kinship as a force in family life, emphasizing a reorientation of affective bonds away from kin and toward spouses and children, leaving kin in early modern Europe with severely diminished roles.[28] Michael Anderson later undermined the diminution of kinship view by demonstrating that people received critical support from kin during the stressful adjustment to urbanization and industrialization.[29] While Tamara Hareven showed families turning to kin in everyday life as well as during major life-course transitions such as migration,[30] the view that ultimately prevailed was one of kinship-crisis, in its simplest form, that people used kin mostly in times of dire need.[31]

During the same three decades family demographers wrestled with the question of whether people in the past had enough kin to live in complex family households (multiple lineal generations or collateral family groups), which were presumed to have been the living arrangements of choice before the pressures of urbanization and industrialization created the mobile nuclear family that could respond easily to changes in the demand for labor. Researchers soon discovered that most people in Western Europe from the fifteenth century onward lived in nuclear families, belying the assertion that industrialization forced a massive structural change in family life, but also

27. Charles Tilly, "Misreading, then Rereading, Nineteenth-Century Social Change", in Wellman and Berkowitz, *Social Structures*, pp. 332–358. For accounts of traditional community life that invalidate Tönnies' views, see Keith Wrightson and David Levine, *Poverty and Piety in an English Village: Terling, 1525–1700* (New York, 1979); David I. Kertzer and Dennis P. Hogan, *Family, Political Economy, and Demographic Change: The Transformation of Life in Casalecchio, Italy, 1861–1921* (Madison, WI, 1989); David Warren Sabean, *Property, Production, and Family in Neckarhausen, 1700–1870* (Cambridge, 1990); and Leslie Page Moch, *Moving Europeans: Migration in Western Europe Since 1650* (Bloomington, IN, 1992).
28. Phillipe Aries, *Centuries of Childhood: A Social History of Family Life*, trans. Robert Baldick (New York, 1962); Edward Shorter, *The Making of the Modern Family* (New York, 1975); and Lawrence Stone, *The Family, Sex, and Marriage in England, 1500–1800* (New York, 1977).
29. Michael Anderson, *Family Structure in Nineteenth-Century Lancashire* (Cambridge, 1971).
30. Tamara K. Hareven, *Family Time and Industrial Time: The Relationship Between the Family and Work in a New England Industrial Community* (New York, 1982). Hareven echoed many of Raymond Firth's and Elizabeth Bott's findings for Londoners in the 1950s and 1960s: Bott, *Family and Social Network: Roles, Norms, and External Relationships in Ordinary Urban Families* (London, 1957); and Firth, Jane Hubert, Anthony Forge et al., *Families and Their Relatives: Kinship in a Middle Class Sector of London: An Anthropological Study* (London, 1969).
31. Peter Laslett, "Family, Kinship, and Collectivity as Systems of Support in Pre-Industrial Europe: A Consideration of the 'Nuclear-Hardship' Hypothesis", *Continuity and Change*, 3 (1988), pp. 153–175; Charles Wetherell, Andrejs Plakans and Barry Wellman, "Social Networks, Kinship, and Community in Eastern Europe", *Journal of Interdisciplinary History*, 24 (1994), pp. 639–663, recast Laslett's nuclear-hardship as kinship-crisis.

raising the issue from one of demography to one of culture. Did people in the past choose to live in nuclear families or did demographic constraints thwart their desire to live in extended families? The discovery of complex household forms in Southern and Eastern Europe only confounded the matter. Some demographers asserted that both pre- and post-industrial demographic regimes provided people with sufficient numbers of kin to make complex family living arrangements possible; others maintained that this only happened in the nineteenth century.[32] Although neither position prevails and family historians and family demographers continue to pursue separate research agendas,[33] the critical question for an HSNA of historic European kinship is how general demographic constraints created genealogical, and hence kinship, structures that affected the possibilities for different living arrangements and the composition of personal community networks.

Historians have routinely uncovered people interacting with kin when conveying or receiving property, or at demographic events such as births, marriages and deaths that create or destroy kin. Indeed, traditional social historical evidence dealing with property and population only serves to reinforce high level generalizations that people used and valued kin and kinship, and that kin rendered support at times of need. Yet beyond this, historians have not systematically analyzed such behavior. SNA and the personal community model help to reformulate questions about historic kinship in ways that provide a concrete research agenda.

First, questions about kinship may be recast in terms of genealogical structure. Exactly how many people in a given locale were actually related? A satisfactory answer to this extremely difficult question will alone confirm or deny the impression that almost everyone was related to almost everyone else in the isolated rural communities of the traditional European past.[34] In network terms, the issue is a matter of kinship density: again, the proportion of all possible ties that actually exist. Kinship density, in turn, can suggest

---

32. Steven Ruggles, "Availability of Kin and the Demography of Historical Family Structure", *Historical Methods*, 19 (1986), pp. 93–102; idem, *Prolonged Connections: The Rise of the Extended Family in Nineteenth-Century England and America* (Madison, 1987); and David I. Kertzer, "The Joint Family Household Revisited: Demographic Constraints and Household Complexity in the European Past", *Journal of Family History*, 14 (1989), pp. 1–15.

33. Steven Ruggles, "Family Demography and Family History: Problems and Prospects", *Historical Methods*, 23 (1990), pp. 22–33, is the most explicit statement of the division.

34. For comments on the issue by family historians, see, for example, Andrejs Plakans, "Identifying Kinship Beyond the Household", *Journal of Family History*, 2 (1977), pp. 3–27; and David I. Kertzer, "Kinship Beyond the Household in a Nineteenth-Century Italian Town", *Continuity and Change*, 7 (1992), pp. 103–121. Among family demographers, the issue is inextricably tied to simulations. See, for example, James E. Smith, "The Computer Simulation of Kin Sets and Kin Counts", in John Bongaarts, Thomas Burch and Kenneth Wachter (eds), *Family Demography: Methods and Their Applications* (Oxford, 1987); Ruggles, *Prolonged Connections*; and Wendy Post, Frans van Poppel, Evert van Imhoff and Ellen Kruse, "Reconstructing the Extended Kin-Network in the Netherlands with Genealogical Data: Methods, Problems, and Results", *Population Studies*, 51 (1997), pp. 263–278.

whether there was any structural basis for kin to act collectively to assist when disaster befell a relative? In short, was kinship density high enough to support the kinship-crisis view of traditional social welfare?

Second, the personal community model provides specific questions about historic kinship based on substantial empirical research on contemporary egocentric networks. Was the place of kin in past personal communities different from that in the contemporary world? Was individual social support as specialized as it is today? From this network analytic perspective, historians need not ask if people had cousins or grandparents, but rather whether they had siblings, parents or adult children since these are the most important ties in the contemporary world. Answers to these structural questions will then allow specific instances of economic and social support to be placed in context and cross-temporal comparisons drawn. In sum, an HSNA of kinship can refocus the community question because the notion of personal communities makes better analytic sense than any simple vision of historical kinship or undifferentiated community support.[35] An HSNA of historic kinship also promises to rejoin the concerns of family historians and family demographers.

A CASE STUDY

The landed estate of Pinkenhof in the Russian Baltic province of Livland, now part of Latvia, during the late eighteenth and nineteenth centuries provides a case study for a preliminary HSNA of kinship.[36] Agricultural estates such as Pinkenhof served as the principal economic units in the Baltic agrarian regime, and were themselves subdivided into estate lands and peasant farmsteads whose size and number changed very little over time. Pinkenhof's peasants operated farmsteads for themselves and provided corvée labor as serfs on estate lands before emancipation in 1819, and labor as farmstead rents after that. Migration was controlled and peasants did not

---

35. See Tamara K. Hareven, "The History of the Family and the Complexity of Social Change", *American Historical Review*, 96 (1991), pp. 95–124; and Glen Elder, "Families and Lives: Some Developments in Life Course Studies", in Hareven and Andrejs Plakans (eds), *Family History at the Crossroads: A Journal of the Family Reader* (Princeton, 1987), pp. 179–199.
36. The following discussion draws largely on Andrejs Plakans and Charles Wetherell, "The Kinship Domain in an East European Peasant Community: Pinkenhof, 1833–1850", *American Historical Review*, 93 (1988), pp. 367–371; idem, "Family and Economy in an Early Nineteenth-Century Baltic Serf Estate", *Continuity and Change*, 7 (1992), pp. 199–223; Wetherell *et al.*, "Social Networks, Kinship, and Community in Eastern Europe"; Plakans and Wetherell, "Migration in the Later Years of Life in Traditional Europe", in David I. Kertzer and Peter Laslett (eds), *Old Age in Past Times: The Historical Demography of Aging* (Berkeley, 1995), pp. 156–174; and Wetherell and Plakans, "Intergenerational Transfers of Headships over the Life Course in an Eastern European Peasant Community, 1782–1850", *History of the Family*, 3 (1998), pp. 333–349. All provide fuller discussions of Eastern European kinship, serfdom and emancipation, as well as mobility, the peasant economy and living arrangements in Pinkenhof from 1782 to 1850.

gain the right to own land until the early 1860s. Like thousands of other such estates in the Baltic before the mid-nineteenth century, Pinkenhof was a relatively isolated, rural community with a largely immobile population, just what Tönnies thought characterized the traditional European world.

Evidence about kinship in Pinkenhof comes from a series of nominal censuses, or so-called "revisions of souls", taken in the Russian Empire between 1795 and 1850. All contain some relational data about the farmstead head and his or her immediate family and co-resident kin, but the 1850 revision is unique. It includes relational information about all members of each enumerated farmstead, where people had been in 1833, the year of the last revision, thus allowing inter-farm movement to be tracked, and when people had died or migrated during the period between the two revisions. The essential information extracted from the revisions for reconstructing kinship was data on birth, death and parentage. Because the revisions identified the marital status of all and the parentage of most peasants, kinship could be computed to five lineal and collateral steps. If one knows, for example, that Janis is both the brother of Maris and the father of Andrejs, then by following a few simple rules it is easy to reckon that Maris is Andrejs' father's brother, or uncle, and all of Maris' children are Andrejs' cousins. Together, the 1833 and 1850 revisions provide enough information about each individual to allow the population to be completely reconstructed from 1833 to 1850 and kindreds assembled for the 1,569 people living on the estate in 1850.[37]

Each peasant in Pinkenhof in 1850 had an average of nine relatives, which represented less than 1 per cent of the entire population.[38] Although possibly understated by 10 per cent, the kinship density in Pinkenhof was so low that it offers little guidance beyond refuting the general assertion of widespread kin connectedness in the traditional European past.[39] But we can go further. Unlike in most of Western Europe, marriage in Pinkenhof did not result in the formation of a separate household; newly married couples tended to reside on the groom's farmstead, creating complex households of two or more nuclear or conjugal family groups. Each farmstead had a designated head who dealt with estate authorities, managed the farmstead's workforce, settled disputes and generally oversaw the farmstead's population. As Pinkenhof farmsteads contained an average of twelve to thirteen people, headship was a position of status, power and responsibility in Baltic peasant society.

37. See Plakans and Wetherell, "The Kinship Domain", pp. 363, 367–371 for a fuller discussion of the evidence.
38. Kin are defined as genealogical relations within three collateral or lineal steps, which incorporates such normal kin types as parents, children, siblings, aunts, uncles, cousins, grandparents and grandchildren. The mean number of kin among the 1,569 residents of Pinkenhof was 9.3 ($s = 9.3$; median = 7). Among the 1,438 peasants with kin, the average was 10.1 ($s = 9.2$; median = 7).
39. Plakans and Wetherell, "The Kinship Domain", p. 368 and n. 24.

Given the importance of farmsteads, kinship ties between residents of different farms provide another view of Pinkenhof's social structure. Formal whole network measures help to describe that structure. Among the 123 farmsteads in Pinkenhof, there were 352 actual ties, for a density of .047, which is to say that only 4.7 per cent of all possible kinship ties actually existed. However, given the additional network notion of reachability to "a kin of a kin" (two steps), Pinkenhof farmsteads possessed ties to an average of 27 or 22 per cent of all other farmsteads.[40] From this perspective at least, kinship in Pinkenhof created a social structure that connected any one farmstead with a fifth of all other farmsteads. Additionally, if adult Pinkenhofers possessed 1,000 active ties, far fewer than in the contemporary world, then the 837 adults over 20 in 1850 probably knew every other adult on the estate. Thus, while individual kinship embeddedness may have been low, kin ties among farmsteads were far more extensive; this in turn suggests structural reasons for supposing that kinship-crisis social support may have been a reality where complex household forms prevailed. Discovering instances of such assistance remains the task of future work.

Assessing the place of kin in the lives of individual peasants remains far more difficult because the evidence at hand reveals only structural possibilities rather than the historical reality. Nonetheless, possibilities come first. Could the peasants of Pinkenhof have constructed personal communities that included kin to the same extent as people in the contemporary world? Using the example of East York, in Toronto, Canada, as a robust point of comparison, the answer is no.[41] Although Pinkenhof's peasants had an average of nine kin, only four to five were other adults. East Yorkers included six kinds of ties in their personal communities: spouses, parents and adult children, siblings, extended kin, coworkers and friends. While most adults in Pinkenhof had kin ties with spouses and parents or adult children, most had only one adult sibling and one extended kin. Table 1 shows that the typical personal community of an adult East Yorker was split half and half between kin and friends. In Pinkenhof, that split would have been closer to one-third/two-thirds because the pool of both immediate and extended kin was smaller.[42] Thus, in order for Pinkenhofers to have assembled personal

40. Wasserman and Faust, *Social Network Analysis*, pp. 107, 159–161. Pinkenhof farmsteads had direct kin ties with an average of 5.7 ($s = 4.7$) other farmsteads, and from these to an average of another 21.4 ($s = 15.6$) farmsteads. Thus farmsteads had ties to an average of 27.1 ($s = 19.8$) additional farms through at most one intermediate step. Short chains of two or less are thought to be highly effective channels of aid and information.

41. Wellman, "The Community Question Re-evaluated", provides a comparison of findings that indicates East York is a good benchmark for the size and composition of contemporary personal communities.

42. Spouses are often excluded from profiles of personal communities because they provide so much more support than any other network member: see, Barry Wellman and Beverly Wellman, "Domestic Affairs and Network Relations", *Journal of Social and Personal Relationships*, 9 (1992), pp. 385–409; Wellman *et al.*, "Networks as Personal Communities". The absence of large pools of

Table 1. *Size and composition of personal communities in Toronto, 1978 and Pinkenhof, 1850*

| | Toronto, 1978 | | Pinkenhof, 1850 | | | |
| | | | Actual | Hypothetical | | |
	N	%	N	N	%	
Spouse	1	8.3	1	1	8.3	
Parent/adult child	1	8.3	1	1	8.3	
Siblings	3	25.0	1	1	8.3	
Extended, kin	1	8.3	50.0	1	1	8.3	33.3
Coworkers	1	8.3		5	2?	16.7	
Friends and neighbors	5	41.7	50.0		6?	50.0	66.7
Totals	12	100.0		9	12	100.0	
Sample N	33			837			

Sources: East York Social Network Study, 1978, Centre for Urban and Community Studies, University of Toronto; Eighth (1833) and Ninth (1850) Imperial Revisions, Central National Historical Archive, Riga, Latvia. Baltic Microfilms, D112, J.G. Herder Institute, Marburg a.d. Lahn, Germany.
Note: Ns, except sample size, are medians.

networks of the size East Yorkers enjoyed, they would have had to include more non-kin. More generally, the pre-modern demographic regime of Pinkenhof clearly limited the number of immediate and extended kin that Pinkenhof peasants could have included in their personal networks, confirming that kinship was structurally different from that in the contemporary world.

The number and kind of adult kin Pinkenhofers possessed varied predictably with age, and in ways that indicate important patterns of kin-life. As Figure 1 displays, adults in their twenties still had parents and siblings; in their thirties they acquired spouses and collateral kin and retained their parents. In their forties, however, Pinkenhof peasants experienced a sea change in their kindreds as they rapidly began losing both siblings and parents at the same time their own children were maturing. By their late fifties, most people had living adult children, but few other kin. Less than one in ten Pinkenhofers over sixty had a living sibling and only one in five had any other extended kin; yet seven in ten had an adult child somewhere on the estate.[43]

The farmstead system of the Baltic agrarian regime further constrained contact with kin. Pinkenhof peasants lived in a "barracks society", in which communal living arrangements prevailed.[44] Housing consisted of structures

immediate kin in Pinkenhof, however, argues for including spouses; for a profile that excludes spouses, see Wetherell *et al.*, "Social Networks, Kinship, and Community in Eastern Europe", esp. Table 1, p. 652.
43. See *ibid.*, Table 2, p. 653.
44. Plakans and Wetherell, "Kinship Domain", p. 371.

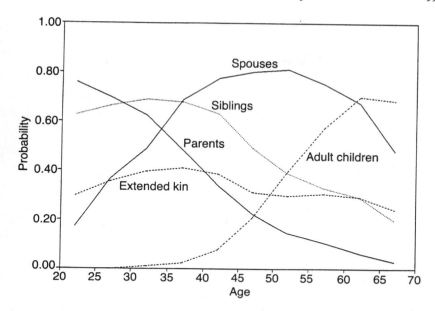

Figure 1. Probabilities of having select kin, by age, Pinkenhof, 1850
Sources: Eighth (1833) and Ninth (1850) Imperial Revisions, Central National Historical Archive, Riga, Latvia. Baltic Microfilms, D112, J.G. Herder Institute, Marburg a.d. Lahn, Germany.
Note: Lines are three-point moving averages.

with large common rooms and perhaps one or two adjoining rooms. People lived, ate and worked together in close, if not intimate, proximity throughout the year. Yet the pool of kin people could use to assemble personal communities that resembled East Yorkers' was even smaller given the possibilities that existed for residents of the same farm. Only slightly more than a third of all adults lived with a parent or an adult child, less than a third with a sibling, and less than an eighth with an extended kin. Fewer than half of young, mostly unmarried, adults in their twenties lived with a parent or sibling – the two most important affective and supportive ties in contemporary personal communities. If Pinkenhof adults formed their strongest ties with their parents, adult children and siblings as they do today, then most of them had to do it off the farm. The situation, however, was decidedly different for a minority of peasants.

Historians have consistently maintained that Baltic peasants valued having kin close at hand and that, given the opportunity, they would live with kin. In part this was a matter of availability, but it was also a matter of ability. Those most able to gather kin together were the heads of Pinkenhof's farmsteads, who possessed the authority to hire and fire the farmstead's workforce. Figure 2 reveals the contrasting situations for heads and their coresident kin on the one hand, and for hired farmhands and their families

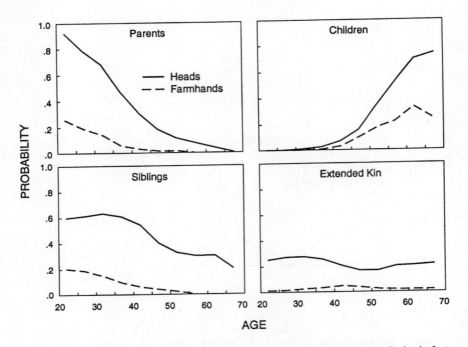

Figure 2. Probabilities of residing with select kin, by age and farmstead status, Pinkenhof, 1850
Sources: Eighth (1833) and Ninth (1850) Imperial Revisions, Central National Historical Archive, Riga, Latvia. Baltic Microfilms, D112, J.G. Herder Institute, Marburg a.d. Lahn, Germany
Note: Lines are three-point moving averages.

on the other. Overall, more than half of those who were either heads themselves or their coresident relatives lived with an adult child, and nearly half with an adult sibling. The experience of hired farmhands stands in stark contrast. Less than 16 per cent had a coresident parent or adult child, less than 10 per cent an adult sibling, and less than 3 per cent an extended kin – not a very bright picture for forming personal communities out of coresident kin.[45]

To establish demographic and residential constraints on the opportunities for forming personal communities from kin does not describe the reality. Certainly the peasants of Pinkenhof had friends and neighbors to whom they could turn for companionship, affection and assistance. To think otherwise would be to deny a world we know existed in the eastern European past. Because the possibilities of assembling personal communities in which kin constituted a significant part were limited, Pinkenhofers probably turned to adults living on their own and nearby farmsteads to form emotionally and socially supportive personal networks. Indeed, if Pinkenho-

45. Wetherell *et al.*, "Social Networks, Kinship, and Community", Table 3, p. 656.

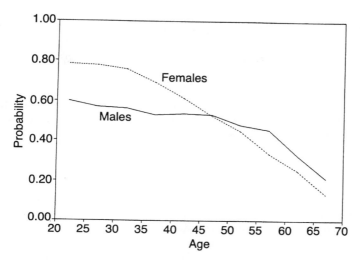

Figure 3. Probabilities of residing with a person of the same sex and age, by gender, Pinkenhof, 1850

Sources: Eighth (1833) and Ninth (1850) Imperial Revisions, Central National Historical Archive, Riga, Latvia. Baltic Microfilms, D112, J.G. Herder Institute, Marburg a.d. Lahn, Germany.

Note: Lines are three-point moving averages.

fers constructed personal communities of any size, they needed to use more non-kin than kin. Whether peasants sought out friends of the same age and sex is difficult to determine, but the society was sufficiently sensitive to age differences to assume Pinkenhofers preferred to make friends with people their own age.

For the most part, adults in Pinkenhof had little trouble finding other adults of the same age and sex somewhere on the estate. Yet, as Figure 3 reveals, living with someone of the same age (defined here as within five years) and gender was a luxury of youth, as adults tended to live increasingly in age-varied circumstances as they grew older.[46] The dynamics of the farm-stead system in Pinkenhof worked to segregate both men and, especially, women from their peers as they aged. Throughout most of their adult years, whether as heads, sons of heads, or farmhands, men tended to live with other men of the same age. The odds, however, were never better than six in ten. Initially at least, women fared better. As daughters of farmstead heads or female farmhands, nearly eight in ten females in their twenties could expect to reside with other women until they married in their late twenties. As they married, moved to other farmsteads with their husbands,

46. The median difference in age between the 33 individuals in the second, 1978 East York Social Network Study, and the 208 people in their intimate personal networks was 5 years (mean = 8.3, $s = 9.4$). East York Social Network Study, 1978, Centre for Urban and Community Studies, University of Toronto. Used with permission.

and started families of their own, women tended to reside less and less with other women their age. After both men and women reached their mid-forties – just as they experienced their sea change in kin life – they became increasingly less likely to live with others of the same sex and age. By the time they reached sixty they were residentially isolated from their peers. If they did not form friendships with the younger adults with whom they increasingly lived, the elderly would have had to maintain their dwindling number of same-age relationships off the farm.[47]

CONCLUSION

This preliminary HSNA of historic kinship reveals three things. First, that individual kinship density was extremely low because the pre-modern demographic regime of Pinkenhof left adults with few immediate or extended kin.[48] Kinship connections between households, however, connected any one farmstead with more than 20 per cent of all the rest, which provides structural reasons for supposing that the kinship-crisis view of historic social support prevailed. Second, individual residents of Pinkenhof did not have enough kin to construct the kind of social networks that exist today. The patterns in the kin life of Pinkenhof adults, with a major shift in the mid-forties from being adult children with siblings to being parents of adult children with few, if any, siblings, indicate that the kin component of past personal networks would have changed significantly over the life course. Third, particular economic and social circumstances of the larger Baltic agricultural regime undoubtedly affected the construction and maintenance of the Pinkenhofer's personal networks. Both the living arrangements and division of power on individual farmsteads worked both to stratify farmstead populations and to force upon them a profound intimacy. Whether peasants considered the five other unrelated adults with whom they lived and worked to be significant members of their personal communities remains impossible to say, but it seems likely that some were also friends who provided sociability, affection and emotional support. The decreasing tendency to live with others of the same sex and age probably worked against forming friendships with other coresident adults over the life course and produced a profound isolation among the elderly.

The analytical imperatives of both the WN and EC approaches in SNA helped to reformulate existing questions about historic kinship in new ways. A WN assessment of individual kinship density effectively belies the assertion of widespread kin connectedness in traditional peasant communi-

---

47. Wetherell *et al.*, "Social Networks, Kinship, and Community", Table 4, p. 658.
48. Plakans and Wetherell, "The Kinship Domain", and Charles Wetherell and Andrejs Plakans, "Fertility and Culture in Eastern Europe: A Case Study of Riga, Latvia, 1867–1881", *European Journal of Population*, 13 (1997), pp. 243–268.

ties. Conceptualizing community as collections of personal relationships, however, provides historians with a blueprint for evaluating when, how and why people in the past used kin and non-kin in the course of their lives. The findings of social network analysts that people need and seek emotional and economic support of different kinds, from different kinds of people, suggest new analytical imperatives. It is not enough now to look solely at how people used kin in times of crisis. Rather, historians need to pursue how people in the past used the kin and friends they had, for different things, throughout the life course, and in the context of the opportunities they enjoyed and the constraints they faced courtesy of demography and culture. Other approaches might be applied to the problem, but HSNA contains the essential perspectives that cannot only advance the debate, but also help historians to meet Tilly's challenge to connect the lives of ordinary people to large-scale change in meaningful ways.

ANNOTATED BIBLIOGRAPHY

Among the works cited, the following serve as especially useful guides, starting points, or examples of HSNA.

Theory/overviews

Blau, Peter M., *Inequality and Heterogenity: A Primitive Theory of Social Structure* (New York, 1977).
A classic statement of structural sensibilities.
Emirbayer, Mustafa, "Manifesto for a Relational Sociology", *American Journal of Sociology*, 103 (1997), pp. 281–317.
Forceful statement on the current state and future needs of relational (largely SNA) thinking in sociology.
Tilly, Charles, "Do Communities Act?", *Sociological Inquiry*, 43 (1973), pp. 209–240.
Landmark essay in HSNA that posed questions about collective political action that analysts are still trying to answer today.
Wellman, Barry and S.D. Berkowitz (eds), *Social Structures: A Network Approach* (New York, 1988).
A comprehensive statement of SNA as a paradigm of social inquiry. Heavily weighted toward the egocentric approach, but includes discussions of the whole network approach. Remarkably clear and readable.

Methods

Borgatti, Steven, Martin Everett and Linton C. Freeman. *UCINET IV*, Analytic Technologies (Natick, MA, 1995).

Comprehensive software package that calculates most network analytic measures. Good documentation.

Wasserman, Stanley and Katherine Faust, *Social Network Analysis: Methods and Applications* (New York, 1994).
A one stop, detailed guide to network analytic methods. Heavy going but comprehensive.

Applications

Bearman, Peter S., *Relations into Rhetorics: Local Elite Social Structure in Norfolk, England, 1540–1640* (New Brunswick, NJ, 1993).
Perhaps the best example of whole network HSNA. Demonstrates that network structure – and hence HSNA – can plausibly explain a major historical event.

Gould, Roger V., *Insurgent Identities: Class, Community, and Protest in Paris form 1848 to the Commune* (Chicago, 1995).
A full-scale HSNA of collective political action that is unusually sensitive to historical context.

Padgett, John F. and Christopher K. Ansell, "Robust Action and the Rise of the Medici, 1400–1434", *American Journal of Sociology*, 98 (1993), pp. 1259–1319.
An HSNA classic that serves forcefully to bring agency into a historical analysis.

International Review of Social History 43 (1998), Supplement, pp. 145–165
© 1998 Internationaal Instituut voor Sociale Geschiedenis

Historical Inference and Event-Structure Analysis

LARRY J. GRIFFIN and ROBERT R. KORSTAD

INTRODUCTION

Event-structure analysis (ESA) is a member of a family of formal analytic procedures designed to analyze and interpret text, in particular the temporal sequences constituting the narrative of a historical event. Its basic purpose is to aid the analyst in "unpacking" an event – that is, in breaking it into constituent parts – and analytically reconstituting it as a causal interpretation of what happened and why it happened as it did.[1] ESA focuses on and exploits an event's "narrativity" – its temporal orderliness, connectedness and unfolding – thereby helping historians and social scientists infer causal links between actions in an event, identify its contingencies and follow their consequences, and explore its myriad sequential patterns. Unlike most other formal analytical techniques, it is completely non-numeric and non-statistical: ESA's value is largely heuristic and centered on how it relentlessly probes the analyst's construction, comprehension and interpretation of the event.[2]

More firmly and self-consciously than do most formal analytical procedures, ESA partially bridges the often damaging methodological chasm separating narrative history and generalizing social science. On the one hand, it borrows from formal social science methodology several features, including

(a) explicit deployment of theoretical concepts and hypotheses about social life;
(b) application, development and validation of causal generalizations;
(c) use of replicable procedures of analysis.

---

1. On "causal interpretation", the best source remains Max Weber, *The Methodology of the Social Sciences* (New York, 1905; reprinted 1949), pp. 113–188, esp. 169. On "unpacking" events, see Philip Abrams, *Historical Sociology* (Ithaca, 1982), pp. 196–226, a remarkably rewarding work for any scholar interested in events, narrative and the history-sociology dialogue. The vast literature on these and similar topics is quite useful. Much that is directly relevant to formal narrative analysis generally and ESA particularly is referenced in Larry J. Griffin, "Temporality, Events, and Explanation in Historical Sociology: An Introduction", *Sociological Methods and Research*, 20 (1992), pp. 403–427; idem, "Narrative, Event-Structure Analysis and Causal Interpretation in Historical Sociology", *American Journal of Sociology*, 98 (1993), pp. 1094–1133; and idem, "How Is Sociology Informed by History?", *Social Forces*, 73 (1995), pp. 1245–1254. Foundational references to event-structure analysis are contained in this essay's annotated bibliography.
2. ESA and other formal analytical strategies have been systematically compared in Larry J. Griffin and Charles Ragin, "Some Observations on Formal Qualitative Analysis", *Sociological Methods and Research*, 23 (1994), pp. 4–21.

By forcing the user to be meticulous in the construction of narratives, to reason causally about unfolding temporal sequences, and to be clear about the bases of causal and interpretive judgements, ESA lays bare the investigator's understanding so starkly – literally, as will be seen, as a diagram of the logic of action – that insights into causal connectedness and significance are intensely sharpened.

On the other hand, ESA mimics in important ways how many historians and historically-oriented social scientists, although themselves drawing on less formal analytical strategies, actually reason to infer causality and meaning from an event. Thus, it requires analysts to

(a) situate events in their historical and cultural contexts and then capitalize on contextual knowledge for explanatory and interpretive purposes;

(b) focus on actors and on social action, thereby fostering appreciation and comprehension of agency; that is, of how women and men actively mold, if in ways they do not always foresee or necessarily wish, their world;

(c) evoke "imaginative reconstruction" of the actor's world and her/his motives, strategies and understandings;[3]

(d) view the precise unfolding of an event as of cardinal importance to its interpretation;

(e) maintain, through the question-and-answer routine illustrated below, fidelity with the interrogatory spirit undergirding much historical reasoning by requiring the analyst to "interrogate" and "cross-examine" events for evidence of causal significance;[4]

(e) adopt the understanding of historical events as configurational, contingent happenings characterized by what philosopher-historian Dale Porter labels "the emergence of novelty";[5]

(f) rely on their substantive judgement and interpretive skill rather than on prefigured (and thus historically "inflexible" or "static") theoretical, logical or statistical algorithms or rules.

ESA's unique analytical efficacy, then, resides in the fact that its very logic

---

3. Samuel Beer, "Causal Explanations and Imaginative Re-enactment", _History and Theory_, 3 (1963), pp. 6–29.

4. "Interrogate" is from E.P. Thompson, _The Poverty of Theory and Other Essays_ (London, 1978), pp. 25–50; "cross-examine" is from Marc Bloch, _The Historian's Craft_ (New York, 1953), p. 64.

5. Dale Porter, _The Emergence of the Past: A Theory of Historical Explanation_ (Chicago, 1981), p. 3. ESA's developer, sociologist David Heise, expresses much the same sentiment when he states that one of the consequences of particular actions are on occasion the production of "new and meaningful sequences of events"; see his "Modeling Event Structures", _Journal of Mathematical Sociology_, 14 (1989), pp. 139–169 (the phrase quoted is on p. 141). Historical contingency has many meanings, but the one that is perhaps best suited to ESA has a temporal basis. Succinctly expressed, it is that prior action often conditions, but does not necessarily determine, subsequent action. One of the most powerful pleas for placing contingency at the very heart of historical analysis is found in Gordon Leff, _History and Social Theory_ (Garden City, NY, 1971), pp. 42–90.

of operation – that is, in what it does and what it demands of the analyst – synthesizes social science and historical methodologies while also empowering each to speak (as it were) with its own "voice". As we demonstrate later in the essay, this synthesis is seen in research practice both through (i) ESA's integration of the theoretically/empirically general and the historically particular so thoroughly as to render their differences largely moot, and (ii) its merger of two modes of inquiry often juxtaposed against each other, explanation and interpretation; with ESA, analysts explain as and because they are compelled to interpret, and they interpret as and because causal explanation is demanded.[6] Because of this methodological "dualism", finally, inferences reached with ESA, though generally interpretive in nature, are strictly replicable. Critics know exactly the causal interpretations, and (often) the logical, empirical and theoretical reasons for them, and can directly challenge any aspect of the analysis, from the selection and written description of actions to be analyzed to their imputed significance and causal connectedness.

WHAT ESA DOES

To illustrate ESA's basic operations and practical effectiveness, we use a slice of the history of the successful United Cannery, Agricultural, Packing, and Allied Workers Union (UCAPAWA) organizing drive at the R.J. Reynolds (RJR) Tobacco plant in Winston-Salem, North Carolina, from 1941 to 1944. The local that resulted from that drive, Local 22, was built and largely sustained by the collective actions of African-American workers, especially women, who made it the primary vehicle for advancing the racial aspirations of Winston-Salem's African-American working class. Incessantly hounded by RJR, damagingly red-baited in the late 1940s, and shunned by white workers, the local lost its contract with RJR in 1948 and disbanded in 1951.[7]

6. Griffin and Ragin, "Some Observations on Formal Qualitative Analysis".
7. The most extensive history of Local 22 is Robert R. Korstad, "Daybreak of Freedom: Tobacco Workers and the CIO, Winston-Salem, North Carolina, 1943–1950" (unpublished Ph.D. dissertation, University of North Carolina at Chapel Hill, 1987). The local has been the subject of numerous publications; see, for example Robert R. Korstad and Nelson Lichtenstein, "Opportunities Found and Lost: Labor, Radicals, and the Early Civil Rights Movement", *Journal of American History*, 75 (1988), pp. 786–811, and Larry J. Griffin and Robert R. Korstad, "Class as Race and Gender: The Making and Breaking of a Union Local in the Jim Crow South", *Social Science History*, 19 (1995), pp. 425–454. Some of the analysis we report here first appeared in Griffin and Korstad, "Class as Race and Gender", and we occasionally paraphrase from that publication. Most of the historical information about Local 22 comes from public newspapers, union newsletters and document collections, federal government reports from several different agencies, and oral histories of participants and other knowledgeable sources. For precise documentation, see Korstad, "Daybreak of Freedom" and Griffin and Korstad, "Class as Race and Gender". The important and growing historical literature on race, gender, class and unionization in the US South has been recently reviewed by Dolores Janiewski, "Southern Honor, Southern Dishonor: Managerial Ideology and the Construction of Gender, Race, and Class Relations in Southern Industry", in

On the eve of the union drive in 1941, RJR operated the largest tobacco manufacturing facility in the world, employing 12,000 unorganized workers. The majority of its workers were African Americans of both sexes, and RJR had long manipulated racial and gender divisions among its workers to thwart unionization. But the UCAPAWA, a left-leaning union affiliated with the CIO, had experienced real, if limited, success in organizing black industrial workers in the South in the late 1930s and moved into Winston-Salem to organize RJR's black workforce in late 1941. Our ESA illustration begins at this point and continues through the first significant collective action by African-American workers in June 1943. In conventional narrative form, here, very briefly, is what happened:

> Using pre-existing African-American organizations, especially the church, UCA-PAWA organizers met with RJR's African-American workers and established the all-black Tobacco Workers Organizing Committee (TWOC) in 1943. TWOC members were strategically placed throughout RJR's productive processes, and the TWOC seized onto both the economic and racial hardships of workers and the war-induced tight labor market to generate support for the union. In the summer of 1943 the rising cost of living and a company directive to speed up production intensified the chronic resentments of RJR's black workers. The ramifications of the speed-up became of immediate concern on the shop-floor on June 17, when an African-American stemmer was belittled by her supervisor for being behind in her work. Just as black women workers, some of them TWOC members, began to discuss the possibility of a protest strike, another African-American worker died on the shop-floor, reportedly after his white foreman refused to let him go home or get medical attention. The TWOC women then spontaneously staged a sit-down strike, which quickly spread. Though the UCAPAWA did not call for a large strike, other African-American workers then also walked off their jobs in solidarity, and, after sustained work stoppage, about six thousand, eight hundred of them (perhaps two-thirds of RJR's black workforce) joined the TWOC.

For use in ESA, this narrative must be condensed and expressed as a chronology consisting of a series of tightly-sequenced short descriptive statements that, in the analyst's interpretation, essentially defines the incident for *formal analysis*. Because ESA is essentially a heuristic aid, however, the analyst should use as much historical information as she or he has in structuring and interpreting the event; as will be demonstrated below, she or he is in no way limited to the actions contained in the formal chronology. Although the software implementing ESA, ETHNO (for "ethnographic analysis"), will accept and process virtually any type of statement, analysts will better harness ESA's "action-centeredness" if they use active voice throughout in the chronology. (As ETHNO diagrams the analyst's understanding of the event's logical structure, it abbreviates the action verb; we often use the

Ava Baron (ed.), *Work Engendered: Toward a New History of American Labor*, (Ithaca, NY, 1991), pp. 70–91, and Rick Halpern, "Organized Labour, Black Workers and the Twentieth-century South: The Emerging Revision", *Social History*, 19 (1994), pp. 361–383.

abbreviations in the text as a form of shorthand.)[8] For the purposes of this exposition, we have reduced the above narrative to the following nine actions:

1. Tar: UCAPAWA/CIO target RJR's African-American workers for unionization.
2. Mee: African-American workers meet with UCAPAWA organizers about unionization.
3. For: UCAPAWA forms all-black TWOC to include strategically placed workers.
4. Spe: RJR speeds up production process.
5. Abu: White foreman abused African-American female for being behind in her work.
6. Die: African American dies on shop-floor allegedly after white foreman refused to permit worker either to leave or to get medical assistance.
7. Sit: African-American female stemmers sit down, stopping production.
8. Stk: Thousands of African-American workers strike.
9. Joi: Almost 7,000 African-American workers join TWOC.

This brief chronology serves as the input into ETHNO, which then transforms it into a series of "yes/no" questions where, quite literally, the analyst is asked if a temporal antecedent ("or a similar event") is required for the occurrence of a subsequent event. ETHNO uses the analyst's responses to diagram a logical structure of action displaying the imputed causal influence and connectedness of all sequences in the chronology. Analysts are strongly advised to keep a written log of ETHNO's questions, their answers and the reasons for their answers. This is essential for subsequent replication and is of immense benefit as the analyst constructs his or her interpretation of the event. Our log, which lists the questions and answers for this analysis, is presented as Table 1.

ETHNO first queried us about the relationship between the first two actions in the chronology (see Table 1). The exact wording of its question was: "Does 'Mee: African-American workers meet with UCAPAWA organizers about unionization' require 'Tar: UCAPAWA/CIO target RJR African-American workers for unionization' (or a similar event)?" For reasons that we discuss later, our response was "Yes", and ETHNO linked the two actions ("target" = "Tar"; "meet" = "Mee") with a line indicating a direct causal tie between an antecedent action (now understood as a cause)

---

8. Generally, the statements in the chronology should conform as closely as possible to ETHNO's constraints: (i) statements should be limited to one line of text (the second line of a two-line description is read by ETHNO as a new action), and (ii) the first word of the statement should be the subject of the sentence (and the actor) and the second word, the verb connoting action. Departures from these rules, though easily made (as we do with the abbreviations), can sometimes lead to needless confusion.

Table 1. *Questions and answers for Local 22 sequence*

Q.1	Does "African-American workers meet with UCAPAWA organizers about unionization" require "UCAPAWA/CIO target RJR's African-American workers for unionization" (or a similar event)? Answer: Yes
Q.2	Does "UCAPAWA forms all-black TWOC to include strategically placed workers" require "African-American workers meet with UCAPAWA organizers about unionization" (or a similar event)? Answer: Yes
Q.3	Does "RJR speeds up production process" require "UCAPAWA forms all-black TWOC to include strategically placed workers" (or a similar event)? Answer: No
Q.4	Does "RJR speeds up production process" require "African-American workers meet with UCAPAWA organizers about unionization" (or a similar event)? Answer: No
Q.5	Does "RJR speeds up production process" require "UCAPAWA/CIO target RJR's African-American workers for unionization" (or a similar event)? Answer: No
Q.6	Does "White foreman abused African-American female for being behind in her work" require "UCAPAWA forms all-black TWOC to include strategically placed workers" (or a similar event)? Answer: No
Q.7	Does "White foreman abused African-American female for being behind in her work" require "African-American workers meet with UCAPAWA organizers about unionization" (or a similar event)? Answer: No
Q.8	Does "White foreman abused African-American female for being behind in her work" require "RJR speeds up production process" (or a similar event)? Answer: Yes
Q.9	Does "White foreman abused African-American female for being behind in her work" require "UCAPAWA/CIO target RJR's African-American workers for unionization" (or a similar event)? Answer: No
Q.10	Does "African American dies on shop-floor allegedly after white foreman refused to permit worker either to leave or to get medical assistance" require "UCAPAWA forms all-black TWOC to include strategically placed workers" (or a similar event)? Answer: No
Q.11	Does "African American dies on shop-floor allegedly after white foreman refused to permit worker either to leave or to get medical assistance" require "White foreman abused African-American female for being behind in her work" (or a similar event)? Answer: No
Q.12	Does "African American dies on shop-floor allegedly after white foreman refused to permit worker either to leave or to get medical assistance" require "African-American workers meet with UCAPAWA organizers about unionization" (or a similar event)? Answer: No
Q.13	Does "African American dies on shop-floor allegedly after white foreman refused to permit worker either to leave or to get medical assistance" require "RJR speeds up production process" (or a similar event)? Answer: No

Table 1. *cont.*

Q.14	Does "African American dies on shop-floor allegedly after white foreman refused to permit worker either to leave or to get medical assistance" require "UCAPAWA/CIO target RJR's African-American workers for unionization" (or a similar event)? Answer: No
Q.15	Does "African-American female stemmers sit down, stopping production" require "UCAPAWA forms all-black TWOC to include strategically placed workers" (or a similar event)? Answer: Yes
Q.16	Does "African-American female stemmers sit down, stopping production" require "White foreman abused African-American female for being behind in her work" (or a similar event)?" Answer: Yes
Q.17	Does "African-American female stemmers sit down, stopping production" require "African American dies on shop-floor allegedly after white foreman refused to permit worker either to leave or to get medical assistance" (or a similar event)? Answer: Yes
Q.18	Does "Thousands of African-American workers strike" require "African-American female stemmers sit down, stopping production" (or a similar event)? Answer: Yes
Q.19	Does "Almost seven thousand African-American workers join TWOC" require "Thousands of African-American workers strike" (or a similar event)? Answer: Yes

and a subsequent action (now understood as a consequence). Diagramed, the causal assumption is:

Tar
|
Mee

We also said "Yes" to question 2 ("Does 'For: UCAPAWA forms all-black TWOC to include strategically placed workers' require 'Mee: African-American workers meet with UCAPAWA organizers about unionization' [or a similar event]?"), and again ETHNO directly connected the two actions as follows:

Tar
|
Mee
|
For

We responded "No" to the next three queries about the relationships between the "Spe: RJR speed-up" and its three antecedents in the chronology ("Tar", "Mee", "For"). Rather than tying "Spe" to any of its temporal antecedents, then, ETHNO instead placed it at the diagram's *logical* (not temporal) origin, indicating that, in our interpretation, the speed-up was exogenous (and unrelated) to what came before it in the chronology.

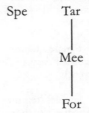

The next two queries asked about possible causal ties between the "white foreman's abuse" ("Abu") and two of its temporal antecedents ("TWOC formation" and the "meeting"). We answered "No" to both questions, as we did to the ninth query about the relationship between "the abuse" and UCAPAWA/CIO's racially-specific "targeting" strategy. Our response to the eighth question asking if "RJR's speed-up" ("Spe") was necessary for the "abuse of a slow worker" ("Abu"), however, was positive. Thus having moved through the five actions in the brief chronology and answered nine questions about relationships between those actions, we have imputed the following structure of action to what had happened in the UCAPAWA organizing drive at RJR as of mid-June 1943:

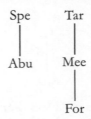

Although quite simple at this stage in the analysis (because the queries have thus far pertained only to the very early history of the still nascent local), the diagram is nonetheless instructive for two interdependent reasons. First, it portrays our causal imputations and our assumptions about how and why the actions are linked as they are, or are not linked at all. Because this feature is at the heart of ESA's utility, we discuss it at greater length in the next section. Second, its very structure has substantive meaning. Building on E.P. Thompson's insight that "(a)ny historical moment is both a result of prior process and an index towards the direction of its future flow",[9] the

9. The deft phrase is from Thompson, *The Poverty of Theory*, p. 47.

analyst can examine the diagram to comprehend better both how the past conditioned the "present" and how the "present", in turn, shapes the range of "future" possibilities and alternatives.

At the precise point in the local's still unfolding history captured by the diagram above (mid-June 1943), for example, a union organizing committee – composed of strategically situated African-American workers – was in place as a structural resource to be activated at any moment by aggrieved workers in their continuing organizing campaign and/or simply as an expression of the job-related discontents of black employees. This fact contextualizes, and thus gives a particular meaning to, the second stream of action – the speed-up induced abuse of an African-American worker by her white supervisor. The two streams of actions (or, as in the case of "TWOC formation", the ongoing institutional consequence of prior actions) are, at the "present" moment, proceeding in parallel fashion rather than conjoined; indeed, they need not ever be causally linked. But the possibility does exist that a future act will wed the class/racial abuse to the fledgling workers' organization, thereby altering the significance of both and producing an effect impossible for either singly to induce. Clearly, then, this is a contingency of great potential importance.

We continue with the remaining actions in the chronology below; first, though, we discuss the rationales for the causal imputations we made above.

CAUSAL ASSUMPTIONS AND SYNTHESIZING KNOWLEDGE

ETHNO's questions are quite obviously premised on temporal order, but, just as obviously, sequence does not necessarily provide answers to them: as was apparent above, we often attribute no causal significance to sequence *per se*. Thus, the difference between our use of ESA and the cognitive act of following the narrative's unfolding is crucial. The determination of causality is a judgement made by the analyst based on a wide array of evidence and theory rather than a "fact" given naturally by the event's or chronology's temporal order. Indeed, to answer ETHNO's questions, and thereby to causally structure the event, we typically counterfactualized the queries about temporal sequence and then synthesized (i) knowledge of the historical particulars of Local 22, especially those pertaining to RJR, its workforce, and the prior organizing efforts there by unions that were mostly white, (ii) general social theory (e.g. about collective action and social movements), and (iii) historical generalizations of one sort or another (e.g. about race and gender in the Jim Crow South, the CIO's racial policies, comparable unionization drives).[10]

---

10. This follows from Max Weber's prescription for the causal analysis of a historical sequence: "The assessment of the causal significance of an historical fact will begin with the posing of the following question: in the event of the exclusion of that fact from the complex of factors which are taken into account as co-determinants, or in the event of its modification in a certain direction,

Thus the tools of the generalizing social sciences – from theoretical deduction and historical generalizations to comparison – equipped us with sensitizing concepts, a theoretical foundation on which to rest our answers to ETHNO's queries, and a set of expectations about how the world might be expected to work. But just as narrative sequence did not necessarily determine inferences about historical causation, neither did the application of generalizing logics or strategies. Instead, what was learned or hypothesized through their use was challenged and often modified by the Local 22's particular context, actors and temporality.

To demonstrate this synthesis at work, consider again the first question ETHNO posed ("Does 'Mee: African-American workers meet with UCA-PAWA organizers about unionization' require 'Tar: UCAPAWA/CIO target RJR African-American workers for unionization' (or a similar event)?"). Expressing the first action as a historical counterfactual and rephrasing the question a bit, we have the following query: "Would 'UCAPAWA organizers have met with RJR's African-American workers about unionization' had the 'UCAPAWA/CIO not targeted RJR's African-American workers for unioniz-ation'?" To answer this question, we had to refrain from being swept away by the unfolding drama of the narrative, discard the taken-for-granted temporal determination of cause-and-effect implicit in the narrative, and, instead, reason causally. Those requirements, in turn, forced us to consider whether the "targeting" was necessary for the "meeting", sufficient for it, or both neces-sary and sufficient. We reasoned, though the diagram suggests otherwise, that the targeting was not sufficient grounds for the meeting because, logically, the simple existence of a possibility (the "targeting" strategy) does not generally bring about its own actuality (the meeting between African-American workers and union representatives). The grievances of the workers, too, were instru-mental in motivating them to meet with UCAPAWA organizers. But the "tar-geting" was necessary, we argue, because without it there would have been no supply of union organizers for African-American workers to meet with. Nor, likely, would there have been a demand for them from the rank-and-file. Why? We know that African-American workers were aggrieved by their working

could the course of events, in accordance with general empirical rules, have taken a direction in any way different in any features which would be *decisive* for our interest?": Weber, *The Methodology of the Social Sciences*, p. 180 (emphasis in original). The use of the historical counterfactual as the fundamental tool in ESA (and as a useful tool in social science more generally) is advanced in Griffin, "Narrative, Event-Structure Analysis and Causal Interpretation in Historical Sociology". Perhaps the most rigorous recent defense of the use of historically-grounded counterfactuals is contained in Geoffery Hawthrone, *Plausible Worlds: Possibility and Understanding in History and the Social Sciences* (Cambridge, 1991), esp. pp. 1–37, 157–187. Hawthrone argues that only "plaus-ible" counterfactuals can have inferential value and that they, in turn, should (a) start from the real world as it was otherwise known before asserting the counterfactual, (b) not require us to "unwind the past", and (c) not unduly "disturb" what we otherwise understand about the actors and their contexts. See also Barrington Moore, *Injustice: The Social Bases of Obedience and Revolt* (New York, 1984), pp. 376–397, for a breathtaking use of the counterfactual.

conditions and their pay, and that they had previously resorted to small-scale protest, but they generally do not seem to have framed their hardships or possible solutions to those hardships in terms of "union". UCAPAWA organizers crucially shaped the frame – which may be fairly defined as "unionization for the economically and racially oppressed" – through which the workers came to understand both their plight and their possible salvation. So the CIO's initial racial targeting strategy also motivated some of RJR's African-American workers to discuss unionization with representatives of a racially liberal and successful union.

To return now to the general methodological issue under discussion, this simple question, premised on a historically plausible counterfactual, impels historians and social scientists to a close engagement with issues queried. That query also demonstrates that ESA, even as it appropriates narrative sequentiality to formulate its questions, requires the analyst to replace temporal order with her or his knowledge/judgement about causal connections and to examine self-critically the foundation and adequacy of that knowledge.

Altogether ETHNO asked us nineteen questions about the brief chronology (see Table I). Q.2 asked if the "TWOC formation" required the initial "meeting". We responded "Yes", reasoning that the early meetings were necessary both to disseminate UCAPAWA's racial, as well as its class, messages and to build trust with African-American workers, who then made the TWOC a reality by joining it. Q.3–Q.5 were not difficult to answer because, as we noted above, RJR's speed-up, though occurring after UCAPAWA began its drive and formed the TWOC, was (from all available evidence) independent of anything the union was doing. Other questions, particular those also suggesting causal independence (Q.9-Q.14), were also easily answered.

Much more difficult, though, were queries such as Q.8 and Q.15-Q.19, which demanded that we juggle and synthesize generalizations and particularities, often in novel ways, as we moved from question to question. Q.8, for example, asked if "RJR's speed-up" was required for the "abuse of a slow worker". There is no unambiguous answer. On the one hand, a production speed-up is not generally necessary for such actions because "slow workers" are routinely chastised by their supervisors, and no doubt many at RJR were prior to the speed-up. On the other hand, the speed-up both (i) signified the heightened import RJR placed on "timely" production, and (ii) genuinely made meeting production quotas more difficult. Given this, the probability that some workers would fall behind and would then be punished by supervisors who were themselves both conveying the new production standards and requiring compliance with them was higher than was true previously. All things considered, then, we answered "Yes".

Space limitations preclude discussion of all nineteen questions. But each had the same formal structure as those described above,[11] and we relied on

---

11. The total number of questions depends both on the number of actions in the chronology and the imputed links between them. The more causal imputations follow a simple sequential chain,

the same general cognitive processes described earlier to address them – that is, we counterfactualized ETHNO's queries and always merged distinct kinds of knowledge and causal and interpretive logics (Verstehen, temporal, theoretic, etc.). After all questions had been answered, the diagram, representing our understanding of how the nine actions constituting the chronology are causally related, is structured as follows:

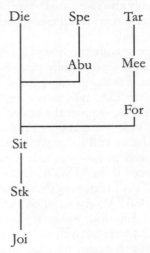

It culminates with the explosive growth of the TWOC during the third week of June 1943 ("Joi", in the chronology and diagram) and shows how this expression of black working-class organization was a consequence of all that preceded it, either directly (the mass strike by thousands of African-American workers that followed the sit-down: "Stk") or indirectly (the causal determinants of "Stk", or the determinants of those determinants).

ETHNO contains other helpful routines but the question-and-answer session just demonstrated is, to our way of thinking, the most valuable.[12] It requires analysts to construct a causal interpretation using their own knowledge and skill and then permits them to examine diagrammatically the logic and implications of that interpretation.

in which action A → B → C, etc., the fewer questions ETHNO asks. Moreover, only direct logical connection is queried; if A is imputed to be a prerequisite of B, and B a prerequisite of C, ETHNO will not ask if A is required for C. The program knows, by logical implication, that this is so, through the causal influence A exerts on B. Although ETHNO does not directly link A and C, the analyst may do so (as we do later in this essay).

12. For example, ESA can assess the logic of the event structure against the program's built-in logic (derived in part from rational choice theory and cognitive anthropology) of how events "ought" to unfold. If a logical discrepancy is discovered, the analyst can choose either to override the diagnostics or alter the event structure to conform to ETHNO's prescriptions. We have found this procedure to be of limited, though occasionally genuine, utility.

USEFUL FEATURES OF THE ESA ANALYSIS

Some features of ESA analysis will be of particular use to those scholars with feet in both the historical and social science camps. Using the analysis of the union organizing drive just completed, we briefly discuss four of them below: contingency, complexity, significance and generalization.

Contingency

Consideration of the reasons for the sit-down strike and how it then quickly led to mass organization adeptly illustrates one of the more important general strengths of ESA, its ability to tease out, display and track the impact of historical contingencies. TWOC's growth ("Joi"), for example, ultimately can be traced back to the UCAPAWA/CIO's early focus on organizing African Americans at RJR ("Tar"), for it was that strategy that both established the possibility of the TWOC's very existence ("For") and led to the meetings between black workers and union organizers ("Mee"). But the diagram (and thus our reasoning) also emphatically denies that mass organization at RJR was either the inevitable or straightforward result of that strategy or of the actions (such as "Mee") that issued directly from it. Indeed, our interpretation suggests that the TWOC would have remained little more than possibility had the sit-down strike by African-American female stemmers not occurred ("Sit"), and that strike, in turn, could not have been predicted from what preceded it or from the extant grievances of the workers. No single structural condition or action, in fact, was sufficient to provoke the sit-down (see the section of the previous diagram relevant to the instigation of the sit-down strike, reproduced below).

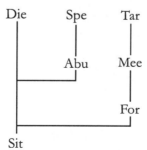

Rather, it was the effect of the complex, contingent (but not necessarily "accidental") confluence of four factors and the meanings female African-American workers placed on them: (i) the prior formation of the TWOC among African-Americans workers ("For"), which provided both the organizational base for collective action and an interpretive frame molding and amplifying the racial, gender and class grievances of those who spontaneously stopped production; (ii) RJR's intensified production pace

("Spe"), which symbolized and exacerbated the long-term grievances of these workers; and (iii, iv) two temporally coterminous, racially-charged "triggering" incidents, the abuse ("Abu") and death ("Die") of black workers.

Neither the sit-down strike nor the mass organization of African-American workers which followed "had to" happen; RJR's aggrieved workers could have accepted their lot, protested individually when and as they could, and remained unorganized. ESA helps us understand why both actions did occur nonetheless, and why they happened when they did. And in doing this, ESA thereby helped us grasp how unionization as a structural possibility was transformed by social action into unionization as a lived reality.

Complexity/Density

Once all of the actions in the chronology have been structured, analysts should examine the diagram with an eye toward seeing if it truly represents their causal and interpretative understandings. If not, ESA permits analysts to alter the structure of the diagram and thereby modify their initial interpretation of the event's unfolding. This seemingly minor technical facility can lead to important substantive and theoretical differences. For example, the "complete" diagram we discussed above (reproduced below)

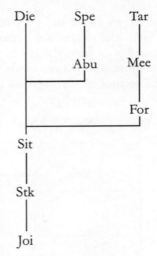

shows quite clearly that among the actions considered here, the only direct determinant of mass membership in the TWOC ("Joi") was the huge strike that preceded it by a few days ("Stk"). That strike, in turn, is seen to have been induced solely by the sit-down strike ("Sit"). In fact, the entire process is represented as simple, unbroken causal chain ("Sit" → "Stk" → "Joi"). Do we really believe this? In fact, we do not: it is unrealistically voluntaristic, permitting spontaneity to replace organization. Logically, for example,

African Americans could join the TWOC only because it already existed, so the TWOC's formation ("For") has to be a direct logical prerequisite of "Joi", as well as an indirect causal antecedent (through "Sit"). Through their appeals to discipline, collective courage and racial solidarity, moreover, TWOC members helped sustain (if they did not actually orchestrate) the massive strike spurred by the sit-down ("Stk");[13] TWOC formation ("For"), therefore, should be considered a direct determinant of the huge strike ("Stk") as well. By linking "For" to both "Stk" and "Joi" in the diagram, we bring into the interpretation the causal weight of pre-existing labor organization, while still permitting the sit-down strike an important role (indeed, as we argue below, a crucial role) in what subsequently happened. The diagram, now revised below, is denser, more complex and, in our opinion, on better theoretical and historical footing.

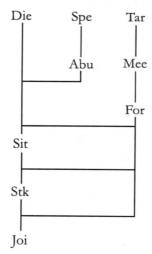

Significance

Earlier, we noted that the structure of ESA's diagrams had substantive import and meaning. These interpretive structures may also be used by the analyst to visualize and thereby better judge the historical significance of particular actions in the event. One way to define "historical significance" in a precise sense is in terms of how an action links past and "present", thereby transmuting the former into the latter, and/or how it portends possible courses of action in the future. Significant actions need not necessarily represent "turning" or "switch" points in the history of an event (these are actions that shunt the event from one sequential path to another),

13. Griffin and Korstad, "Class as Race and Gender".

but they are actions of heightened consequence to the entire sequence because they both serve as the repository of previous actions and funnel the causal force of that past onto subsequent actions, thereby establishing future possibilities.

In the diagram of the UCAPAWA organizing drive, each action is indispensable; there are no truly irrelevant actions, and no historical "dead-end" paths that terminate without consequence. But some actions, nonetheless, are more equal than others. In the chain of historical causation, for instance, union organization at RJR was the culmination of actions instigated by the sit-down strike ("Sit") by African-American females. That action pivotally linked the CIO's national strategy ("Tar") of organizing African Americans, and chronic (e.g. the production speed-up: "Spe") and unforeseen grievances (the racial abuse ("Abu") and death ("Die")), on the one hand, to the thousands of potential African-American unionists at RJR ("Joi"), on the other. The sit-down proved to be the means through which both UCAPAWA institutionalized its presence at Reynolds and African Americans gained, at least for number of years, a powerful voice in the company and in Winston-Salem.[14] Thus can ESA be wielded to peel back layers of significance buried in conventional historical narratives.

Generalization

The analyst may also formally generalize an event's initial, "concrete" logical structure (i.e. those, such as the ones we develop in this essay, that stay very close to, and reproduce analytically, the historical particulars of the event). In this routine (known as "instantiation" in ETHNO), actions in the "concrete" structure are viewed as empirical "instances" of theoretically general concepts and the analysis, still sequential in its interrogatory logic, proceeds at a "higher", theoretically more explicit, level of generality.

Were we to filter the early history of Local 22 through the conceptual lens of general social movement theory, for example, both the first and second actions in the chronology ("UCAPAWA/CIO target RJR's African-American workers for unionization", and "African-American workers meet with UCAPAWA organizers about unionization") might be generalized in meaning and restated as a single action, "Social movement organization (SMO) formulates strategy for interracial organization"; the third action ("UCAPAWA forms all-black TWOC to include strategically placed workers") redefined as "SMO deepens organization resources"; the fourth action ("RJR speeds up production process") generalized to "SMO's target intensifies movement constituency's grievances", and so on. Only those "concrete" actions thought to "instantiate" pertinent theoretical concepts (pertinent to a given theory, that is) would be generalized in meaning and

14. *Ibid.*

thus included in the more parsimonious "general" chronology. This chronology would then be subject to the same sort of question-and-answer routine described earlier. Hence, ETHNO would ask if "SMO deepens organization resources" requires "Social movement organization (SMO) formulates strategy for interracial organization". The analyst's responses, now rooted in historical generalizations and theoretical expectations rather in event particulars, again would be diagramed by ETHNO as ESA began to build a "general" event structure.

Though perhaps of greater utility to the generalizing social scientist than the historian, ESA's proficiency with multiple levels of analysis (and with structuring a tight dialogue between them) is worthwhile to any scholar interested in the broader empirical applicability and conceptual meaning of her or his research. In the hypothetical analysis just described, for example, Local 22's early history is used to construct a "general" causal interpretation of movement-building and that representation, in turn, could be explicitly compared to abstract event structures derived from the historical experiences of other union organizing campaigns and even entirely different kinds of social movements (civil rights and women's movements, etc.).

ESA's "instantiation" routine, finally, is useful even to those who do not wish to extend theoretically or empirically the scope of their analysis beyond the historical particulars of the single event. It can assist them in aggregating similar actions and in otherwise reducing the length of the "concrete" chronology, and it can deepen their conceptual understanding of the specific actions. Because the causal reasoning embedded in the two interpretations can be tested for logical consistency, moreover, ESA can also help analysts detect points in the interpretation where their "concrete" understanding of what happened differs from (or even contradicts) their "general" understanding. In his ESA analysis of a 1930 white-on-black lynching, for example, Griffin uncovered and corrected important substantive problems in his "concrete" causal interpretation because of a logical discrepancy between it and his "general" event structure.[15] Thinking "generally", then, can profoundly enhance thinking "particularly".

CONCLUSION

ESA is a flexible analytical tool: it can be bent to more "theoretical" or more "historical" purposes (to the extent that these really are different or opposite); it can focus intensely on a singular happening or it can be deployed for systematic comparison; it can incorporate the actions of virtually any actor – from living individuals to those of a corporate (e.g. RJR) and collective (e.g. sit-down strikers) nature – and it can be used

---

15. Griffin, "Narrative, Event-Structure Analysis and Causal Interpretation in Historical Sociology".

to unpack events of virtually historical scope or duration, from the most geographically and temporally circumscribed to those unfolding over large blocks of space and time.

It is also an unusual tool in that it requires the analyst to merge disparate ways of thinking and knowing in order to unpack an event and construct a compelling, historically-grounded causal interpretation of it. If we are to grasp the general *in* the particular, and the abstract and logical *in* the chronological – and these are crucial aspects of what the "unpacking" of a narrative entails – we must avoid social science reductionism as well as pure narrativism. Social science explanations of historical events too often rest on and are content with the imposition on history of ahistorical general theory rather than on serious engagements with historical complexity and specificity. Too often what theoretically general social science brings to historical questions are pseudo-explanations, bereft of real utility and often bereft of even the possibility of empirical disconfirmation. But a "return to narrative",[16] if that is understood as merely telling a story, is, as we have documented, also unacceptable as the basis for crafting replicable causal interpretations of events. The real historical utility of narrative, we think, hinges more on viewing its sequences as "witness" to and "testimony" about historical events than as analytically rigorous interpretive accounts of *why* happenings occurred as they did.

ESA, in contrast, demands what E.P. Thompson has called a "disciplined dialogue" between theory and evidence.[17] In particular, it mandates near constant "particularization" of the theoretically general ("what bearing does this generalization have for this particular action? for this particular event?") and the "generalization" of the historically particular ("what is the general meaning and significance of this action? what generally induces action of this sort?"). Narrative is buttressed by ESA's analytical self-consciousness, then, just as social science methodology is historicized in purpose and practice.

None of this is to suggest that ESA is without its own problems, both pragmatic and otherwise. One practical limitation, for instance, is that effective application of ESA becomes quite difficult, and the ETHNO diagram visually chaotic, if chronologies contain a great many statements (roughly, beyond fifty). As we noted earlier, however, analysts are encouraged to range far beyond the chronology as they interpret and structure the event. Chronologies can remain relatively short with no loss of essential information.

16. Compare, for example, Lawrence Stone, "The Revival of Narrative: Reflections on a New Old History", *Past and Present*, 85 (1979), pp. 3–24, with Eric Hobsbawm, "The Revival of Narrative: Some Comments", *Past and Present*, 86 (1980), pp. 3–8.
17. Thompson, *The Poverty of Theory*, p. 43.

Quite likely much more formidable barriers to widespread adoption of ESA are disciplinary conventions and prejudices. Social scientists are apt to suspect ESA is much too similar to the practice of history because it is too "subjective" and too focused on particularity and complexity. Though largely incorrect, this belief is unlikely to be overthrown as long as sociologists and others are invested in scientistic epistemologies of social inquiry.[18] Historians, on the other hand, may believe ESA excessively formal and "model-driven". This belief, too, is unfounded: event structures are not theoretical models imposed on the historical record, but nothing more than explicit depictions of the analyst's interpretations. ESA does not mechanically spit out answers to pressing historical questions, and causality, significance and meaning are not "discovered" through its use. It assumes that the analyst, not the algorithm, possesses the requisite knowledge to anticipate possibilities in a sequence of unfolding action, counterfactualize questions and conditions, explain what happened and interpret meaning. Thus the hard work of interpreting causality and extracting meaning from the event falls, as always, to the investigator.

Nor should historians fret that ESA destroys the tension and drama of narrative flow, reduces "real" persons to theoretical stick-figures, or weighs the story down with needless technicalities and incomprehensible jargon. Because ESA is, first and foremost, for scholarly self-edification – that is, to sharpen, deepen and broaden the analyst's own thinking – the fruits of an ESA analysis need not be present in the text nor impede stylistic facility.[19] The research product would look and read much like any conventional narrative history: it would simply be better history.

To argue, finally, that ESA is irrelevant to the narrativist because causal or interpretive methodology is itself unnecessary begs the issue: all historical inquiry is of necessity indelibly stamped by the methodological presuppositions and practices brought to the research. The real questions to confront, then, are not *whether* or not to use methodology, but *what* methodologies to use, *how* to use them and for *what* purpose, and *how* to communicate what was learned from their use. Few methodologies, formal or informal, either demand or offer so much in these respects as does event-structure analysis.

---

18. See, for example, the extended rebuttal to these and similar criticism of ESA (and interpretive methods more generally) by Griffin and Ragin, "Some Observations on Formal Qualitative Analysis".

19. As previously stated, though our substantive analysis of Local 22 was grounded in ESA, as was the narrative organization of our interpretation, we did not present either the analysis or any of its collateral details (the diagram, etc.). ESA functioned as the unobserved logical backbone of what appeared stylistically to be conventional narrative history: see Griffin and Korstad, "Class as Race and Gender".

ANNOTATED BIBLIOGRAPHY

Foundations of Event-Structure Analysis

Event-structure analysis was developed by sociologist David Heise. Though devoid of any linkage to historical inquiry/reasoning, he and his colleagues' early expositions of the methodology are detailed, generally accessible, and essential to all who consider ESA.

Corsaro, William and David Heise, "Event Structure Models from Ethnographic Data", *Sociological Methodology, 1990* (1990), pp. 1–57.
Heise, David, "Computer Analysis of Cultural Structures", *Social Science Computer Review*, 6 (1988), pp. 183–196.
Heise, David, "Modeling Event Structures", *Journal of Mathematical Sociology*, 14 (1989), pp. 139–169.
Heise, David, and Elsa Lewis, *Introduction to ETHNO* (Raleigh, NC, 1988). This is the ESA-ETHNO computer manual; it is invaluable.

ESA and Historical Reasoning

Griffin, Larry J., "Narrative, Event-Structure Analysis and Causal Interpretation in Historical Sociology", *American Journal of Sociology*, 98 (1993), pp. 1094–1133.
This was the first, and still most fully developed, attempt to wed ESA's logic and mode of operation to issues of causal interpretation, narrative, historical causation, comparative method, etc. Much of the article is devoted to the explication of ESA and includes a long, detailed substantive application of ESA to a 1930 lynching in Mississippi.

ESA: Applications, Explorations and Extensions

Brown, Cliff and John Bruggemann, "Mobilizing Interracial Solidarity: A Comparison of the 1919 and 1937 Steel Industry Labor Organizing Drives", *Mobilization*, 2 (1997), pp. 47–70.
Using ESA, Brown and Bruggemann formally compare the event-structures of the two organizing drives in steel to comprehend better why one failed (1919) and one succeeded (1937).
Griffin, Larry J. and Robert R. Korstad, "Class as Race and Gender: The Making and Breaking of a Union Local in the Jim Crow South", *Social Science History*, 19 (1985), pp. 425–454.
In our previous publication on Local 22, we relied on but did not report the ESA analysis. This example thus shows how ESA may be used solely as a heuristic aiding the analyst to interpret the event and to structure her or his narrative of its history.
Griffin, Larry J., Paula Clark and Joanne Sandberg, "Narrative and Event:

Historical Sociology and Lynching", in Fitzhugh Brundage (ed.), *Under Sentence of Death: Lynching in the New South* (Chapel Hill, NC, 1997).
Griffin *et al.* argue that ESA is a useful tool to understand why some "lynchings-in-the-making" were averted and others completed.

Isaac, Larry, Debra Street and Stan Knapp, "Analyzing Historical Contingency with Formal Methods: The Case of the 'Relief Explosion' and 1968", *Sociological Methods and Research*, 23 (1994), pp. 114–141.
Isaac *et al.* productively apply ESA to an unusual "event", the tumultuous year 1968.

Kiser, Edgar, "The Revival of Narrative in Historical Sociology: What Rational Choice Can Contribute", *Politics and Society*, 24 (1996), pp. 249–271.
Criticizing much of the "new narrativism" in sociology for its inductivism, Kiser urges the wedding of narrative analysis (including ESA) to a powerful deductive frame, rational choice theory.